The Social Sciences
in International
Agricultural Research

The Social Sciences in International Agricultural Research

Lessons from the CRSPs

edited by
Constance M. McCorkle

Lynne Rienner Publishers • Boulder & London

Published in the United States of America in 1989 by
Lynne Rienner Publishers, Inc.
1800 30th Street, Boulder, Colorado 80301

and in the United Kingdom by
Lynne Rienner Publishers, Inc.
3 Henrietta Street, Covent Garden, London WC2E 8LU

Library of Congress Cataloging-in-Publication Data
The Social sciences in international agricultural research : lessons
 from the CRSPs / edited by Constance M. McCorkle.
 Bibliography: p.
 Includes index.
 ISBN 1–55587–133–X (alk. paper)
 1. Agriculture—Economic aspects—Developing countries—Research.
2. Agricultural innovations—Economic aspects—Developing countries.
3. Agriculture—Social aspects—Developing countries—Research.
4. Agricultural innovations—Social aspects—Developing countries.
I. McCorkle, Constance M. (Constance Marie)
HD1417.S567 1989
338.1'09172'4—dc20   89–32083
                                                            CIP

British Cataloguing in Publication Data
A Cataloguing in Publication record for this book
is available from the British Library.

Printed and bound in the United States of America

The paper used in this publication meets the requirements of
the American National Standard for Permanence of Paper for
Printed Library Materials Z39.48–1984.

*To the many agricultural scientists, be they social or
biological/technical, who, despite personal, professional,
and other sacrifices, have chosen to enlist in the
fight against global hunger and famine*

Contents

List of Tables and Figures

TABLES

FIGURES

Acknowledgments

As the chapters in this volume document, many individuals and institutions have contributed to make this innovative "cross-CRSP" and cross-disciplinary publication a reality. However, special recognition is due the USAID/Title XII Small Ruminant Collaborative Research Support Program's (SR-CRSP) Sociology Project (Grant No. DAN-1328-G-SS-4093-00), housed in the Department of Rural Sociology at the University of Missouri–Columbia (UMC) and directed by Michael F. Nolan, professor of rural sociology and associate dean in the College of Agriculture at UMC. With additional support from the University of Missouri, the SR-CRSP Sociology Project team conceived and funded a conference designed to stimulate CRSP researchers to document their experiences on these integrative new programs to combat world food problems.

Among the contributors to this volume, special thanks go to Billie DeWalt for his early input into the conference concept, and to Joyce Turk, SR-CRSP project officer in the Agency for International Development, for her unstinting support throughout the lengthy process that brought the project to fruition.

Thanks are also due Julia X. Grimes, intern and information officer on the SR-CRSP Sociology Project, for her help in copyediting and proofing. Last, but by no means least, the editor is profoundly grateful to Judy Gieselman, administrative assistant in the UMC College of Agriculture Dean's Office. She served as production manager for the book—translating between almost mutually unintelligible word-processing languages, shepherding the manuscript through numerous drafts with superhuman patience, and coordinating with the publisher. Without her efforts, publication would not have been possible.

Constance M. McCorkle

Foreword:
Social Scientists and the CRSPs

Joyce M. Turk

Agriculture is everywhere a social activity. Naturally, researchers must thoroughly understand the dynamics of agrobiological systems before improvements or alterations can be made in any part of a system. But equally important, they must also understand the sociocultural and socioeconomic dynamics of such systems.

Interdisciplinary and intercultural communication is the key to agricultural change and development. Like a complex net, communication must be woven and cast among researchers, producers, consumers, and legislators—not only in developing countries (DCs), but also in the donor nations. The weavers of this net are the social scientists. When this communication is successful, multidisciplinary relationships that are all too often disjointed become fruitful interdisciplinary alliances.

In the Collaborative Research Support Programs (CRSPs), sponsored by the U.S. Agency for International Development (USAID), anthropologists and sociologists match sociocultural with agrobiological events in production systems and promote cross-disciplinary communication. They not only link researchers with researchers, and researchers with producers, consumers, and legislators, they also interrelate the roles of crops and livestock as cash and food commodities in both international and domestic socioeconomic contexts.

While producers perceive their systems as a whole, technical and biological scientists selectively focus on discrete areas of production. Social scientists help to balance research biases by promoting collaboration between producers and scientists, leading agrobiological research in sociologically meaningful directions. By translating abstract research goals into practices that are socially, culturally, and economically acceptable to producers, social scientists forecast the impact of research results. In this way, research design becomes more site-specific, focused, realistic, and practical.

For the past decade, CRSP anthropologists and sociologists have been working to build more sensitive social consciousness into biological research. Their work is documented here. *The Social Sciences in International Agricultural Research* records their tangible and positive contributions to the innovative agricultural research and development (R&D) conducted in the CRSPs. Each chapter presents provocative accounts of the roles these social scientists have in designing, targeting, and implementing a collaborative research support effort. This book reviews procedures used to develop technologies for farmers, describes on-farm research, and addresses the policy context of agricultural research in relation to the cultural, social, and economic realities of smallholder producers.

Coupled with commentary by collaborating CRSP technical and biological scientists, the book also addresses problems encountered by social scientists in integrating their skills into programs of international agricultural R&D. While they have sustained an image as "cultural cartographers," social scientists are entitled to the same professional recognition accorded physical and biological scientists. This volume clearly and concretely demonstrates why. They have a critical impact on international agricultural R&D and the success of collaborative research.

For example, the description by INTSORMIL (International Sorghum/Millet CRSP) social scientists of an integrated crop-livestock production system in Sudan improved the design of subsequent research on sorghum and millet by guiding decisions regarding which varieties and features of these grain crops to investigate (Coughenour and Reeves this volume). Likewise, in Honduras, INTSORMIL anthropologists conducted revealing research on the role of sorghum within the food system and assessed the acceptability of improved varieties to local populations (DeWalt and DeWalt this volume).

CRSPs point out the value of learning and sharing with other disciplines and with small farmers. By including farmers as colleagues in the research process, these programs find production methods that are cost-effective and sometimes unconventional. For example, CRSP social scientists have highlighted the value and potentials of indigenous technical knowledge coupled with modern scientific inputs. The Small Ruminant CRSP's (SR-CRSP) investigation of the use of native plants in managing animal health in Peru is illustrative (McCorkle this volume). Research by Bean/Cowpea CRSP social scientists on animal draft power in Botswana has directly benefited female farmers who lacked access to oxen for field preparation. These findings led to design of a minimum tillage ridger/planter for use with donkeys—animals that women could more easily obtain and handle (Ferguson this volume).

The latter example raises the question: Who benefits from agricultural research in developing countries? When anthropologists and sociologists are not included in the planning process, usually the answer is the more prosperous producers. But thanks to social science inputs, the CRSPs do not just ask, "Will small farmers benefit?" These programs also ask, "*Which* small farmers will benefit?" For example, biological scientists on the SR-CRSP in Peru initially targeted for research only commercially oriented livestock cooperatives and enterprises. However, baseline data collected by SR-CRSP social scientists showed that peasant communities are equally important producers of livestock. As a result, limited program resources were efficiently reallocated to work with both kinds of producers (Jamtgaard this volume).

Thus, social scientists on the Small Ruminant and other CRSPs strengthen the technical capabilities and successes of biological researchers by encouraging them better to address the range of needs among more, and more different, types of smallholder populations. In addition, social scientists help to make program research achievements as a whole more visible and easily understood, as their preparation of this book demonstrates.

The CRSP concept is unique among donors in international agricultural R&D (Lipner and Nolan this volume). Planners in USAID recognize the tremendous opportunities that the CRSP design affords U.S. universities and host country research institutions in creating and sustaining close and long-term scientific rapport. Traditional projects are too short (3–5 years) to address issues in production agriculture adequately. The nontraditional CRSP design allows for long-term programs and, with them, greater potential for long-term successes.

CRSP accomplishments demonstrate the excellence of this concept. For example, a vaccine for contagious caprine pleuropneumonia developed through the SR-CRSP will benefit goat producers worldwide. In Kenya, the introduction of dual-purpose (meat and milk) goats promises producers supplemental income, as well as improved nutrition through the consumption of goat's milk, which is far less expensive than cow's milk. On the SR-CRSP in Morocco, research on ovine genetics and breeding has shown that lamb crops can be increased 150% simply by crossing two indigenous breeds. In the Middle Atlas Mountains, producers are already adopting this practice. Few traditional agricultural projects have yielded such quantitative successes.

The CRSPs' dual objective is to improve food production and consumption in DCs and to strengthen research capabilities both in DCs and in the United States. These programs link the expertise of U.S. agricultural universities to DC needs worldwide. By supporting the CRSPs, USAID therefore also supports U.S. land grant institutions. This means that U.S. farmers benefit, too. U.S. institutions involved with CRSPs conduct research on priority areas in which the United States has a continuing interest, thus stimulating a reverse flow of technology useful to U.S. agriculture.

U.S. farmers also directly benefit through substantially increased commercial exports of agricultural products, as recent trade statistics show. In many countries, U.S. assistance has increased agricultural production, rural incomes, and ultimately trade. Peanuts are a prime example. In collaboration with food scientists, Peanut CRSP social scientists have analyzed food demand and food policies to differentiate growth markets for peanut products in the Caribbean (Wheelock et al. this volume). Such research can further stimulate the upward trend in U.S. peanut exports since 1980.

In sum, the findings and achievements of these innovative and scholarly programs attest to the shrewd decisions and foresighted vision of USAID planners. Unfortunately, past patterns of development assistance do not bode well for such initiatives as the CRSPs. International donors traditionally cite income and income distribution problems in DCs as the primary cause of inadequate nutrition. They thus give less attention and lower priority to agricultural production problems, relegating basic agricultural research to the academic community. Such an approach only exacerbates long-term economic problems.

In an era of shrinking foreign aid budgets, it is important that the multiple advantages of CRSPs be made clear so that these worthy efforts can successfully compete for funding against more traditional programs. By comparison to the latter, the CRSP model does a better job of using existing resources, mobilizing additional support, concentrating on what is achievable in improving DC livestock and crop production and food consumption, and sustaining natural resources. Part of the strength of these programs in addressing their objectives lies in their inclusion of anthropologists and sociologists.

Abbreviations

AAMU	Alabama Agricultural and Mechanical University
ARC	Agricultural Research Center(s)
BIFAD	Board for International Food and Agricultural Development
CARDI	Caribbean Agricultural Research and Development Institute
CC	Comunidad Campesina (Peru)
CEPLAES	Centro de Planification y Estudios Sociales (Ecuador)
CGIAR	Consultative Group on International Agricultural Research
CIAT	Centro Internacional de Agricultura Tropical
CIP	Centro Internacional de la Papa
CIMMYT	Centro Internacional de Mejoramiento de Maíz y Trigo
CRM	Centro de Rehabilitación de Manabí (Ecuador)
CRSP	Collaborative Research Support Program
DC	Developing Country
DCCN	Dirección de Comunidades Campesinas y Nativas (Peru)
DGEA	Dirección General de Economía Agrícola (Mexico)
DGOR	Dirección de Comunidades Campesinas y Nativas
EMBRAPA	Empresa Brasileira de Pesquisa Agropecuaria
FAO	Food and Agriculture Organization
FBS	Food Balance Sheet(s)
FRC/ARC	Food Research Center/Agricultural Research Corporation (Sudan)
FSR(&E)	Farming Systems Research (and Extension)
FSSP	Farming Systems Support Project
GAO	General Accounting Office
ha	Hectare(s)
HAPS	Household Agricultural Production Study
IADS	International Agricultural Development Service
IARC	International Agricultural Research Center
ICRISAT	International Center for Research in the Semi-Arid Tropics
ICTA	Instituto de Ciencias y Tecnología Agrícola (Guatemala)
IDRC	International Development Research Center
IFAD	International Fund for Agricultural Development

IFPRI	International Food Policy Research Institute
IICA	Instituto Interamericano de Cooperación para la Agricultura
IITA	International Institute of Tropical Agriculture
ILCA	International Livestock Center for Africa
INCAP	Institute for Nutrition for Central America and Panama
INIA	Instituto Nacional de Investigaciones Agrícolas (Mexico)
INIAP	Instituto Nacional de Investigaciones Agropecuarias (Ecuador)
INIFAP	Instituto Nacional de Investigaciones Forestales, Agrícolas, y Pecuarias (Mexico)
INIPA	Instituto Nacional de Investigación y Promoción Agropecuaria (Peru)
INTSORMIL	International Sorghum and Millet CRSP
IRHO	Institut de Recherches pour les Huiles et Oleagineux
IRRI	International Rice Research Center
JCARD	Joint Committee on Agricultural Research and Development
JRC	Joint Research Committee
kg	Kilogram(s)
MAP	Mexican Agricultural Program
ME	Management Entity (of a CRSP)
MOU	Memorandum of Understanding
MSU	Michigan State University
mt	Metric Ton(s)
NAS	National Academy of Sciences
NASULGC	National Association of State Universities and Land Grant Colleges
NRLP	Niger Range and Livestock Project
OEA	Organización de Estados Americanos
OSS	Office of Special Studies (Mexico)
PATF	Project Advisement Task Force
PI	Principal Investigator (of a CRSP project)
PIP	Program of Investigation in Production (Ecuador)
R&D	Research and Development
SAS	Statistical Analysis System
SAT	Semi-Arid Tropics
SD	Standard Deviation
SPSS	Statistical Package for the Social Sciences
SR-CRSP	Small Ruminant CRSP
TAC	Technical Advisory Committee
TC	Technical Committee
UCD	University of California-Davis
UCLA	University of California-Los Angeles

UMC	University of Missouri-Columbia
UN	United Nations
USDA	United States Department of Agriculture
USAID	United States Agency for International Development
UTM	Universidad Técnica de Manabí (Ecuador)
WHO	World Health Organization
WID	Women in Development
WILRTC	Winrock International Livestock Research and Training Center (now Winrock International Institute for Agricultural Development)
WSARP	Western Sudan Agricultural Research Project

Introduction: Anthropology, Sociology, and Agricultural R&D

Constance M. McCorkle

This volume has multiple messages for a diversity of readers. At one level, it serves to document some of the many scientific achievements of an innovative approach to agricultural R&D—the Collaborative Research Support Programs, or CRSPs.[1] Five of these dynamic programs are represented here: the Bean/Cowpea, Sorghum/Millet, Nutrition, Peanut, and Small Ruminant CRSPs.

The book's primary aim, however, is more ambitious. By drawing on research from these five CRSPs, it outlines the wide-ranging kinds of contributions that the most "social" of the social sciences, anthropology and sociology, make to both the concept and the conduct of agricultural R&D. Of course, other social and behavioral sciences have important roles to play in this arena, e.g., political science, human geography, social psychology, communications, and especially economics and agricultural economics.[2] But within the development community, anthropology and sociology have taken the lead in the delicate task of relating agricultural R&D to the overall well-being of its intended beneficiaries. This is the final test of success in any development endeavor.

In the pages that follow, CRSP scientists, biological/technical as well as social, spell out the many ways that input from anthropology and sociology can and does directly enhance the focus, design, implementation, and evaluation of agricultural R&D. More broadly, they document the imperative need for social research in any efforts at directed change and development.

At the same time, the chapters that follow illustrate how anthropology and sociology have grown in scope, relevance, and maturity through their engagement in agricultural R&D, as these disciplines have ventured forth from the halls of academe to confront the problems of rural peoples throughout the world.

A final, further aim of this book is to share some of the hard-won lessons learned about working in a collaborative, cross-national, and cross-disciplinary mode. Both present and future professionals in any field that is

1

active in international development can profit from the candid retrospectives and hands-on insights tendered here.

THE SOCIAL SCIENCES IN AGRICULTURAL R&D

While the place of sister social sciences like economics is now well recognized in international agricultural R&D, the value of anthropology and sociology has often been poorly understood. As relative latecomers, the roles of these disciplines have sometimes been subject to misapprehensions among biological/technical coworkers. Understandably, few non–social scientists are familiar with the specialized methods, theories, or even the long-standing subject matters within anthropology and sociology that relate to agriculture. In consequence, they are often uncertain as to how social research can profitably inform development programs, as Rhoades (1983, 1986), McCorkle and Gilles (1987), and many others have observed. And with some exceptions (e.g., Cernea 1985, Colfer 1987, DeWalt 1985, IRRI 1982, Lacy 1985, McCorkle et al. 1989, Michael Butler 1987, Nolan 1985, Rhoades 1984, and especially Zambia/CIMMYT 1986), until recently neither have social scientists been particularly adept at explicitly and systematically enunciating their hands-on relevance to agricultural R&D.

Along with tight R&D budgets, uncertainty about social science roles has led to complaints that inclusion of social research is a superfluous expense. It has even been argued that "socially sensitive" members of other disciplines can perform any necessary social analyses just as well as anthropologists or sociologists (see the exchange between Simmonds 1985 and Cernea and Guggenheim n.d. and accounts in Hamilton 1973, Rhoades 1983, and van Dusseldorp 1977). At worst, social research has been seen as an impediment to technological progress, with what some consider excessive emphasis on such issues as equity, empowerment, risk, and sociocultural appropriateness. (For exceptionally forthright discussions, see Horowitz 1988 and Hammett 1973).

An even more pervasive and pernicious notion of anthropologists' and sociologists' roles in agricultural R&D is that they are solely facilitators (Flinn 1988) and "farmer convincers." Typically, social scientists have been assigned service functions. They perform various administrative and statistical chores, ex ante diagnostic studies, and ex post evaluations of project outcomes. Frequently, too, they are assigned the job of finding ways to increase the adoption rates of new agricultural technologies—technologies that may have been devised with little or no input either from social scientists or from producers themselves (see Chapter 6 in this volume). In this capacity, anthropologists and especially rural sociologists[3] are charged with cajoling recalcitrant human "software" into adopting project-generated "hardware."

Fortunately, such myopic views of social science roles have been expanding in the face of evidence that technology cannot be indiscriminately designed, developed, delivered, or sustained in ignorance of the specific human ecologies in which it is to be used. As the contributors to this book point out, assigning anthropologists and sociologists only fragmented functions as facilitators and extension strategists is of limited utility. The real value of social research is obtained when it is included in the R&D process from start to finish.

It is noteworthy that a careful study of 68 World Bank projects found that attention to social issues pays off in financial as well as human terms. Projects that incorporated proper social science inputs yielded economic rates of return more than twice as high as those without such inputs (Kottak 1985). Drawing on the wealth of CRSP experience, the contributors to this volume spell out what these inputs are, and where, when, and how they should be integrated into all phases of the R&D process so as to best advance development goals. In broad terms, their observations can be summarized as follows.

Planning and Research Design

Anthropologists and sociologists have critical roles to play in preproject planning and design. They help to ensure that a good fit exists between the social ends of development and the proposed technological means; that data collected by diverse disciplines are analytically compatible; that project site selection is well reasoned; that plans for field operations are socioculturally feasible; and that still other design and start-up needs are met. Authors Anne Ferguson, Dorothy Cattle, and Michael Paolisso and Michael Baksh in particular present some telling examples from the Bean/Cowpea and Nutrition CRSPs of how omitting social inputs at this phase would have meant costly redesign later on, loss of client credibility and cooperation, and possibly project failure.

Targeting

To be successful in both human and technical terms, development projects must accurately conceptualize, define, and locate beneficiary populations. As specialists in the delineation of human groups, anthropologists and sociologists bring to this critical task unique skills and sophisticated methodologies. They can therefore translate the often vague initial definitions of target groups into workable socioeconomic, cultural, sex, age, etc., categories.

Chapter 11, by Keith Jamtgaard, offers a dramatic example of this targeting function. Jamtgaard describes how, by applying powerful statistical tools to a national database, sociologists on the Small Ruminant CRSP/Peru were able to operationally clarify the program's mandate to focus on small-holder stockraisers. The benefits to the program were multifold. Research was reoriented to incorporate what was in fact the nation's largest group of stockowners, a group that was not initially slated for study or assistance! This resulted in a reallocation of resources that was simultaneously more efficient and more comprehensive, with broader potentials for outreach and impact. Moreover, by utilizing an existing data set, the analysis was performed at a very modest cost. The savings to the program in terms of time, money, and possible embarrassment are incalculable.

Similarly, anthropological analyses of biosocial and socioeconomic characteristics of study populations on the Nutrition and Sorghum/Millet CRSPs were critical for determining which rural groups were at greatest nutritional risk and therefore required priority program attention (Chapters 5, 6, and 7). Moreover, as documented throughout this book, careful targeting is equally important in ensuring that a new technology or practice can realistically be disseminated to those for whom it is designed. In sum, a clear understanding of target-group composition and dynamics is a necessary first step in identifying interventions appropriate to different producer and consumer categories. This is the domain *par excellence* of the social sciences.

Fieldworking

As a rule, sociologists and especially anthropologists conduct their investigations in more intimate, sustained contact with rural communities than do scientists of other disciplines. This research strategy generates a wealth of in-depth information useful for understanding producers' current practices and the rationales behind them.

In the process, fieldwork often leads to discoveries of "lost" or unappreciated local knowledge and practice. Examples include the folk veterinary skills and pharmaceuticals of Quechua Indians in highland Peru (Chapter 12), the acumen of Ecuadorian farmers in manipulating complex interrelationships among agricultural variables like plant spacing and weed control (Chapter 8), and the unsuspected diversity and creativity in rural Hondurans' diet and cuisine (Chapter 5).

Often, too, fieldwork reveals important factors that have been overlooked in a priori planning and research design, as Paolisso and Baksh (Chapter 7) discovered in investigating links between nutritional status and biosocial or socioeconomic status in Kenya, or as Gerald Wheelock et al. (Chapter 10) found in assessing competing biogenic and sociogenic hypotheses about the causes of aflatoxin contamination in Caribbean peanuts.

As these and other contributors indicate, when brought to the attention of biological/technical colleagues, such field-based insights can reorient agricultural R&D in profitable ways. Ground-breaking basic research may be stimulated by the need to scientifically validate producers' own ethnoscientific practices or by new, unanswered questions. Applied research may be rerouted in more context-sensitive and sustainable directions.

Integrating

Like producers themselves, anthropologists and sociologists generally take a more holistic view of the agricultural enterprise than do other scientists. Failure to integrate complex and sometimes competing components operating at multiple levels of agricultural systems runs the risk that development projects may end up "robbing Peter to pay Paul," with no real net benefits to the intended beneficiaries.

Thus, a major social science contribution consists of ensuring that, while focusing on one commodity or development need, the *whole* agricultural system is addressed, including the complex tradeoffs that producers make among plant crops, livestock, and other productive activities (Chapters 1 and 5). Similarly, in the realm of consumption, social scientists integrate biomedical information with the social and economic roles, cultural beliefs, cropping systems, etc., that generate the nutritional behaviors and outcomes under study (Chapters 5, 6, and 7).

Generally, too, social scientists are more keenly aware of the need to look beyond the farm gate to community, regional, national, and international contexts in which producers and their farming systems are embedded, to assess whether proposed interventions are workable in these, as well as purely technological, terms. A good example is the careful socioeconomic studies by Peanut CRSP sociologists to predict both potentials and problems posed by domestic and international markets for Sudanian and Caribbean peanut products (Chapter 10).

Translating and Brokering

Closely related to the two preceding activities is anthropologists' and sociologists' ability to effectively translate or broker communication among different disciplines, institutions, and policymaking and donor entities, and between scientists and producers in all phases of agricultural research, technology development, and transfer. In this capacity, they constitute a conduit for productive dialogue—often as not serving as "researcher convincers" rather than "farmer convincers"—in the iterative feedback and feedforward necessary to successful R&D.

Virtually all the contributors speak to this task. To give just a few examples, Bean/Cowpea CRSP sociologists in Ecuador noted the simple need to get local cultivar names straight so as to collect accurate and comparable baseline data (Chapter 9). More subtle complexities of translating between emic and etic, between anthropological and biological, knowledge systems were tackled by social scientists on the Small Ruminant CRSP/Peru in promoting cooperative research between village stockraisers and CRSP veterinarians and animal scientists (Chapter 12). On the Sorghum/Millet CRSP in Sudan, sociologists and anthropologists worked to define information networks among producers, extensionists, and national and international R&D establishments (Chapters 3 and 4). And on the Nutrition CRSP in Kenya, anthropologists played a key role in establishing interactive forums for dialogue among community participants, village leaders, and junior and senior field staff, as well as between social and biological scientists (Chapter 6).

Social scientists' translating and brokering roles have high payoffs in terms of smoother project functioning and greater project success, the result of giving a voice to all stakeholders in the R&D enterprise. Perhaps Joyce Turk's "Foreword" and Hendrik Knipscheer's closing commentary most clearly enunciate this very real, albeit sometimes less tangible, contribution of the social sciences.

Monitoring, Guiding, and Evaluating

As Knipscheer, Tommy Nakayama (Chapter 14), Michele Lipner and Michael Nolan (Chapter 1), and others note in this book, monitoring, guiding, and evaluating constitute one of the most visible and immediate rationales for including social scientists on R&D teams in the first place. Timely social science inputs from ongoing data collection, analysis, and monitoring are essential for deploying project resources efficiently and appropriately and for making in-field course corrections.

For example, social scientists on the Bean/Cowpea CRSP in Ecuador (Chapters 8 and 9) saved program time and money by helping to pinpoint regions where these crops were most prevalent; by guiding research toward problems most important to producers (improved seed storage techniques) and away from inappropriate technology (fertilizers); and by reorienting breeding agendas to varieties that readily fit into existing crop rotations. Similarly, anthropological studies on the Sorghum/Millet CRSP in Honduras were instrumental in redirecting breeding research to focus on sorghum varieties instead of hybrids. Drawing on livestock R&D in Africa, R. E. McDowell (Chapter 15) also describes a number of compelling cases of how timely social scientific advice forestalled problems in, for example, distributing crossbred animals, assisting women in dairy production and marketing, and training producers in the use of new ox-drawn technologies.

Because of these kinds of insights and skills, CRSP social scientists are frequently charged with coordinating and monitoring the interdisciplinary field testing of new technology. Drawing on baseline data, which they have played a major role in collecting, they have primary responsibility for monitoring and evaluating the flow of benefits to the intended beneficiaries. As Matt Silbernagel (Chapter 13) candidly observes, this information often determines whether a project is cancelled or continued. Evaluation information is equally if not more important for improving the formulation of future development programs and policies (Chapter 5).

Training and Institution Building

Anthropologists and sociologists have played a variety of roles in training CRSP participants in techniques for teamworking, field interviewing, and meeting farmers (Chapters 1, 6, and 9); recommending training needs for groups as diverse as extensionists, merchants, and women; and mounting workshops and conferences (Chapters 3 and 8). Interestingly, several authors observe that one of their most important, if less explicit, "training" contributions may have been in urging both U.S. and host country scientists out of their labs and research stations into direct dialogue with rural producers and consumers.

As noted earlier, anthropologists and sociologists are experts in delineating human organizational and institutional structures. Therefore they play key roles in interpreting the operational and training needs of entities like national agricultural research centers, extension services, universities, etc., and in planning for their growth and strengthening (Chapters 9 and 10). These roles are exemplified in Chapter 4 on the Sorghum/Millet CRSP's study of the Sudan Agricultural Research Center and in the Small Ruminant CRSP's work to establish or reinforce social science research units in host country institutions (Chapter 1).

Policymaking

With insights gained from exercising all the roles and skills listed above, social research can make decisive contributions to the formulation of development policy and to bringing the R&D process full circle to the conceptualization of future programs. Illustrating from the disappointing, even distorting, history of U.S. policies for agricultural development in Mexico, Billie DeWalt (Chapter 2) cogently argues the case for building a more "macro," theoretically informed, and politically conscious level of social analysis into the policy process itself, above and beyond the relatively micro-level application of social analysis *in* specific projects and programs. There is urgent need for a theoretically grounded and critical social science *of* agriculture to examine the underlying assumptions, values, and social risks behind policy agendas and to inform agricultural policy reform in an ever-shrinking globe. Ultimately, this is the most important contribution of the social sciences to agricultural R&D.[4]

VICE VERSA: AGRICULTURAL R&D
IN THE SOCIAL SCIENCES

Although this book's overarching aim is to determine how anthropology and sociology contribute to agricultural research and development, the converse question is equally important. That is, how does agricultural R&D contribute to research in, and the development of, anthropology and sociology? Biological/technical scientists have not been the only ones to harbor confusions and misgivings about the place of anthropology and sociology in this arena. So have many social scientists.

Their concerns have centered on a variety of moral, political, and intellectual issues, including the humanistic implications of interfering in the lives of others; ethical qualms about supplying information to powerful agencies that may misuse it; compromised scientific objectivity by virtue of direct involvement in action-oriented programs; restricted scientific freedom due to client demands; and loss of professional prestige, funds, and promotions, given the often "second class" status of development or applied studies in academia and the historical stereotypes of such work as "the shabbier side" (Schaedel 1964:190) of the discipline or even as "virtual academic prostitution" (Miniclier 1964:189).

This is not the place to recapitulate the lengthy history of debates surrounding such issues.[5] Suffice it to say that these views have been rapidly changing (Almy 1977) as growing numbers of anthropologists and sociologists have enlisted in initiatives like the CRSPs. Strengthening and broadening their fields' concepts, tools, subject matters, critical perspectives, and functions (Bowen 1988, Chambers 1987) and sometimes placing development specialists "at the cutting edge of the discipline" (van Willigen 1986:xiv), this move has benefited nearly every facet of disciplinary activity.

Empirical and Theoretical Resources

Participation in development initiatives has provided social scientists more and more varied opportunities to exercise their craft. This has made for an invigorating infusion of comparative data from every part of the globe—data that would have gone otherwise uncollected. These fresh empirical resources can be (and have been) marshalled by the academic community to refine or expand existing analyses of nearly all aspects of social change and development, as well as to fashion new theoretical constructs responding to the needs of a social science of agriculture (Chapter 2).

To list but a few examples that come immediately to mind: global theories of change and development; explications of the role of risk, uncertainty, and "peasant rationality" in such theories; macro-micro linkages; advances in cultural ecological theory and investigation of the social control and management of natural resources; decision-making modeling; the relatively neglected study of agricultural transformation and consumption as versus production and distribution; and the sociopolitically sensitive analysis of research institutions and development assistance bureaucracies and policies. Some of these contributions of agricultural R&D to the social sciences are reflected in this book; many more are detailed in a literature too vast to reference here.[6]

Methodology

Perhaps inevitably, new methodologies and new uses for old methodologies can be expected to arise in the course of data collection and fieldwork in any discipline. But there is evidence that the demands of interdisciplinary, problem-solving or programmatic R&D (Chapter 1) add considerable impulse to this process (Appleby 1988).

For example, in response to basic information needs on the Nutrition CRSP, program anthropologists helped pioneer the addition of a new technique, time allocation studies, to their disciplinary toolkit (Chapter 7). Sociologists on the Bean/Cowpea CRSP created a new microcomputer program to measure landholding inequities among small farmers (Chapter 8). Confronted with an empirically unanswered research question on the Small Ruminant CRSP, program sociologists devised a novel use for a familiar methodology by applying cluster analysis (commonly employed in marketing research) to features of agricultural production systems (Chapter 11).

Research Approaches

Collaboration in such R&D enterprises as the CRSPs enhances disciplinary knowledge in anthropology and sociology by stimulating innovative research approaches (Chapter 1). This volume illustrates a few of the many new perspectives that have emerged in the social sciences as a result of their engagement in agricultural R&D initiatives—like the participative research paradigm discussed by Knipscheer (Chapter 16), the interdisciplinary study and application of indigenous agricultural technical knowledge highlighted by McCorkle (Chapter 12), or the formulation by DeWalt and DeWalt (Chapter 5) of an NSR (nutrition systems research) framework to complement FSR (farming systems research) models (Chapters 3 and 8).

Subject Matters

Although some of the authors (for example, Coughenour and Reeves, Ferguson, and Lipner and Nolan) note understandable difficulties in relating their CRSP work to orthodox research themes within their academic fields, in fact one of the most vital contributions of such R&D programs to anthropology and sociology (or indeed, any discipline) is the discovery of exciting and important new *non*traditional subject matters. The very nature of these R&D endeavors, interdisciplinary and problem oriented, offers rich opportunities for expanding the intellectual horizons and the "real world" relevance of all participating disciplines, guiding them into territories heretofore systematically unexplored.

A good example of the new directions that can arise from interdisciplinary synergisms is the Small Ruminant CRSP's definition of two novel subject matters: veterinary anthropology (see Mathias-Mundy and McCorkle forthcoming and McCorkle 1986, as well as Chapter 12 of this volume) and the sociology of range management (Gilles 1982a,b, in progress). Collaborative work in these areas has changed the way that both social and biological/technical scientists view the conduct and content of their disciplines. Similarly, problem-solving demands on the Bean/Cowpea CRSP and many other projects have led to the recognition that development goals cannot be achieved without serious scientific attention to a new, pandisciplinary research theme—the vital roles of women in agriculture and other development arenas (Chapter 8).

Disciplinary Definition

The emergence of such hybrid subject matters is hardly surprising in disciplines that already nurture subfields like medical anthropology and sociology, cultural ecology, economic anthropology, and so forth. But again, the more intense and sustained cross-fertilization of scientific fields in R&D programs like the CRSPs accelerates and amplifies the evolution of research approaches and domains.

It is no accident that the mid-to-late 1970s witnessed the redefinition of anthropology and sociology to incorporate the subdisciplines of agricultural anthropology and the sociology of agriculture. Spanning the developed as well as the developing world, and now formally recognized with their own professional organizations, newsletters, and sessions at national meetings, these subdisciplines testify to the contributions of agriculturally oriented research to the social sciences. At the same time, they represent a major step forward on the road to a social science *of* agriculture and all that this implies for more astute development policy and praxis.

Training and Curricula

Neither is it any accident that throughout the United States, departments of anthropology (DeWalt and DeWalt 1985) and, to a lesser extent, sociology and rural sociology (Hansen et al. 1982, Koppel and Beal 1983) are redesigning their instructional programs to include agricultural and other development studies. Some have followed the advice of McDowell (Chapter 15) and Silbernagel (Chapter 13) and encouraged students to take courses in other disciplines relevant to international development. These new training options will better prepare future social scientists to grapple with the debates with which this section began.

DISCIPLINARY AND INTERDISCIPLINARY R&D

The final aim of this book is to share some of the lessons that CRSP scientists—social and biological/technical alike—have learned about the professional rewards and difficulties of doing interdisciplinary,[7] collaborative R&D. The contributors to the book are not the first to note the many challenges of such endeavors; numerous authors have tackled this subject.[8] With relatively few exceptions, however (e.g., Byerlee and Tripp 1988, Cock 1979, Heberlein 1988, Horton 1984, Knop et al. 1985, Rhoades et al. 1986), this large and growing literature rarely integrates views from both social and biological scientists on the often uneasy interaction among disciplines teamed together in agricultural development.[9]

In a conscious move to go beyond such narcissistic dialogue to a more balanced perspective, CRSP biological/technical scientists were asked to contribute their critical commentary on this as well as other issues. Their reactions in Part 6 offer one of the most candid discussions to be found in print. Together with their colleagues in anthropology and sociology, representatives from the fields of agricultural economics, agronomy, animal science, and food and nutrition science outline a number of problems, and some solutions, in the conduct of interdisciplinary, applied research.

Mutual Ignorance

The four authors in Part 6, along with Lipner and Nolan in Chapter 1, aptly identify mutual ignorance of the workings of one another's fields as one of the paramount barriers to interdisciplinary R&D. They cite differences in professional terminology, research methods, publication styles and audiences, research topics, and even philosophies. Drawing on their CRSP experiences, they suggest some immediate solutions to this problem, including sustained interdisciplinary interaction across all program phases, mutual education, and even "semispecialization" in one another's disciplines. A longer-term solution lies in restructuring graduate training curricula for practitioners of all disciplines, to make their programs of study more cross-departmental.

Applied Versus "Pure" Research, and Professional Advancement

Development-oriented research is distinct from discipline-specific, "pure" research. It is problem oriented, applied, and, if it is to have a positive impact in the "real world," of necessity interdisciplinary. Unfortunately, as Knipscheer, Lipner and Nolan, Silbernagel, and others point out, this is not the kind of research that wins kudos within traditional disciplinary and academic structures.

In consequence, scientists of any discipline who tackle development problems often find themselves professionally penalized. They must serve two masters simultaneously if they are to advance in their careers. Perhaps the most realistic, immediate solution to this problem is to leave room for disciplinary research within the development agenda. A longer-term but less likely solution is to build into university and other research institutions new kinds of reward systems, appointment structures, and subcenters that give full support and recognition to outstanding applied research.

Balancing Social and Biological Research

The question of how to allocate scarce resources between social and biological research is glossed as a "territoriality" or "turf" conflict by some of the contributors. Biological/technical scientists are notorious for their tendency to commit massive resources to designing and promoting a technology without adequate evidence that it will in fact meet producers' needs. Social scientists are infamous for their proclivity to conduct endless surveys and field studies that may not supply this evidence in a clear or timely fashion. For both groups, these tendencies are exacerbated by the applied vs. pure quandary.

To achieve a balanced allocation of resources between technology design and the social research necessary to target and validate it, the contributors urge equal structural status and joint decision-making powers between social and biological/technical components; continual interaction among all disciplines to cooperatively identify problems and information needs arising in ongoing research; periodic program reviews, both internal and external; and maintenance of a tight focus on project goals to ensure that *all* research activities advance the entire team's efforts (Chapters 1, 6, 14, 15, and 16). Most of these suggestions are not new, but the CRSP experience adduces evidence that they work.

CONCLUSION

As a number of contributors observe, resolving the tensions between social and non-social sciences in agricultural R&D takes time, effort, negotiation, compromise, and a new way of thinking about research and development. But, based on a decade of experience with the CRSP model, the firm consensus is that it is well worth the effort. The ultimate reward is better research, whether social or non-social, and certainly better "development" for the human groups to whom these efforts are directed.

The hope is that this volume will promote increased understanding of the value of anthropology and sociology/rural sociology, not as disciplinary isolates but yoked with other concerned sciences to combat the ever more pressing problems of global hunger and malnutrition.[10] Our aim will have been achieved if this book speaks in comprehensible and actionable ways to those who formulate, design, and direct development assistance; to biological/technical scientists who are members of interdisciplinary teams; to academic social scientists who would like to better understand the work of their development-oriented colleagues and to instruct their students in this exciting and growing area; and to individuals of all fields who may be planning careers in international development.

NOTES

Preparation of this chapter was supported by the USAID Title XII Small Ruminant Collaborative Research Support Program under Grant No. DAN-1328-G-SS-4093-00 through the SR-CRSP Sociology Project. Additional support was provided by the University of Missouri-Columbia. The author would like to thank Mike Nolan, Jere Gilles, Patricia Vondal, and especially Alessandro Bonanno for their helpful comments on a draft of the chapter. All sins of omission or commission are, of course, the author's own.

1. Throughout this chapter, *agriculture* should be understood as referring to four component areas: production, transformation (processing for storage, consumption, sale, etc.), consumption (including nutrition), and distribution (marketing or other forms of exchange). Also note that, when used in reference to a CRSP, *project* and *program* denote distinct levels of operation; in other contexts, however, these terms are used interchangeably. Finally, *R & D* signifies the full range of scientific activity, from basic through applied research to technology development, assessment, and dissemination, as well as the intellectual, planning, or policy decisions that give rise to these activities.

2. As in any agricultural R&D effort, economics has formed an indispensable part of the CRSPs, often working in close conjunction with anthropology and sociology. Hence, many of its contributions are documented here (see especially Chapters 8, 10, and 16). However, for the purposes of this volume, economics has been classed as a technical science. This heuristic finds a precedent in the Rockefeller Foundation report (1977:2) that "for the sake of simplicity . . . adopts the frequent Latin convention of classifying the 'social' sciences as separate from the 'economic' ones." (Of course, anthropology and sociology are "technical sciences" as well, in that they have their own methodologies, subject matter specialities, and so forth.)

3. In large part, this is a result of sociologists' early and extensive

attention to the study of adoption and diffusion of agricultural technology. The classic example is Rogers 1983.

4. Although policy analysis and disciplinary theory building are not a central theme of this book, in the broadest sense they constitute the ultimate mandate of the social sciences in truly international (i.e., domestic as well as foreign, First as well as Third World) agricultural R&D. Rural sociologists in particular have spoken to this urgent need for a global and policy-relevant "sociology of agriculture." For a sampling of some of this cutting-edge work, see Bonanno 1989; Busch and Lacy 1983, 1986; Buttel et al. forthcoming; Christenson 1988; Friedland et al. forthcoming; Friedmann and McMichael 1989; Goodman and Redclift 1982; Kloppenburg 1988; Newby 1983; van der Ploeg 1989; various publications of the Institute for Food and Development Policy; and the journal *Agriculture and Human Values*, notably 4(1) and 5(1-2).

5. For anthropology, see, e.g., Eddy and Partridge 1987, Grillo 1985, or Hoben 1982. Falk and Gilbert 1985 reference some of these tensions for rural sociology, although that discipline's origins as an applied science generate different concerns from those of anthropology.

6. A large and growing collection of anthologies, monographs, and articles present studies that illustrate the contributions of agriculture to social science research and theory. At the same time, this body of literature also suggests many of the contributions of anthropology and sociology to agricultural R&D, albeit often only implicitly. These studies are far too numerous to list here. However, a few representative examples of recent anthologies focusing exclusively or largely on anthropology and agricultural development include Barlett 1980, Bennett and Bowen 1988, Brokensha et al. 1980, Grillo and Rew 1985, Jones and Wallace 1986, Smith and Reeves 1989, and the monograph series of the Institute for Development Anthropology and of the Society for Economic Anthropology. Many sociologists have also published in these volumes. For some suggestive syntheses and useful bibliographies, see Bennett 1988, Buttel 1987, 1989, and Campbell and Campbell 1986.

7. A distinction is commonly drawn between multi- and interdisciplinary R&D. In the former, disciplinary research is conducted more or less independently, with results then aggregated or merged in some fashion across disciplines. In the latter, teams of scientists from diverse fields work together in a specific locale or on a specific problem. The CRSPs offer examples of both approaches (see Chapter 16). For the sake of simplicity, however, "interdisciplinary" is employed throughout this introduction.

8. Specifically for the social sciences in agricultural and natural resource development, see, e.g., Brady 1984, Brush 1986, Campbell et al. 1981, DeWalt and DeWalt 1985, Esslinger and McCorkle 1985, McArthur 1987, and Messerschmidt 1988, along with the references cited at the outset of this chapter.

9. It is noteworthy that at least two international conferences on interdisciplinary R&D have been held, and a new pandisciplinary association devoted to this subject is planned (see, e.g., Chubin et al. 1986 and Epton et al. 1983).

10. Although the focus here is on agricultural R&D, virtually all of the social science roles and contributions outlined in these pages apply *mutatis mutandis* to other development arenas as well.

REFERENCES

Almy, Susan W. 1977. Anthropologists and Development Agencies. *American Anthropologist* 79(2):280–292.

Appleby, Gordon. 1988. Personal communications with McCorkle on the variety of techniques and methodological refinements emerging from social scientists' increasing involvement in development work.

Barlett, Peggy F. (ed.). 1980. *Agricultural Decision Making: Anthropological Contributions to Rural Development*. New York and London: Academic.

Bennett, John W. 1988. Anthropology and Development: The Ambiguous Engagement. In *Production and Autonomy: Anthropological Studies and Critiques of Development*. Monographs in Economic Anthropology No. 5. John W. Bennett and John R. Bowen, eds., pp. 1–29. Lanham, MD: University Press of America.

Bennett, John W., and John R. Bowen (eds.). 1988. *Production and Autonomy: Anthropological Studies and Critiques of Development*. Monographs in Economic Anthropology No. 5. Lanham, MD: University Press of America.

Bonanno, Alessandro. 1989. *Sociology of Agriculture: Labor, Technology and Development in an International Perspective*. New Delhi and London: Concept Publishing.

Bowen, John R. 1988. Power and Meaning in Economic Change: What Does Anthropology Learn from Development Studies? In *Production and Autonomy: Anthropological Studies and Critiques of Development*. Monographs in Economic Anthropology No. 5. John W. Bennett and John R. Bowen, eds., pp. 411–430. Lanham, MD: University Press of America.

Brady, Nyle C. 1984. Title XII in Retrospect and Prospect. *The Rural Sociologist* 4(4):269–277.

Brokensha, David, D. M. Warren, and Oswald Werner (eds.) 1980. *Indigenous Knowledge Systems and Development*. Lanham, MD: University Press of America.

Brush, Stephen B. 1986. Basic and Applied Research in Farming Systems: An Anthropologist's Appraisal. *Human Organization* 45(3):220–228.

Busch, Lawrence, and William B. Lacy. 1983. *Science, Agriculture, and the Politics of Research*. Boulder: Westview Press.

Busch, Lawrence, and William B. Lacy (eds.). 1986. *The Agricultural Scientific Enterprise*. Boulder: Westview Press.

Buttel, Frederick H. 1987. The Rural Social Sciences: An Overview of Research Institutions, Tools, and Knowledge for Addressing Problems and Issues. *Agriculture and Human Values* 4(1):42–65.

———. 1989. The Sociology of Agriculture: Current Conceptual Status. *The Rural Sociologist* 9(2):16–31.

Buttel, F. H., O. F. Larson, and G. W. Gillespie, Jr. Forthcoming. *The Sociology of Agriculture*. Wesport, CT: Greenwood.

Byerlee, Derek, and Robert Tripp. 1988. Strengthening Linkages in Agricultural Research Through a Farming Systems Perspective: The Role of Social Scientists. *Experimental Agriculture* 24(2):137–151.

Campbell, Mary F., and Rex R. Campbell. 1986. *Sociology of Agriculture Bibliography, 1975–1985*. Columbia, MO: University of Missouri, Department of Rural Sociology, College of Agriculture, UMC Extension, and the Missouri Agricultural Experiment Station.

Campbell, Rex R., Michael F. Nolan, and John F. Galliher 1981. Reflection on Title XII: The Case of Sociology in the Small-Ruminants Collaborative Research Support Program. *The Rural Sociologist* 1(1):2–10.

Cernea, Michael M. (ed.). 1985. *Putting People First: Sociological Variables in Rural Development*. New York: Oxford University Press, for The World Bank.

Cernea, Michael M., and Scott Guggenheim. n.d. Is Anthropology Superfluous in Farming Systems Research? Paper distributed at the 1985 FSR&E Symposium, Kansas State University, Manhattan, KS.

Chambers, Erve. 1987. Applied Anthropology in the Post-Vietnam Era: Anticipations and Ironies. *Annual Review of Anthropology* 16:309–407.

Christenson, James A. 1988. Social Risk and Rural Sociology. *Rural Sociology* 53(1):1–24.

Chubin, Daryl E., Alan L. Porter, Frederick A. Rossini, and Terry Connolly (eds.). 1986. *Interdisciplinary Analysis and Research: Theory and Practice of Problem-Focused Research and Development*. Mt. Airy, MD: Lomond.

Cock, James H. 1979. Biologists and Economists in Bongoland. In *Economics and the Design of Small Farmer Technology*. Alberto Valdés, Grant Scobie, and John L. Dillon, eds., pp. 71–82 [with Comment by Reed Hertford]. Ames: Iowa State University Press.

Colfer, Carol J. Pierce. 1987. An Anthropologists [sic] Role in the Tropsoils Project. *FSSP Newsletter* 5(1):15–18.

DeWalt, Billie R. 1985. Anthropology, Sociology, and Farming Systems Research. *Human Organization* 44(2):1985.

DeWalt, Kathleen M., and Billie R. DeWalt. 1985. Issues in Training and Selection of Anthropologists in Multidisciplinary Settings. Paper presented to the Society for Applied Anthropology, 13–17 March, Washington, DC.

Eddy, Elizabeth M., and William L. Partridge (eds.). 1987. *Applied Anthropology in America*. New York: Columbia University Press.

Epton, S. R., R. L. Payne, and A. W. Pearson (eds.). 1983. *Managing Interdisciplinary Research*. New York: John Wiley & Sons.

Esslinger, Donald L., and Constance M. McCorkle. 1985. Communications in FSR Team-Building: The Interdisciplinary Research Team. In *Proceedings of Kansas State University's 1985 FSR&E Symposium—Management and Methodology*, pp. 158–175. Manhattan: Kansas State University.

Falk, William W., and Jess Gilbert. 1985. Bringing Rural Sociology Back In. *Rural Sociology* 50(4):561–577.

Flinn, William L. 1988. The Social Sciences in the Small Ruminant CRSP. Paper presented at the SR-CRSP Strategic Planning Conference, Raleigh, NC, 12–15 January.

Friedland, W. H., L. Busch, and F. H. Buttel (eds.). Forthcoming. *The New Political Economy of Agriculture*. Chapel Hill: North Carolina State University Press.

Friedmann, H., and P. McMichael. 1989. The World-Historical Development of Agriculture: Western Agriculture in Comparative Perspective. *Sociologia Ruralis* 19:in press.

Gilles, Jere L. 1982b. Planning Livestock Development: Themes from International Systems. *Agricultural Administration* 11:215–225.

———. 1982b. *The Sociology of Range Management: A Bibliography and Guide to the Literature*. CPL Bibliography No. 87. Chicago: Council of Planning Librarians.

————. (ed.). In progress. Pastures, People, and Productivity: Essays in the Sociology of Range Management.

Goodman, D., and M. Redclift. 1982. *From Peasant to Proletarian.* New York: St. Martin's.

Grillo, Ralph. 1985. Applied Anthropology in the 1980s: Retrospect and Prospect. In *Social Anthropology and Development Policy.* ASA Monographs 23. Ralph Grillo and Alan Rew, eds., pp. 1–36. London: Tavistock.

Grillo, Ralph, and Alan Rew (eds.). 1985. *Social Anthropology and Development Policy.* ASA Monographs 23. London: Tavistock.

Hamilton, James W. 1973. Problems in Government Anthropology. *Proceedings of the Southern Anthropological Society* 7:120–131.

Hammett, Ian. 1973. The Role of the Sociologist in Local Planning. *Journal of Development Studies* 9(4):493–507.

Hansen, David O., Paul Van Buren, and J. Mark Erbaugh. 1982. Sociology and the U.S. Agency for International Development: Contributions, Constraints, and Contradictions. *The Rural Sociologist* 2(3):154–162.

Heberlein, Thomas A. 1988. Improving Interdisciplinary Research: Integrating the Social and Natural Sciences. *Society and Natural Resources* 1(1):5–16.

Hoben, Allan. 1982. Anthropologists and Development. *Annual Review of Anthropology* 11:349–375.

Horowitz, Michael M. 1988. Anthropology and the New Development Agenda. *Development Anthropology Network* 6(1):1–4.

Horton, Douglas E. 1984. Social Scientists in Agricultural Research: Lessons from the Mantaro Valley Project, Peru. Ottawa: IDRC.

IRRI (ed.). 1982. Report of an Exploratory Workshop on the Role of Anthropologists and Other Social Scientists in Interdisciplinary Teams Developing Improved Food Production Technology. Los Baños, Phillipines: IRRI.

Jones, Jeffrey R., and Ben J. Wallace (eds.). 1986. *Social Sciences and Farming Systems Research: Methodological Perspectives on Agricultural Development.* Boulder: Westview Press.

Kloppenburg, Jack. 1988. *First the Seed.* New York: Cambridge University Press.

Knop, Ed, Maya ter Kuile, Willard Schmehl, and Mary Beebe. 1985. Making the Mixed-Discipline Farming System Model Work: Issues and Management Insights from U.S. and Egyptian Projects. Paper presented to the 1985 FSR&E Symposium—Management and Methodology, Kansas State University, Manhattan, KS.

Koppel, Bruce, and George Beal. 1983. Graduate Education for International Development: A Second Report on a Study of American Rural Sociology. *The Rural Sociologist* 3(1):2–10.

Kottak, Conrad Phillip. 1985. When People Don't Come First: Some Sociological Lessons from Completed Projects. In *Putting People First: Sociological Variables in Rural Development.* Michael M. Cernea, ed., pp. 325–356. New York: Oxford University Press, for The World Bank.

Lacy, William B. (ed.). 1985. Collection: The Roles of Sociologists in Two AID Programs. *The Rural Sociologist* 5(4):273–299. [Includes five articles on sociology in the Sorghum/Millet, Bean/Cowpea, Peanut, and Small Ruminant CRSPs plus the FSSP.]

Mathias-Mundy, Evelyn, and Constance M. McCorkle. Forthcoming. *Ethnoveterinary Medicine: An Annotated Bibliography.* Ames: Center for Indigenous Knowledge and Rural Development, Iowa State University.

McArthur, Harold J., Jr. 1987. The Role of Anthropologists in Agricultural Development: Process over Product. Paper presented to the Society for Applied Anthropology, 8–12 April, Oaxaca, Mexico.

McCorkle, Constance M. 1986. An Introduction to Ethnoveterinary Research and Development. *Journal of Ethnobiology* 6(1):129–149.

McCorkle, Constance M., and Jere L. Gilles. 1987. Stereotypes and Roles of Social Scientists in International Agricultural Development. *The Rural Sociologist* 7(3):216–224.

McCorkle, Constance M., Michael F. Nolan, Keith Jamtgaard, and Jere L. Gilles. 1989. Social Research in International Agricultural R&D: Lessons from the Small Ruminant CRSP. *Agriculture and Human Values* 6(3):in press.

Messerschmidt, Donald A. 1988. Social Science Activities in the F/FRED Project: A Background and Discussion Paper. Washington DC: Office of Rural and Institutional Development, Bureau for Science and Technology, USAID.

Michael Butler, Lorna. 1987. Contributions of Anthropologists and Sociologists to Farming Systems Research and Extension Teams. Paper presented to the Rural Sociological Society, 12–15 August, Madison, WI.

Miniclier, Louis. 1964. The Use of Anthropologists in the Foreign Aid Program. *Human Organization* 23(3):187–189.

Newby, Howard. 1983. The Sociology of Agriculture: Toward a New Rural Sociology. *Annual Review of Sociology* 9:67–81.

Nolan, Michael F. 1985. Lambs to the Slaughter or Wolves in Sheep's Clothing? Some Comments on the Role of Rural Sociology in International Agriculture Programs. In *Rural Sociologists at Work: A Festschrift for M.E. John.* Bob Bealer, ed., pp. 54–61. University Park, PA: The M. E. John Memorial Lecture Series Fund.

Rhoades, Robert E. 1983. *Breaking New Ground: Anthropology in Agricultural Research—The Case of the International Potato Center.* Lima: CIP.

———. 1984. *Breaking New Ground: Agricultural Anthropology.* Lima: CIP.

———. 1986. Using Anthropology in Improving Food Production: Problems and Prospects. *Agricultural Administration* 22:57–78.

Rhoades, Robert E., Douglas E. Horton, and Robert H. Booth. 1986. Anthropologist, Biological Scientist and Economist: The Three Musketeers or Three Stooges of Farming Systems Research? In *Social Sciences and Farming Systems Research: Methodological Perspectives on Agricultural Development.* Jeffrey R. Jones and Ben J. Wallace, eds., pp. 21–40. Boulder: Westview Press.

Rockefeller Foundation. 1977. Society, Culture, and Agriculture: A Workshop on Training Programs Combining Anthropology and Sociology with the Agricultural Sciences. New York: The Rockefeller Foundation.

Rogers, Everett M. 1983. *The Diffusion of Innovations.* New York: Free Press.

Schaedel, Richard P. 1964. Anthropology in AID Overseas Missions: Its Practical and Theoretical Potential. *Human Organization* 23(3):190–192.

Simmonds, Norman W. 1985. Farming Systems Research: A Review. World Bank Technical Report No. 83. Washington, DC: The World Bank.

Smith, Sheldon, and Ed Reeves (eds.). 1989. *Human Systems Ecology: Studies in the Integration of Political Economy, Adaptation, and Socionatural Regions.* Boulder: Westview Press.

van der Ploeg, J. D. 1989. *Labor Markets and Agricultural Production*. Boulder: Westview Press.

van Dusseldorp, D. B. W. M. 1977. Some Thoughts on the Role of Social Sciences in the Agricultural Research Centres in Developing Countries. *Netherlands Journal of Agricultural Science* 25:213–228.

van Willigen, John. 1986. *Applied Anthropology: An Introduction*. South Hadley, MA: Bergin & Garvey.

Zambia, Republic of, and CIMMYT (eds.). 1984. Report of an ARPT/CIMMYT Networkshop on the Role of Rural Sociology and Anthropology in Farming Systems Research and Extension. Networking Workshop Report No. 6. Chilanga, Zambia: Adaptive Research Planning Team, Ministry of Agriculture and Water Development, Mount Makulu Central Research Station.

1

Dilemmas of Opportunity: Social Sciences in CRSPs

Michele E. Lipner and Michael F. Nolan

Formal involvement of social scientists in agricultural development projects largely began in the late 1960s, after the first critical questions concerning the unanticipated social consequences of the green revolution were raised. Such works as *Blossoms in the Dust* by Kusum Nair (1961) stimulated inquiries as to whether purely technological approaches could solve world hunger problems. While recognizing that the green revolution had achieved enormous gains in food production, critics such as Nair also observed that it came at a rather large social cost. Coupled with some notable failures in other agricultural development projects, the "unanticipated consequences" of the green revolution caused development planners to look for ways to improve their track record. Sociologists and anthropologists came to be perceived as the "silver bullet" that would cure all development planning ills. Perhaps the apex of this wave of good feeling was reached in the 1970s when the U.S. Agency for International Development (USAID) began to require that all proposed USAID projects include an assessment of their economic and social soundness at the project paper stage. If nothing else, this provided a considerable number of employment opportunities for sociologists and anthropologists, as social soundness analyses were not something USAID was particularly adept at doing "in-house."

In the same period, Title XII and the Collaborative Research Support Programs (CRSPs) were initiated. They evolved from the changing directions of U.S. international development efforts in the early 1970s. At the time, policymakers and researchers were becoming increasingly aware that development efforts often overlooked the needs of small-scale farmers and the rural poor who compose the vast majority of the population in developing countries (DCs). Earlier models of international agricultural assistance, such as the modernization approach, emphasized technology transfer and diffusion. However, these approaches began to be perceived as increasing, rather than decreasing, the gaps between rich and poor and urban and rural sectors (Mickelwait et al. 1979). In 1973, in response to these concerns, Congress passed the New Directions mandate, which amended the Foreign Assistance Act of 1961.

The new legislation specified that more emphasis should be placed on "expanding their [the poor's] access to the economy through services and institutions at the local level, increasing labor-intensive production, spreading productive investment from major cities to small towns and outlying areas . . . by sharing American technical expertise, farm commodities and industrial goods and less on large-scale capital transfer" (Mickelwait et al. 1979:3). The implications of the mandate were twofold. First, the "poorest of the poor" were formally acknowledged and targeted for development programs. Second, there was a shift from technology transfer toward host country self-determination. As stated in Section 102, Chapter 1:

> United States bilateral development assistance should give the highest priority to undertakings submitted by host governments which directly improve the lives of the poorest of their people and their capacity to participate in the development of their countries (cited in Mickelwait et al. 1979:3).

New Directions represented a major step in expanding the scope and focus of development. Yet its larger significance perhaps lay in sensitizing U.S. foreign policy to host country needs and goals rather than imposing rigid guidelines on how development programs would or should be implemented. Within months of its passage, critics of the legislation (notably land grant universities) expressed concern that implementation still concentrated too heavily on capital transfer rather than on research and institution-building as intended in the mandate. Coupled with the concern that USAID budget reductions in the early 1970s were slowly diminishing university participation in development activities abroad, there was a concerted effort through legislative channels to reverse these trends and expand the parameters of development assistance (Comptroller General 1981).

This push for additional legislation had its roots in two institutions. First, there was a belief within USAID that world food problems could be solved only through basic research to create a new and/or expanded knowledge base of local conditions. Second, Congress moved to bring together the expertise of U.S. agricultural universities and USAID in implementing development assistance (Luykx 1978). Both initiatives were in part motivated by the success of the 1887 Hatch Act, which created the U.S. system of state agricultural experiment stations. The Hatch Act recognized the primacy of research in solving agricultural problems; it thus allocated federal funds to land grant universities to conduct research relevant to domestic agricultural issues. Using the Hatch Act as a model, support grew to mobilize the scientific and technical expertise of land grant institutions within a formal policy framework aimed at eliminating world hunger.

Along with a major lobbying effort by the land grant universities, these initiatives resulted in passage of the International Development and Food Assistance Act of 1975, formally submitted to Congress by Senator Hubert Humphrey and Representative Paul Findley. The Humphrey-Findley Bill amended the Foreign Assistance Act of 1961 by adding Title XII—Famine Prevention and Freedom from Hunger. Title XII specified:

> Congress declares that, in order to prevent famine and establish freedom from hunger, the United States should strengthen the capacities of United States land grant and other eligible universities in program-related agricultural institutional development and research, consistent with sections 103 and 103A, should improve their participation in the United States Government's international efforts to apply more effective agricultural sciences to the goal of increasing world food production, and in general should provide increased and longer term support to the application of science to solving food and nutrition problems of the developing countries (U.S. Congress 1975:23).

USAID was responsible for the overall administration of Title XII. To ensure adherence to the spirit of the legislation, however, Congress authorized the president to appoint a Board for International Food and Agricultural Development (BIFAD). The board would be a permanent participant in Title XII planning, program development, and budgeting. BIFAD became a fully functioning, seven-member unit in early 1977. Shortly thereafter, it created two advisory committees to implement Title XII policy. The Joint Research Committee (JRC) was responsible for all research to promote the discovery of new knowledge and the development of technology useful to DCs. The Joint Committee on Agricultural Development (JCAD)[1] was given responsibility for adapting research results and technology to the needs of developing countries. Title XII mandated the creation of collaborative research programs that addressed issues of food production, distribution, storage, marketing, and consumption. Thus, collaborative research fell under the purview of the JRC. In 1977, the JRC met to discuss how collaboration would be organized and managed. Its deliberations gave birth to the Collaborative Research Support Programs.

OVERVIEW OF THE CRSPs

The CRSPs were charged with creating structures to facilitate collaboration among U.S. land grant universities, USDA, international agricultural research centers (IARCs), DC institutions, and other research entities "on a problem-oriented basis in a common research and development program to solve a priority food and nutrition problem" (Hutchinson 1977:49).

While the JRC was granted authority to organize CRSPs, general guidelines were provided within the language of Title XII. Congress made it clear that this development mode should: be directly related to the food and agricultural needs of developing countries; be carried out within developing countries; be adapted to local circumstances; provide for the most effective interrelationship among research, education, and extension in promoting agricultural development in developing countries; and emphasize the improvement of local systems for delivering the best available knowledge to the small farmers of such countries (22nd U.S. Congress Section 220b (c), cited in Comptroller General 1981:3-4).

In the organizational phase of CRSPs, the JRC identified a number of priority research areas. As of 1987, eight such areas have been incorporated into fully functioning Collaborative Research Support Programs (Table 1.1). All are still operative, with the exception of the Nutrition CRSP, which was planned for only five years and is presently in a close-out stage. To date, 40 U.S. land and sea grant universities, as well as other institutions, have officially collaborated with 66 host country institutions in 30 countries.

Although each CRSP has a unique research agenda, they all share certain basic organizational assumptions. In the early 1970s, however, these assumptions represented major departures from USAID's previous research strategy. First, whereas earlier agricultural R&D programs had relied on

TABLE 1.1. ESTABLISHMENT OF THE COLLABORATIVE RESEARCH SUPPORT PROGRAMS

Program	Date Established	Funding through 1985[a] (in millions)
Small Ruminant	Oct 1978	45.2
Grain Sorghum/Pearl Millet	Jul 1979	34.0
Bean/Cowpea	Oct 1980	21.3
Tropical Soils Management	Sep 1981	19.9
Nutrition	Dec 1981	14.8
Peanut	Jul 1982	15.9
Pond Dynamics/Aquaculture	Sep 1982	5.6
Fisheries and Stock Assessment	Jul 1985	1.7

Source: NASULGC n.d.

[a]Includes AID, U.S., and host country contributions.

yearly budgetary allocations, CRSPs received firm 5-year budgetary commitments, with the opportunity for extensions. Thus, USAID formally recognized that research is not only vital to successful development, but also that it is long-term in nature. Second, as their name implies, CRSPs are collaborative ventures between and among scientists and researchers in U.S. universities, IARCs, and host country institutions. As part of this collaboration, U.S. participants are required to match 25% of the cost of any project funded by a CRSP. Similarly, host country institutions are expected to contribute to the cost of the research, either financially or in kind. Third, CRSPs are explicitly multidisciplinary, bringing together scientists from numerous social and biological fields in a cooperative working relationship with common objectives. Some sense of the breadth and depth of both the collaborative and the multidisciplinary foundations of CRSPs is given in the following overview of the five CRSPs represented in this volume.

ORGANIZATIONAL STRUCTURE OF CRSPs

Structurally, each CRSP is intended to be autonomous, with its own administrative board, a program director housed in a management entity (ME) office, and a technical advisory committee. While funds flow from USAID/Washington, resource allocation decisions are made by the CRSP participants. Thus, each CRSP reflects a complicated negotiation process among scientists and administrators from varying disciplines and institutions. A total of eight programs have emerged, all developed from the same mold, but with distinct personalities and agendas representing the concerns and interests of their project participants.

What follows is a brief summary of the technical and administrative structures of the five programs represented in this volume: the Small Ruminant, International Sorghum/Millet, Bean/Cowpea, Nutrition, and Peanut CRSPs. Only their *formal* multidisciplinary and collaborative relationships are overviewed (see Table 1.2). However, it should be noted that many other informal links exist that expand the scope of CRSP research and the potential for meaningful results. For instance, while one of the formal disciplinary components of the Small Ruminant CRSP (SR-CRSP) is rural sociology, anthropology also forms an integral part of the program's social science research. While the Sorghum/Millet CRSP has formal collaborative relationships with four host countries, plus the Centro Internacional de Agricultura Tropical (CIAT), in actuality, informal collaborative research projects are under way in over 13 DCs. Often informal collaborative relationships are as important as formal ones in realizing CRSP objectives.

In interpreting Table 1.2, some caution should be exercised. First, the columns in the table are ordered alphabetically and are independent of each other. Second, only very general structural comparisons can be made across CRSPs since each program has its own unique set of organizing principles. For example, the SR-CRSP was planned around four ecological zones, with any particular site having a complete array of discipline-based projects (e.g., a rural sociology project, an economics project, a veterinary health or range management project) deemed essential to study small ruminant production at that site. In this program, "projects" and "disciplines" are nearly synonymous. By contrast, other CRSPs tended to organize themselves around broadly framed projects that often included scientists from a number of disciplines. Such projects might well be the only ones operating at a particular overseas site. Thus, while Table 1.2 and the following summary descriptions[2] capture certain key organizational structures of the various CRSPs, the reader should refer to individual CRSP publications for more detail about how sites, disciplines, projects, and institutions are melded into a coherent program.

Small Ruminant CRSP

The goal of the SR-CRSP is to improve milk, meat, and fiber production of sheep, goats, and alpaca in order to increase the food supply and raise the income of smallholders in developing countries. The scope of work is organized by production systems (intensive versus extensive) and ecological zones. Based on these considerations, research activities have been developed in five countries. In the program planning stage, it was determined that research should include all disciplinary aspects of the production process— from animal genetics and reproduction studies aimed at improving local breeds, to feasibility studies aimed at determining socioeconomic constraints on improving small ruminant production and utilization. At its height, the SR-CRSP included 10 disciplines and 13 U.S. institutions. However, recent funding cuts have curtailed activities both in the United States and abroad. Only one SR-CRSP discipline operates across all five sites: sociology. Others are involved in specific projects in one or more countries.

On an administrative level, each participating U.S. institution is responsible for at least one disciplinary component of the research agenda. Each also has a principal investigator (PI), who oversees the conduct of her/his disciplinary research at home and abroad. In the case of institutions housing two disciplinary activities, PIs are assigned to each research component. A technical committee (TC) is responsible for addressing research concerns and making recommendations to the program board concerning budgetary matters. The committee consists of one PI from each SR-CRSP discipline. The board is composed of one member from each participating U.S. institution and host country. Within this framework, the social science component has full participatory privileges with its

TABLE 1.2. FORMAL ORGANIZATIONAL COMPONENTS OF THE FIVE CRSPs[a]

U.S. Institutions	Disciplinary Areas	Host Countries

Small Ruminant CRSP -- University of California-Davis, ME

U.S. Institutions	Disciplinary Areas	Host Countries
U. of California-Davis	Agricultural Economics	Brazil
California Polytechnic U.	Animal Breeding and Genetics	Indonesia
Colorado State U.	Animal Health	Kenya
U. of Missouri-Columbia	Animal Nutrition	Morocco
Montana State U.	By-products and Nutrition	Peru
North Carolina State U.	Production Systems	
Ohio State U.	Range Management	
Texas A&M U.	Reproductive Physiology	
Texas Tech U.	Rural Sociology	
Tuskegee Institute	Systems Analysis	
Utah State U.		
Washington State U.		
Winrock International		

INTSORMIL -- University of Nebraska, ME

U.S. Institutions	Disciplinary Areas	Host Countries
U. of Arizona	Agronomy/Physiology	Botswana
Kansas State U.	Economics	Honduras
U. of Kentucky	Entomology	Niger
Mississippi State U.	Food Quality and Utilization	Sudan
U. of Nebraska	Plant Breeding	
Purdue U.	Plant Pathology	
Texas A&M U.	Sociology/Anthropology	

Bean/Cowpea CRSP -- Michigan State University, ME

U.S. Institutions	Disciplinary Areas	Host Countries
Boyce Thompson Institute for Plant Research	Agronomics	Botswana
	Economics	Brazil
U. of California-Davis	Entomology	Cameroon
U. of California-Riverside	Food Technology/	Dominican Rep.
Colorado State U.	Nutrition	Ecuador
Cornell U.	Genetics and Plant Breeding	Guatemala
U. of Georgia	Sociology and Anthropology	Honduras
Michigan State U.		Kenya
U. of Nebraska		Malawi
U. of Puerto Rico		Mexico
Washington State U.		Nigeria
U. of Wisconsin		Senegal
		Tanzania

Nutrition CRSP -- University of California-Berkeley, ME

U.S. Institutions	Disciplinary Areas	Host Countries
U. of California-Berkeley	Anthropology	Egypt
U. of California-Los Angeles	Data Management	Kenya
U. of Connecticut	Medicine	Mexico
Purdue U.	Nutrition	
(U. of Arizona)	Psychology	
(U. of Kansas)		

Peanut CRSP -- University of Georgia, ME

U.S. Institutions	Disciplinary Areas	Host Countries
Alabama A&M U.	Breeding and Cultural	Burkina Faso
U. of Georgia	Practices	Caribbean
North Carolina State U.	Entomology	Niger
Texas A&M U.	Food Technology	Nigeria
(Purdue U.)	Plant Pathology	Philippines
	Socioeconomics	Senegal
		Sudan
		Thailand

[a]All institutions, disciplines, and host countries that have been formally
involved in the five CRSPs at any point in the life of the programs are
listed. Items in parentheses represent subcontractor institutions.

biologically oriented counterparts, on both the technical and administrative bodies governing SR-CRSP activities.

International Sorghum/Millet CRSP

The primary objective of INTSORMIL is to develop technology for increasing the production and utilization of grain sorghum and pearl millet worldwide. To this end, both formal and informal collaborative research activities have been initiated around seven multidisciplinary objectives involving eight U.S. universities and 17 host country institutions. Formal collaborative relationships have been established with four host countries and with CIAT, which conducts agronomic research throughout Central and South America. Since INTSORMIL's inception in 1979, research agendas have been modified and budgetary constraints have reduced both the number and disciplines of program participants. Yet, INTSORMIL continues to stress the need for multidisciplinary research and multi-institutional input to alleviate major constraints to improved sorghum and millet production.

Administratively, technical and operational concerns are addressed by a committee composed of representatives from each disciplinary component that is active in the program at the time. Thus, all disciplines are fully integrated into the decision-making process. The program board is comprised of one member from each participating institution. An added committee, the Ecological Zone Council, plans and implements identified host country and U.S. collaborative research activities based on ecogeographic zones. The council consists of one representative from each zone with ongoing INTSORMIL activities, plus one member at large. In sum, the administrative bodies of INTSORMIL are structured so as to integrate and give full voice to disciplinary, institutional, and host country concerns. Although the social sciences are presently being phased out of the International Sorghum/Millet CRSP, historically they have been structurally incorporated into the administrative process.

Bean/Cowpea CRSP

The primary goal of the Bean/Cowpea CRSP is to improve the availability and utilization of beans and cowpeas in DCs. The University of Puerto Rico, the Boyce Thompson Institute for Plant Research, and nine other U.S. institutions have taken the lead in developing collaborative research programs in 13 host countries, primarily in Africa and Latin America. In addition, collaborative research has been carried out with the Instituto de Nutrición de Centroamérica y Panamá (INCAP), the International Institute of Tropical Agriculture (IITA), and CIAT. Originally, 18 priority projects involving six disciplines were identified and implemented in 13 host countries. Presently,

13 research projects are in operation, three of which focus on social science issues (Ferguson this volume).

The Bean/Cowpea CRSP has rotating membership on a technical committee, and a board to direct program activities. The committee is comprised of seven members—five from participating U.S. institutions, one host country representative, and a grain legume specialist from either CIAT or IITA. The board is composed of five U.S. institutional participants representing disciplinary concerns of the program. While membership is rotated, certain disciplines are given a permanent voice in decisionmaking: food technology/nutrition, entomology, and crop production. Within this framework, the interests of the social sciences are represented on the technical committee by a Women in Development (WID) coordinator from Michigan State University who holds ex officio status.

Nutrition CRSP

Unlike the other seven CRSPs, the Nutrition CRSP was designed as a terminal 5-year program. It focuses on issues related to marginal human food intake in DCs characterized by different subsistence commodity foods. Nutrition CRSP studies follow a standardized research design overseen by four U.S. universities across three sites. Five functional research components are included in the program design: resistance to disease, reproductive lactation, work productivity, cognitive development, and social competency. This CRSP is expected to yield results that will determine whether comparable human nutrition problems exist across regions. Also, findings from the Nutrition CRSP should prove instrumental in helping set food policy in DCs.

Technical matters pertaining to the Nutrition CRSP are addressed by the Scientific Coordination Board, composed of one representative from each host country and U.S. institution, including subcontractors. Since each site is allocated one vote on the board, unlike INTSORMIL and the SR-CRSP, emphasis is placed on site rather than disciplinary concerns when technical issues must be resolved.

Peanut CRSP

The primary goal of the Peanut CRSP is to maximize the production and utilization of peanuts in DCs. To this end, the program planning entity identified 13 constraints to peanut production, targeting six as priority research concerns. Twelve projects involving five disciplinary domains have been initiated in Africa, Latin America, the Caribbean, and Southeast Asia. Four U.S. universities serve as lead institutions on the Peanut CRSP. Unlike the other four CRSPs described here, the social sciences were never considered a separate disciplinary component of the Peanut CRSP. Rather, social science activities were integrated into the food science component at Alabama A&M University or initiated under a separate contractual agreement between Purdue University and the ME office at the University of Georgia.

The Technical Committee of the Peanut CRSP is composed of the PIs from each lead U.S. university. The board is likewise composed of one representative from each participating U.S. university. Within this framework, the PI from Alabama A&M is the principal spokesperson for the social sciences. However, in order to ensure that the social sciences have a voice in program decisionmaking, the outside review team that evaluates the progress of the Peanut CRSP includes a social scientist.

SOCIAL SCIENCES IN THE CRSPs

The multidisciplinary structure of CRSPs arguably represents one of their greatest assets. This approach to international agricultural R&D implies that truly effective development must utilize expertise from many different fields. It assumes that study of "the whole" must include its many parts; conversely, study of a part must take into account the whole. Thus, whether the research topic be small ruminants or human nutrition, useful results can be achieved only by examining all factors—sociological, biological, technological, economic—that may impede or encourage change.

The success of the CRSPs in incorporating the multidisciplinary concept into their research agendas has been variable. Clearly, such integration takes time and patience on the part of researchers and administrators alike. While individuals are willing to commit themselves to a concept and an ideal, actual implementation often requires negotiation and compromise, as a number of the chapters in this volume attest. Even prior to the birth of CRSPs, this issue has been particularly relevant for sociologists and anthropologists. Proving that their disciplines are worthy of an equal partnership with biological sciences in international agricultural programs has taken years, and the process is still incomplete. However, the CRSP mode of agricultural research has gone far toward demonstrating, refining, and institutionalizing the need for multidisciplinary work. Moreover, it has offered social scientists more, and more varied, opportunities than did many technical assistance programs in the past.

As the preceding section has suggested, the social sciences have been incorporated into the individual CRSPs in several different ways. The first two CRSPs (Small Ruminant, Sorghum/Millet) were constructed with explicit social science projects built into the program plan. Some of the later CRSPs (e.g., Peanut, Bean/Cowpea) included social science components as part of more broadly framed biological projects. This distinction is not trivial. If incorporated as separate and autonomous entities with their own subgrants, social science projects are automatically accorded a certain visibility and institutional status. The principal investigator on such projects is therefore a member of the program technical committee, and her/his institution is represented on the CRSP's governing board. This status does not automatically accrue to the social sciences when they form subcomponents of other projects. Structurally, when social sciences are accorded full project standing, they enjoy more legitimacy and power. Yet, as components that cannot themselves produce new technology, CRSP social science projects are particularly vulnerable to reduction or elimination when budgets shrink.

The roles of sociologists and anthropologists within the CRSP structure were not clearly defined at the outset. In part, this is due to the fact that social impacts are so much more difficult to anticipate, measure, and predict than, say, economic or agronomic effects. To illustrate from the SR-CRSP's experience, the pervasive view in the program's early stages was that social scientists' primary responsibility was to determine how best to transfer biological scientists' innovations to the limited resource farmer (McCorkle and Gilles 1987, Nolan 1985). Only with persistence and persuasion did this view change, ultimately evolving into a recognition that the production of research innovations should itself be informed by social science research. In those early days, all SR-CRSP scientists, social and biological alike, tended to see the world very much through disciplinary blinders. It was not until members of each discipline gained some degree of self-assurance that we began to function more as a team on projects, rather than merely as a collection of representatives of disciplines competing for scarce resources.

For example, SR-CRSP biological scientists working in Peru initially concentrated their efforts on small ruminant production systems associated with large cooperatives. However, research by SR-CRSP social scientists, who were working in peasant communities (where the poorest of the poor reside) revealed that peasant systems of animal husbandry were very different from those of cooperatives. Moreover, SR-CRSP sociologists demonstrated that peasant communities accounted for more than half of the total small ruminant production in Peru (Jamtgaard 1986). These findings were communicated to the other program scientists, and research activities were subsequently reoriented to give more attention to community production systems. Establishing this kind of constructive dialogue between social and biological scientists early in the program resulted in greater agreement on the appropriateness of research topics vis-à-vis the CRSP mandate to improve the well-being of small producers.

As CRSPs matured, social scientists also came to play an increasingly important role in what can be termed "integration," or the interpretation of research results within a broader production context. On the SR-CRSP, the reason for this was very simple: the animal scientists, by and large, were not particularly sensitive to production issues beyond the animal units they were studying. In general, the biological scientists were all specialists in livestock-related disciplines such as range management, veterinary medicine, animal breeding, genetics, or nutrition. Thus, they tended to ignore the plant-crop components in farming systems. Yet, farmers routinely make trade-offs among crops, livestock, and human resources. It fell to SR-CRSP sociologists and anthropologists to ensure that the *whole* farming system was clearly conceptualized, particularly insofar as cultivation impacted on the livestock sector, and to determine the dynamics of trade-offs between the two (Primov 1982).

For example, social scientists provided an early insight into the farming system of Andean agropastoral communities. They found that one of the primary purposes of small ruminant production systems was to maximize the production of collectable manure rather than wool or meat (Jamtgaard 1984, McCorkle 1983). This meant that in contemplating possible changes in the production system, biological scientists needed to take cognizance of what the farmers were trying to achieve. For example, a range management strategy that called for animals to graze far from the community would probably have little chance of being adopted because the herds could not be returned to a family corral at night to deposit their manure for later collection.

In the same vein, social scientists were often called upon to coordinate the testing and implementation of new technologies in the field. Because the research of biological scientists tended to be "station oriented," social scientists were among the first to collect data directly from farmers and to act as a bridge between the on-station biological work and the small farm setting. Later, when on-farm testing of biological innovations commenced, social scientists played a pivotal role in establishing a mechanism for testing and evaluating results. Often it was their responsibility to establish lines of communication among the biological scientists as well as between the biological scientists and the farming communities in which the on-farm research was to be done. For example, coordination of village farmer meetings on the SR-CRSP in Indonesia was the responsibility of the collaborating in-country sociologist (Knipscheer and Suradisastra 1986).

This multiplicity of integrative, communicative, and evaluative roles (McCorkle et al. forthcoming) leads to what is probably the greatest dilemma faced by social scientists within programs such as the CRSP: the types of knowledge they are asked to produce.

SOCIAL SCIENCE, BIOLOGICAL SCIENCE, AND KNOWLEDGE PRODUCTION

Following Bonnen (1986:5), three broad types of knowledge resulting from scientific research can be identified. The first, "disciplinary knowledge," consists of theory and methods used to explain the fundamental class of phenomena of concern to such disciplines as physics, botany, economics, and philosophy. It serves to push back the frontiers of knowledge in that discipline. The second, "subject-matter knowledge," is multidisciplinary information useful to decisionmakers in solving a set of problems. This type of knowledge is organized under such headings as marketing, animal nutrition, or farm management. Most departments in colleges of agriculture are organized around subject-matter knowledge systems. Finally, "problem-solving knowledge" intervenes between subject-matter knowledge and decisionmaking. As Bonnen writes:

> Before even multidisciplinary, subject matter knowledge has direct relevance to a specific problem, it must be fashioned into multidisciplinary, problem solving knowledge . . . i.e., "should" or "ought" statements to which knowledge of values is essential (1986:5).

The gulf between disciplinary or even subject-matter research objectives and problem-solving (programmatic) research objectives is especially large for social scientists within CRSPs, although it impacts biological scientists as well. While R&D programs may seek to blend the three knowledge types, it is our impression that CRSP biological scientists have been more successful than have social scientists in melding disciplinary and problem-solving research goals. Even where this has not been possible, as in studies on the genetic origins of prolificacy in sheep, the biological scientists have consistently devoted a higher percentage of their budgets to research agendas that produce disciplinary or subject-matter knowledge versus only problem-solving knowledge.

By contrast, because of the multiplicity of roles explicitly and implicitly assigned to them, social scientists have found it difficult, if not impossible, to engage in disciplinary or even subject-matter research. Politically, this has been difficult because of the relatively weak position of social science projects within most CRSP research and administrative structures. This sometimes required social scientists to forsake their own scientific interests for the interest of the program. In some CRSPs, social scientists became increasingly identified as key actors in the process of on-farm testing and evaluation; hence a greater proportion of their budgets was allocated to these activities. On the SR-CRSP, discussions have even been held as to whether it is the intrinsic role of the sociology project to pull together "technology packages" combining the research of all disciplines working at a particular site. Yet, such program goals and research expenditures often do not contribute to any disciplinary goals that the social science projects might have had at the outset. Opportunities for publication and disciplinary recognition deriving from these kinds of activities are correspondingly limited since they are often seen as insufficiently academic.

The challenge for both biological and social scientists within this organizational framework is to understand each other's motivations and to reach some agreement on appropriate program responsibilities. This can be accomplished only through dialogue and negotiation. The perception of some biological scientists that social scientists should play a "service" role in what is essentially "their project" clearly must be altered. Likewise, social scientists must be willing to work with biological scientists to understand their disciplinary perspectives and to act as guides to contextualize their work within the "human" experience. Meeting biological scientists at their own level is essential so that social scientists can be effective. This implies a rudimentary knowledge of biological terminology, research methods, and approaches to problem solving. In addition, both groups will need to surrender some of their disciplinary objectives for the greater problem-solving goals of the program.

CONCLUSION

After nearly a decade's work with CRSPs, it seems appropriate to ask how and if the social sciences have made a difference. Unfortunately, the answers are not straightforward; and they involve considerable post hoc analysis and anecdotal information. Moreover, the question can be posed at multiple levels—e.g., research, training, institution-building, and program or project versus personal levels.

It is difficult to cite examples wherein one piece of sociological research directly altered the course of a biological project. On the SR-CRSP, however, we believe that the sustained interaction of our Sociology Project team with program biological scientists has redirected the work of the latter in significant ways, causeing them to look at issues that might otherwise have been ignored. In many respects, however, we feel our greatest contribution has been to stimulate contact between biological scientists and farmers. In a number of cases, this has been an eye-opening experience for both groups.

A further evaluation question is: How can we effectively measure our contribution to institutional development? In the case of the SR-CRSP, a social science research unit has been established in every collaborating host country with which we are working. Although often understaffed, the creation of such units nonetheless marks a significant step in the direction that host country research programs are likely to take in the future. This could be one of the most lasting contributions of the CRSP social science projects.

Additional evaluation questions deserve consideration. First, as a result of participation in CRSPs, have we, as social scientists enhanced our credibility within our home institutions and colleges of agriculture? Have we, as a group, developed skills in working with biological scientists on other international or domestic food production issues? Finally, how has the CRSP experience impacted our own long-term career development?

In reflecting on our experience, it is relatively easy to remember the countless frustrations, the incredible amount of time invested in initiating any overseas work, and the inadequate resources we had to fulfill the responsibilities given to us. But when we ask ourselves whether we made a difference, it is people and professional linkages we must first think about. On the SR-CRSP, the relationships our project team has developed with biological researchers, host country scientists, USAID mission personnel, and the students who have come to study at our U.S. universities, as well as our continuing ties within the Sociology Project team, are among our most enduring contributions. While we may never know for certain whether we as social scientists have exerted an influence on all aspects of our CRSP, we do know that the CRSP certainly had a major influence on us. In some cases, it radically altered the careers of some program social scientists, launching them in new directions they had not previously considered.

In a more positive vein, we believe we *have* stimulated our biological science colleagues to recognize that "bringing people in" to commodity-oriented projects increases their chance of success. Certainly this is the case within the SR-CRSP. It is easier now than it was five or six years ago to sell such concepts as farming systems research, on-farm testing, and studies determining who benefits. In sum, our contributions clearly consist of more than just a change in our personal worldviews. The chapters in this volume seek to document these contributions in a variety of contexts. It is hoped they will allow those who follow us to learn from our experience and perhaps, too, from a few of our mistakes.

NOTES

Preparation of this chapter was conducted under USAID Title XII Grant No. DAN-1328-G-SS-4093-00, with additional support from the University of Missouri-Columbia. Both authors share equal responsibility and credit for the information and insights presented in this chapter.
1. In 1982, the JRC and JCAD merged into the Joint Committee on Agricultural Research and Development (JCARD).

2. Information regarding the five CRSPs was obtained from the following sources: for the SR-CRSP, Blond n.d.; for INTSORMIL, Winn n.d. and personal communications with Joan Frederick, administrative officer for the ME; for the Bean/Cowpea CRSP, the 1984 Annual Report (ME, eds.) and personal communications with Ann Ferguson, WID Coordinator at MSU, and Barbara Webster, PI at the Department of Agronomy and Range Science, UCD; for the Nutrition CRSP, NASILGC n.d. and personal communications with AID/Washington Program Officer Samuel Kahn; and for the Peanut CRSP, the ME's 1987 report on program years 6, 7, and 8, and personal communication with Program Director Tommy Nakayama.

REFERENCES

Bean/Cowpea CRSP ME. n.d. 1984 Annual Report. East Lansing: Bean/Cowpea CRSP, ME. Michigan State University.

Blond, R. D. (ed.). n.d. Partners in Research: A Five Year Report of the Small Ruminant Collaborative Research Support Program. Davis, CA: SR-CRSP ME, University of California–Davis.

Bonnen, James T. 1986. A Century of Science in Agriculture: The Lessons for Science Policy. Fellows Lecture, American Association of Agricultural Economics, Reno, NV.

Comptroller General. 1981. AID and Universities Have Yet to Forge an Effective Partnership to Combat World Food Problems. Report to the Congress of the United States, No. ID 82-3. Washington, DC: GAO.

Hutchinson, F. E. 1977. The Role of the Joint Research Committee (JRC) in Serving the Board for International Food and Agricultural Development. In *Proceedings of the Conference: The U.S. University and Title XII*. Olga Stavrakis and Sally Nelson, eds., pp. 47–53. St. Paul: University of Minnesota.

Jamtgaard, Keith. 1984. Limits on Common Pasture Use in an Agro-Pastoral Community: The Case of Toqra, Peru. SR-CRSP Technical Report No. 42. Columbia: Department of Rural Sociology, University of Missouri.

————. 1986. Agropastoral Production Systems in Peruvian Peasant Communities. In *Selected Proceedings of Kansas State University's 1986 Farming Systems Research Symposium—Farming Systems Research and Extension: Food and Feed*, pp. 751–765. Manhattan, KS: Kansas State University.

Knipscheer, H. C., and K. Suradisastra. 1986. Farmer Participation in Indonesian Livestock Farming Systems by Regular Research Field Hearings (RRFH). *Agricultural Administration* 22:205–216.

Luykx, Nicholas. 1978. *Title XII Famine Prevention and Freedom From Hunger*. Washington, DC: Bureau for Development Support, AID.

McCorkle, Constance M. 1983. The Technoenvironmental Dialectics of Herding in Andean Agropastoralism. SR-CRSP Technical Report No. 30. Columbia: Department of Rural Sociology, University of Missouri.

McCorkle, C. M., and Jere L. Gilles. 1987. Stereotypes and Roles of Social Scientists in International Agricultural Development. *The Rural Sociologist* 7(3):216–224.

McCorkle, Constance M., Michael F. Nolan, Keith Jamtgaard, and Jere L. Gilles in press. Social Research in International Agricultural R&D: Lessons from the Small Ruminant CRSP. *Agriculture and Human Values*.

Mickelwait, Donald R., Charles F. Sweet, and Elliott R. Morss. 1979. *New Directions in Development: A Study of U.S. AID*. Boulder: Westview Press.

Nair, Kusum. 1961. *Blossoms in the Dust*. New York: Praeger.

NASULGC (National Association of State Universities and Land Grant Colleges). n.d. *Partners in Agricultural Research . . . U.S. Universities and Developing Countries. Collaborative Research Support Programs (CRSP)*. Washington, DC: NASULGC.

Nolan, Michael F. 1985. An Overview of Sociology in the Small Ruminant CRSP. *The Rural Sociologist* 5(4):280–284.

Peanut CRSP ME. 1987. Peanut Collaborative Research Support Program (CRSP): Program for Years 6, 7, and 8. Georgia Experiment Station: University of Georgia.

Primov, George. 1982. Small Ruminant Production in the Sertão of Ceará, Brazil: A Sociological Analysis. SR-CRSP Technical Report No. 15. Columbia: Department of Rural Sociology, University of Missouri.

U.S. Congress. 1975. International Development and Food Assistance Act. Report No. 94-442 to accompany H.R. 9005, 94th Congress, First Session. Sections 296–300. Washington, DC: Committee of the Whole House.

Winn, Judy F. n.d. INTSORMIL: Fighting Hunger with Research. Lincoln, NE: INTSORMIL ME.

PART 1

Sorghum/Millet CRSP

2

Halfway There: Social Science *in* Agricultural Development and the Social Science *of* Agricultural Development

Billie R. DeWalt

This chapter examines the contribution of the social sciences to international agricultural development efforts and suggests ways in which this contribution might be enhanced. Although there has been substantial progress involving agricultural economics in the agricultural R&D process, the full value of social research in this realm has still to be recognized. A social science *of* agricultural development has not yet been incorporated into the international agricultural research centers (IARCs), the Collaborative Research Support Programs (CRSPs), USAID, or other similar efforts. While we can praise the efforts of social scientists working in agriculture, I will argue that an effective social science of agricultural research and development is even more important in such settings.

To illustrate, I present a particular case, the history of Mexico's agrarian change, outline how it has been affected by the Mexican Agricultural Program (MAP) established by the Rockefeller Foundation during the early 1940s; by its successors, the National Institute of Agricultural Research (INIFAP) and the International Maize and Wheat Improvement Center (CIMMYT); and by collaborative work between INIFAP and U.S. universities, most recently under the auspices of the International Sorghum/Millet Project (INTSORMIL). This case illustrates that a social science of the agricultural development process has been consistently and explicitly excluded from consideration, and that this has been a small part of the reason why technological modernization of Mexico's agriculture has been accompanied by continuing underdevelopment.[1]

SOCIAL SCIENCES IN AGRICULTURAL DEVELOPMENT

While many early efforts could be cited, the social sciences have only relatively recently been incorporated into international agricultural R&D. Their tardy arrival relates partially to disciplinary concerns within those

Copyright Society for Applied Anthropology (1988). Reprinted with revisions by permission from *Human Organization*, vol. 47, no. 9.

social sciences most relevant to international agricultural development. Rural sociologists were preoccupied with consolidating their own particular niche in the U.S. land-grant system and thus focused principally on domestic concerns. Anthropologists tended to view "culture as if it were cast in concrete" (Whyte 1984) and often characterized themselves as defenders of traditional cultures. Anthropologists also often adopted an elitist attitude as pure scientists of the study of humans and their culture, seeing agriculture as too basic and mundane for their attention (see Netting 1974, Rhoades 1985:4). Agricultural economics was viewed as more immediately relevant and was incorporated much earlier, but even then there was little consciousness among biological scientists as to what was expected of economists. Ruttan's experiences when he reached the International Rice Research Institute are exemplary.

> When I arrived at IRRI, I was shown to an office in the very attractive new institute complex. The office was conveniently located near the library. It had a brass plate in the door with the label Agricultural Economics. In the weeks that followed, however, neither the director nor the associate director of IRRI conveyed to me a very clear idea of why they needed an agricultural economist or what contribution they expected from the economics unit at IRRI (Ruttan 1982:308–309).

In spite of a slow start, social scientists have gained a toehold in international agricultural development. Perhaps the most important reason behind their incorporation was the Foreign Assistance Act passed by the U.S. Congress in the 1970s. The bill includes legislation that has come to be called the New Directions mandate because it emphasizes considerations of equity rather than economic growth. The mandate highlights the importance of measures to increase income redistribution, the selection of labor-intensive appropriate technologies to help generate employment, participation of beneficiaries in the decision-making process, and adaptation of programs to local social, ecological, and cultural conditions. Further amendments have added an emphasis on helping people meet their "basic needs" of adequate nutrition, shelter, clothing, health care, and education (Hoben 1980:356). A special section on agricultural research in the act states:

> Agricultural research carried out under this Act shall (1) take account of the special needs of small farmers in the determination of research priorities, (2) include research on the interrelationships among technology, institutions, and economic, social, environmental, and cultural factors affecting small farm agriculture, and (3) make extensive use of field testing to adapt basic research to local conditions (Foreign Assistance Act 1979, Section 103(a)).

The passage of this legislation had several impacts favorable to the involvement of social sciences. One was that social soundness analyses of projects within USAID became required in 1975. Second, USAID missions were required to produce Country Development Strategy Statements that included analysis of the socioeconomic conditions of the poor and the reasons for their deprivation. Third, the Title XII amendment, "Famine Prevention and Freedom from Hunger," established U.S. universities as resources for increasing food production and distribution in developing countries. This clause led to the development of the CRSPs. Fourth, the Percy Amendment on Women in Development elevated women and their special concerns into the consciousness of development planners. Fifth, the emphasis on small farms and the extensive use of field testing in agriculture in turn led to an emphasis on farming systems research (FSR). The New Directions mandate thus brought socioeconomic and equity issues to the forefront of USAID and essentially demanded the involvement of social scientists. In terms of anthropology alone, the effects were quite dramatic. The number of anthropologists working in USAID quickly jumped from only one in the early 1970s to 22 by 1977 (Hoben 1980:364).

The currents affecting USAID were also felt in other agricultural R&D settings. One of the most significant concomitants was the creation of the Rockefeller Foundation "Social Science Research Fellowship in Agricultural and Rural Development" in 1974. By 1984, 33 scientists (21 of whom were anthropologists) had been placed in the IARCs (Rhoades 1985:5). Also, increased attention was given to FSR in the international centers (DeWalt 1985b, CGIAR n.d.:Part IV, Chapter 16:13–14). Presently, several have established farming systems types of programs; three (IRRI, ILCA, and CIMMYT) have economics programs; all but one have economists working in some capacity; and two—CIMMYT and CIP—employ anthropologists as senior scientists.[2]

Several recent books have documented the role that the social sciences can play in agricultural research and development. These include *The Role of Anthropologists and Other Social Scientists in Interdisciplinary Teams Developing Improved Food Production Technology* (IRRI 1982), *Coming Full Circle:Farmers' Participation in the Development of Technology* (Matlon et al. 1984), *Breaking New Ground:Agricultural Anthropology* (Rhoades 1985), and *Putting People First:Sociological Variables in Rural Development* (Cernea 1985).[3] Nevertheless, what social science has contributed thus far is only part of what it could conceivably contribute. The vast majority of efforts to date fall under the rubric of what I call social sciences *in* agriculture.[4] What I mean by this is: how social scientists contribute to the improvement of project functioning, usually by providing descriptive information that facilitates the identification, diffusion, and adoption of new technology created by biological scientists.

This is what has come to be expected of social scientists in international agricultural R&D. For example, Horton (1984:11) reports that on CIP projects in the Mantaro Valley of Peru, "anthropologists and sociologists proved to be extremely effective in delimiting agroecological zones, classifying farm types, appraising the socioeconomic viability of alternative technologies, and conceptualizing new approaches to research and training." A review of the achievements and potential of the IARCs contains an appraisal of what social scientists have to offer in FSR: "The purpose in such work is to assist in the identification of effective changes to and designs of practices, techniques, enterprises, activities and policies that are acceptable to and appreciated by the target groups in farming systems research" (CGIAR n.d.:Part IV,Chapter 16:14). A very similar list of research problems appropriate to anthropologists and sociologists is found in the IRRI report mentioned above (1982:98).

Because they are first and foremost *technology generation programs*, the IARCs, FSR types of programs, and the CRSPs have created a small but significant role for social science in agriculture. Technical scientists assume that the agricultural technology generated can help solve the problems of small farmers in developing countries. The role of social scientists is thus to further the goals of the biological agricultural scientists in agriculture by acting as, in effect, *cultural brokers* between farmers and researchers. This is made most explicit in Rhoades and Booth's (1982) model for generating "acceptable agricultural technology." In their farmer-back-to-farmer model, social scientists should come to an understanding of farmers' perspectives and needs, communicating these to other scientists who use the findings to design better, more appropriate technology. Ideally, the technology is next tested and adapted on-farm. Social scientists then observe farmers' reactions and communicate their evaluations to the technical scientists, at which point the cycle can begin again.

In this model, social science provides an important service to both farmers and researchers by brokering the communication between them. Particularly in organizations such as CIP, where social scientists have been thoroughly incorporated into multidisciplinary teams to address technological problems, the model works very well (DeWalt 1983, Rhoades 1985). This service-oriented research, however, is only a part of what social science has to offer. In my view, equally and perhaps more important is a social science *of* agriculture.

THE SOCIAL SCIENCE OF AGRICULTURE

Several important issues are being only minimally addressed by social sciences in agriculture. First, issues of equity are being partially addressed through attention to the special technological needs of small farmers. Yet, there is very little effort to monitor the benefits of new technology to small farmers versus other elements of the population. While much is made of paying attention to the small farmer, it is still not clear that the technology being generated is in fact small-farmer biased.

Second, the New Directions mandate and other statements have stressed the need to promote labor-intensive technology to generate employment. However, indications are that jobs in the agricultural sector are being lost rather than generated (e.g., DeWalt 1985a, 1985c). Does this have to do with the technology being generated, with government policies that run counter to the goals of agricultural R&D, or with other trends that are unrelated to agriculture? Much more research is needed regarding the interrelationships of technology with the institutional structures and the economic, social, and cultural settings within which it will be used—as the Foreign Assistance Act mandated.

Finally, minimal attention has been paid to assessing the social and ecological soundness of new technology and programs. Those social soundness analyses that have been done are often largely pro forma; questions have been raised about whether ecological analyses have any impact on the kinds of projects funded (Rich 1986). In any case, such analyses have seldom been carried out by social scientists affiliated with any of the major agricultural R&D institutions. Instead, they are typically done by outside consultants hired by USAID, the World Bank, and other donor organizations specifically to satisfy the legislated requirement.

These are the sorts of issues that can be meaningfully addressed only by a social science *of* agricultural development. What I mean by this is the study of the interaction of the natural environment, sociocultural patterns, market conditions, government policy, and technological systems in order to identify agricultural research and/or extension priorities, to determine appropriate institutional structures and responsibilities for research and extension, to predict the consequences of agricultural change, and to identify government, agency, and institutional policies that will facilitate the development of more just and equitable social systems. Rather than performing a service-oriented role within a system in which policies have already been established, a social science of agriculture should provide an ongoing critique (both positive and negative) of R&D programs; it should also be a key element in the *formulation of policies* that will guide and direct them.

This focus explicitly recognizes that research itself is fundamentally a political process (Busch 1986). This process applies both to social and non-social agricultural research. Therefore, a major purpose of a social science *of* agriculture should be to examine the larger structure within which agricultural technology is generated and used, and explicitly to address issues of who is likely to gain or lose from the technologies being developed.

Unfortunately, this kind of research is viewed with suspicion by many biological scientists in agricultural development, most of whom still see themselves as doing "pure" research for its own sake and/or for the good of humankind. What is not recognized is that an "apolitical" stance is itself a very powerful political statement. In dismissing much of social research as "too political" and, in effect, suppressing a social science of agriculture, the research system has made some very clear political choices.

This can be demonstrated with data from Mexico, the country in which institutional efforts to apply agricultural research and technology to the solution of food and agriculture problems were first made. This case is especially interesting because we can see a consistent pattern of choices about issues of equity and social science involvement in research, starting with the Rockefeller Foundation's Mexican Agricultural Program in the 1940s and 1950s, carrying through CIMMYT's efforts beginning in the 1960s, and affecting the work of the INTSORMIL in the 1980s. A failure to incorporate social understanding, planning, and monitoring into the technology-generation program may have exacerbated, rather than alleviated, the problems of rural Mexico.

THE MEXICAN CASE: TECHNOLOGICAL MODERNIZATION WITHOUT DEVELOPMENT

During the early 1940s, the Rockefeller Foundation began discussions with the Mexican government about sponsoring a new research program to raise agricultural productivity and improve human nutrition in Mexico by applying modern technology. The foundation established the Mexican Agricultural Program (MAP) to work with an Office of Special Studies (OSS) within the Ministry of Agriculture in 1943. The purpose of the OSS

> was to increase the production of varieties, the improvement of the soil and the control of insect pests and plant diseases. A corollary goal was to train young men and women in agricultural research and in the development of techniques for promoting the rapid adoption of the new technology (Wellhausen 1976:128–129).

Because maize and wheat together accounted for over 70% of Mexico's cultivated land and were the most important food crops, primary emphasis was placed on them. The MAP, OSS, and their successors are very important in the annals of agricultural research. They mark the beginning of attempts to apply research breakthroughs made in U.S. and other Western agriculture to less developed parts of the world, thereby establishing the precedent for the IARC system (Plucknett and Smith 1982).

For this reason, it is important to understand the positive and negative aspects of the development of the Mexican Agricultural Program. Jennings (n.d.) has produced an interesting and controversial history of MAP. He points out that only a few individuals questioned the directions that the Rockefeller Foundation program was taking soon after its establishment. Two criticisms of this program, however, were quite prophetic.

First, during the early 1940s when MAP was just beginning, an outstanding cultural geographer of Latin America, Carl Sauer, recommended that agricultural research be directed toward the rural poor. He noted that the nutritional and agricultural practices of small Mexican farmers were quite sound, and that their main problems were economic rather than cultural. Sauer cautioned against attempts to recreate the model of U.S. commercial agriculture in Mexico.

> A good aggressive bunch of American agronomists and plant breeders could ruin the native resources for good and all by pushing their American commercial stocks. . . . And Mexican agriculture cannot be pointed toward standardization on a few commercial types without upsetting native economy and culture hopelessly. The example of Iowa is about the most dangerous of all for Mexico. Unless the Americans understand that, they'd better keep out of this country entirely. This must be approached from an appreciation of native economies as being basically sound (quoted in Oasa and Jennings 1982:34).

However, influential people in the Rockefeller Foundation dismissed Sauer's warnings as merely an appreciation of the quaint customs of the Mexican peasantry and a resentment of any attempt to change them.

A second question arose concerning the political, economic, and social effects of the new technologies being developed by MAP. A report prepared in 1949 by John Dickey (then president of Dartmouth College) noted:

> For example, I can imagine that this program before long might begin to have a considerable impact upon the whole land use policies of Mexico, and I am perfectly sure that within three to five years the program will raise some very acute problems with respect to the political control of these benefits. . . . These very benefits may introduce fresh economic disparities within the Mexican economy, which will present political problems not now even dimly perceived by many Mexicans (cited in Oasa and Jennings 1982:36).

Rather than suggesting research and other measures to cope with such potential problems, Dickey's recommendation was to avoid the issue: "it would be unfortunate for all concerned, especially for the program itself, if the foundation is heavily in the picture when this growth in social tensions takes place" (cited in Oasa and Jennings 1982:36). Dickey recommended that the foundation confine its responsibility to scientific experiments so that it would not be identified with any problems arising from the effects of the new technologies.

The posture adopted by Dickey and the Rockefeller Foundation in Mexico is similar to that taken later by the IARCs. Some of the most thoughtful individuals in the CGIAR centers are very careful to indicate that they deal in intermediate goods (germplasm, training, and other expertise) that national programs then use to produce the final results that are disseminated to farmers within their countries. Given the difficult political contexts and funding constraints under which the IARCs operate, this is an understandable position. In this way also, the centers can deflect potential criticisms concerning the political, economic, and social effects of the new technology they create. But this posture leads agricultural science to continue to treat rural underdevelopment as a *technical problem* rather than one stemming from a combination of factors of which technology is only one aspect.

Thus, just as the warnings of people such as Sauer went unheeded, and just as the agricultural research system tried to dissociate itself from the socioeconomic and political problems that Dickey identified, and just as the Rockefeller Foundation's Program continually ignored calls for the involvement of social scientists in MAP, so the social science *of* agriculture was ignored when CIMMYT and the other IARCs were established. The "image of neutrality" (Jennings n.d.) that agricultural scientists in Mexico in the 1940s and 1950s cultivated as assiduously as their experimental plots continues to the present day. Although Mexico has achieved some remarkable success in modernizing its agriculture, the process has led to substantial social, economic, and political problems. These issues are addressed more fully elsewhere (Barkin and DeWalt 1985; DeWalt 1985a; DeWalt and Barkin 1986, Hewitt de Alcántara 1976), but some of the main concerns are summarized here.

Mexico's First Green Revolution: Wheat

There is little question that MAP succeeded in increasing the productivity of some of Mexico's crops. As Figure 2.1 demonstrates, average wheat yields have more than quadrupled since MAP's establishment in 1943. Production increased from an average of only 425,000 tons per year in the early 1940s to over 4,500,000 tons in 1984. A large part of this increase was due to two plant-breeding breakthroughs applied by the Rockefeller Foundation and the OSS—the creation of semidwarf spring wheats and of varieties insensitive to differing day lengths (Borlaug 1983).

However, these "miracle seeds" were only part of the story. As Wellhausen (1976) and Hewitt de Alcántara (1976) have emphasized, the

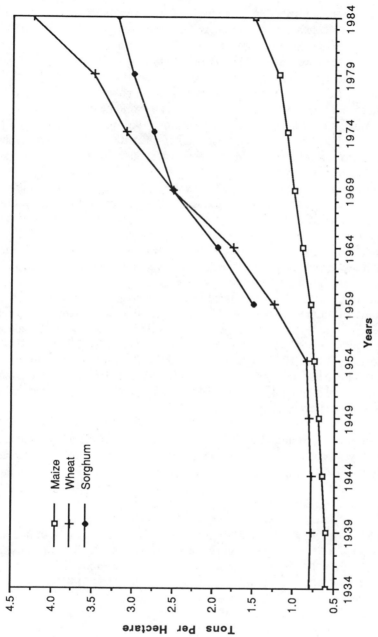

FIGURE 2.1. YIELDS OF MAIZE, WHEAT, SORGHUM 1934-1984

seeds also required irrigation, more fertilizer, more effective control of weeds and insects, mechanization, and better land management. These were often subsidized by the Mexican government. The government also invested in other infrastructure, most notably roads, railroads, and storage facilities necessary to effectively market the new wheat varieties. Finally, wheat production did not substantially increase until the government established a guaranteed price that was considerably above the world market price for wheat at the time. This subsidy, which lasted from 1954 to 1964, amounted to about 250 million pesos per year (Hewitt de Alcántara 1976:308-309). Thus, the first green revolution was to a considerable extent subsidized by a drain on the Mexican treasury.[5]

As one might expect, given the extensive hydrological, technological, and chemical inputs required, wheat was and is generally grown by larger, commercial farmers or by those small farmers or *ejidatarios* with access to credit. In 1977, 82% of the land in wheat was irrigated, 98% was fertilized, and improved seeds were used on about 91% of the hectares (ha) planted (Barkin and Suárez 1983:84). Larger landowners generally benefited most from the miracle wheat (Hewitt de Alcántara 1976).

While average yields continued to increase (Figure 2.1), the first green revolution sputtered during the 1960s and 1970s. Land planted in wheat peaked in the subsidy years of the late 1950s (Figure 2.2). Over 950,000 ha were planted in 1957, but an average of fewer than 750,000 were planted between 1975 and 1980. It was only in the early 1980s, with substantial increases in guaranteed prices, that this figure began to rise again. Because of ever-expanding demand, the country has had to import large quantities of wheat in almost every year since 1970.

The maize program of MAP and its successors never achieved the same level of technological and genetic improvements as did the wheat program. Average yields of maize have not increased nearly as rapidly as those of wheat (Figure 2.1). Consequently, maize production has followed a rather bumpy trajectory; the amount of land planted in maize has never again reached 1966 levels (Figure 2.2). Principally because maize yields remain low, farmers have turned to other crops that are economically more competitive. Maize continues to be grown mainly by small farmers using rudimentary techniques, few inputs, and traditional varieties of seed. The result is that between 1980 and 1984, maize imports represented almost one-quarter of national production, rising as high as 35% in 1980 and 1983 (Barkin and Suárez 1986:Table 19).

Two of the main architects of MAP and CIMMYT have admitted that, in retrospect, much more attention should have been paid to breeding maize varieties that would meet the needs of the resource-poor small farmers who grow the crop in rainfed areas (Borlaug 1983:691; Wellhausen 1976:150).[6] However, the point is that there were many calls for just such programs

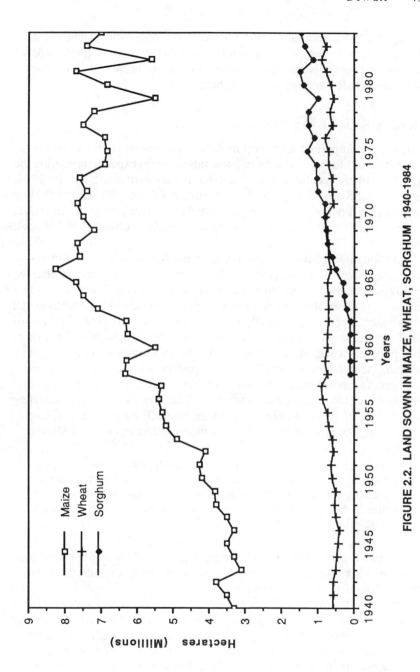

FIGURE 2.2. LAND SOWN IN MAIZE, WHEAT, SORGHUM 1940-1984

during the 1940s and 1950s by both social and non-social scientists; calls that were largely ignored until recently. Perhaps the greatest irony for MAP and its successors is that their major impact has been with a crop only belatedly included in their work—sorghum.

Mexico's Second Green Revolution: Sorghum

Sorghum, an important food crop in Africa, was unknown in the traditional agriculture of Mexico. Aside from a few unsuccessful experiments during the first half of the century, it was not cultivated systematically. In 1944, however, OSS agronomists began experimental work with the crop. They hoped that a drought-tolerant sorghum would help areas marginal for maize, those in which rainfall was either limited or poorly distributed (Pitner et al. 1954:1).

Although sorghum did not figure in the Mexican diet, promoters of sorghum research did not consider this a problem. They pointed out that the grain could be used by livestock, as it was in the United States. Still, a few doubts were raised about the wisdom and appropriateness of sorghum research for Mexico. For example, during program discussions in 1956, the head of MAP's poultry project noted that if MAP's objective was improved nutrition, then putting animals into the food chain between plants and people might be an inefficient use of grains. Even then, poultry was competing for grains with people, and he wondered "whether this is sound in Mexico" (quoted in Jennings n.d.:108). The question was raised, but like other questions dealing with the social goals and objectives of the research program, it was largely ignored. In 1957, the Rockefeller Foundation's annual report on MAP noted:

> Interest in sorghums has grown considerably during the last year principally because of the rapid expansion of the livestock industry, especially pork and poultry production. As a result of recent heavy demand, the price of sorghum grain in Mexico City has increased (Rockefeller Foundation 1957:77).

In short, as the demand for sorghum grew, MAP's emphasis on food grains was lost, along with its original goal of creating sorghum varieties for marginal, rainfed areas of the country.

In 1958, the government began to collect statistics on sorghum for the first time. The crop's history since then is nothing short of spectacular (Figure 2.2). Between 1965 and 1980, when the land under cultivation in Mexico was growing at a rate of 1.5% per year, the area planted in sorghum was increasing by 13% per year. By 1984, sorghum occupied over 1.6 million hectares—about one fourth the area of maize, and about 50% more than the area of wheat, the miracle crop of the first green revolution (Figure

2.2). In 1986, sorghum occupied the second largest area of any crop sown in Mexico, and the country has become the fifth largest producer in the world. Despite this, Mexico is not self-sufficient in sorghum. In some recent years, there has been a demand for 50% more sorghum than is produced nationally. Moreover, Mexico has become the second largest importer of sorghum from the United States.

Two principal factors fueled this second green revolution (DeWalt 1985a). First, sorghum production in Mexico benefited technologically from hybrids developed in Texas in the 1950s (Quinby 1971:17-19), which MAP worked to adapt to local conditions. Mexican farmers quickly recognized these hybrids' productivity and began replacing maize with sorghum or introducing sorghum into newly opened areas. As Figure 2.1 shows, the average yields of sorghum are about 80% higher than those of maize. Where the two crops have been directly compared under similar technological circumstances, sorghum yields were 40% higher on irrigated lands and 89% higher on rainfed lands (Montañez and Aburto 1979:145).

The second reason why sorghum is so popular among Mexican farmers is that it requires much less labor than does maize. The biggest advantage is that sorghum harvesting is mechanized; combines replace the many workers that still hand-pick maize in most of Mexico. The sorghum goes directly from the combine into trucks that haul it to markets where it is purchased— usually by one of the multinational livestock feed producers. Mechanized planting and cultivating of sorghum (or maize) reduces labor requirements by approximately 50%. Combine harvesting of sorghum reduces the remaining need for labor by roughly another 50% (DeWalt and Barkin 1986). Mechanization and sorghum cultivation have had a substantial effect on farming and employment in rural Mexico. Both large and small farmers have found mechanization attractive because of the decreased wages they have to pay. Unfortunately, the result is declining rural employment opportunities and rising rural out-migration.

To give just a small indication of the magnitude of this process, Tables 2.1 and 2.2 present data from research in four sorghum-producing areas in Mexico.[7] Out-migration in search of work has been substantial in all four; 66% to 95% of household heads in the communities have at one time or another left the village to work; many have joined the flow of illegal migrants to the United States. In the case of these four communities, more people have gone to work in the United States than to Mexico City. The same is true of their sons and daughters. As Table 2.2 demonstrates, 37% to 56% of the children over the age of 15 have had to leave their communities to live and work elsewhere. The favorite destination in every community but one (El Porvenir) is the United States. Such patterns may have developed anyway, but mechanized production of sorghum has certainly exacerbated them.

TABLE 2.1.   OUTSIDE WORK EXPERIENCE FOR HOUSEHOLD HEADS FROM FOUR
COMMUNITIES IN RURAL MEXICO

	Las Bateas, Michoacan (N = 83)		Derramaderos, S.L. Potosí (N = 60)		El Porvenir, Tamaulipas (N = 75)		Quebrantadero, Morelos (N = 97)	
	N	%	N	%	N	%	N	%
Have worked outside community	55	66	57	95	51	68	59	61
WHERE[a]								
Mexico, rural	31	37	39	65	48	64	12	12
Nearby city	12	14	22	37	24	32	20	21
Mexico City	8	10	3	5	1	1	14	14
U.S., rural	21	25	48	80	17	23	6	6
U.S. city	14	17	27	45	6	8	15	15

[a]Percentages sum to more than 100% because several people have worked in
multiple locations.

TABLE 2.2.   PRESENT RESIDENCES OF CHILDREN AGE 15 BORN TO HOUSEHOLD HEADS IN
FOUR RURAL COMMUNITIES

Place of Residence	Las Bateas, Michoacan		Derramaderos, S.L. Potosí		El Porvenir, Tamaulipas		Quebrantadero, Morelos	
	N	%	N	%	N	%	N	%
Home community	116	51	98	44	101	63	142	55
Nearby city	24	11	7	3	17	11	5	2
Same state	22	10	11	5	20	13	23	9
Other states	12	5	28	12	12	8	27	11
Mexico City	9	4	6	3	0	0	30	12
U.S.	44	19	71	32	9	6	30	12

With the technological changes that occurred in Mexican agriculture, grain production in Mexico by 1980 was approximately eight times greater than in 1940, while population only trebled during this period (DeWalt 1985a: 44–45). Given such data, one would have predicted in 1940 that Mexico would have solved its food availability problems.

Such is not the case, however. The modernization of Mexican agriculture, especially since 1965, has been characterized by phenomenal growth in the livestock sector, especially among pigs, chickens, and cattle (Table 2.3). This expansion has taken place through increasingly "industrialized" production. As part of this process, growing numbers of animals have been inserted into the food chain between grains and people—just as the head of the MAP poultry program warned in the 1950s. The expansion of sorghum production must be evaluated in this context because sorghum accounts for approximately 74% of all industrialized livestock feed sold in Mexico (DeWalt 1985a:43).

Land use in Mexico has been changing even more rapidly than Dickey might have expected; the fastest-growing sectors of Mexican agriculture have been feed grains and oil seeds (Yates 1981). The basic grains for direct human consumption (i.e., maize, beans, and wheat) have been increasingly displaced by soy, alfalfa, sorghum, oats, and other cultivars intimately related to "modern" agricultural and livestock production (Table 2.3).

Enormous quantities of natural resources are now devoted to meat production. The proportion of cropland devoted to livestock production rose from about 5% in 1960 to over 23% in 1980 (Barkin 1982:66-67); and 64% of the national territory reportedly is used to produce only 3,140,000 tons of meat, a yield of only 24 kg per hectare (García Sordo 1985:8). The proportion of grain fed to animals has increased from 4.8% in 1960 (Meissner 1981) to over 32% in 1980 (DeWalt 1985a). More recently the Programa Nacional de Alimentación estimated the proportion of feed grain to be as high as 48% of the total apparent grain consumption (*UnoMasUno* 10 January 1985:1). Mexican nutritionist Chávez has likened this use of grain to the miracle that Christ performed with the loaves and the fishes, but in reverse (Chávez 1982:9).

The social benefits of the use of cropland, grains, and the 74 million hectares of pasture (DeWalt 1985a:51) devoted to producing livestock are very poorly distributed. Although per capita consumption of meat is about 42 kg per year (DGEA 1982a:16), the government itself reported that in 1980 over 25 million Mexicans (more than 35% of the population) *never* eat meat, and less than 30 million drink milk regularly (see also Redclift 1981:13-14). Although many occasionally consume eggs and milk, it is clear that the distribution of animal products is sharply skewed toward the upper- and middle-income groups (González Casanova 1980). Malnutrition is widely accepted as one of the country's gravest public health problems. When in

TABLE 2.3.   ANNUAL RATES OF GROWTH OF SOME IMPORTANT INDICATORS FOR
              UNDERSTANDING THE AGRICULTURAL SITUATION IN MEXICO

	Hectares	Hectares	Annual Percent
Basic Grains (1,2)	1965	1982	
Maize	7,718,371	5,744,249	-1.7
Beans	2,116,858	1,581,000	-1.7
Wheat	858,259	1,017,359	1.0
Rice	138,065	156,317	0.7
Feeds (1,2)			
Alfalfa	106,252	242,379	5.0
Oats (feed)[a]	16,550	251,716	28.1
Grain sorghum	314,373	1,275,212	8.6
Cultivated pastures		2,044,527	39.7
Oilseeds (1,2)			
Safflower	58,805	189,045	7.1
Sesame	267,234	91,013	-6.5
Soy	27,466	375,238	16.6
Animals (3)[b]	(tons)	(tons)	
Pigs	572,894	1,365,414	8.2
Chickens	215,485	482,491	8.4
Cattle	624,956	1,200,544	6.1
	1940	1982	
Cultivated Area (4)	5,900,000	16,000,000	2.4
Irrigated Area (4)	1,700,000	16,000,000	2.4
Population	19,763,000	71,464,000	3.1

Source: (1) DGEA 1981, (2) DGEA 1983a, (3) DGEA 1982b, (4) DGEA 1983b.

[a]These figures date from 1971, the year in which data on oats for feed began to be collected.

[b]These figures date from 1972, when the DGEA first began collecting data on animal production.

1980 the Mexican government launched its short-lived drive for food self-sufficiency, the Sistema Alimentario Mexicano (Austin and Esteva 1987), it estimated the daily calorie and protein intake of 19 million Mexicans (more than 27% of the population) fell below that required for physical well-being (summarized in Redclift 1981:13-14). Another source reported that about 40 million Mexicans (more than half of the population) are seriously undernourished (Universidad Nacional Autónoma de México/Instituto Nacional de Nutrición study cited in 18 August 1984 issue of *UnoMasUno*).

Thus, the modernization of Mexican agriculture has not been accompanied by an improvement in the conditions of life for most rural Mexicans. There is substantial unemployment or underemployment in rural areas; many Mexicans migrate to cities or to the United States to try to earn a livelihood; and widespread undernutrition and malnutrition exist despite the huge increases in grain production in the country.

CONCLUSIONS

I should emphasize that MAP and its successors were not the major causes of the problems plaguing Mexico's agriculture and food systems. Government policies and priorities have been the principal factors in creating what is widely recognized as one of the most unequal societies in the world (González Casanova 1980). Yet MAP and its successors continually skirted the crucial agrarian and social issues that were evolving contemporaneously with their agricultural research. The MAP research program created new technology that fit into a Mexican agricultural system in which small farmers became increasingly unable to compete. Social scientists and others warned the agricultural research establishment of the dangers inherent in such efforts. But rather than heed these warnings and employ social scientists to identify appropriate technology for small- and medium-size farmers so as to avoid potential pitfalls in new technology, program decisionmakers and biological scientists considered social research irrelevant or simply dismissed it. When, in the late 1950s and early 1960s, a MAP agricultural economist began to advocate more attention to the needs of small farmers, he was replaced by other investigators less prone to raise such issues (Jennings n.d.).

Some social science research was initiated within CIMMYT in 1970, although the Economics Program was not established until 1979. However, the individuals staffing this program have never focused on the potential social and economic consequences of technology as part of their research mandate. Instead, most of their efforts have centered on identifying appropriate technologies for defined sets of farmers and on devising methods to disseminate technologies developed at CIMMYT (Oasa and Jennings 1982:38–39). CIMMYT's Economics Program today clearly follows the tradition of social science *in* agriculture, as a service-oriented appendage to the maize and wheat programs. In this, they have been quite successful. Their work in on-farm research and FSR methodologies is outstanding (Byerlee et al. 1980; Byerlee et al. 1982; Collinson 1983). A good indication of their status within the system is that the former director of the Economics Program has now become director general of CIMMYT. A social science *of* agriculture, however, is excluded from this and other programs in the IARCs.[8]

The situation in the IARCs carries over to the CRSPs. When I presented some of the data in this chapter to a 1984 meeting at CIMMYT on Sorghum in Latin American Farming Systems, a meeting I co-organized (Paul and DeWalt 1985), the reaction of my INTSORMIL colleagues and their Mexican collaborators was very hostile. The response was quite surprising because, from my perspective, my recommendations resulting from this work were relatively innocuous. I recommended that research focus on sorghums that could be used for direct human consumption and on drought-tolerant varieties for marginal, rainfed areas of the country (DeWalt and Barkin 1985). These were the original goals of OSS and MAP scientists—to increase food availability in the country and to cultivate sorghums for the marginal areas where maize was not viable. Instead, the vast majority of the research on sorghum in Mexico focuses on hybrid sorghums, which are suitable only for animal feed and irrigated zones of the country.[9]

U.S. and Mexican biological scientists at the INTSORMIL conference at CIMMYT were proud of their accomplishments and of the success of sorghum in the country; they viewed my research as a direct attack on them and their work. Given these kinds of reactions, it may not be possible for anthropologists and sociologists to do both social science *in* and *of* agriculture simultaneously. The sometimes critical perspective of the latter may preclude the acceptance of social researchers by their biological, agricultural scientist colleagues involved in technology creation. This is unfortunate because there should be room for a self-critical perspective within the IARCs, the CRSPs, and other such organizations. When criticism comes from outside the system, it is often destructive and leads to vituperative and unproductive debate.

A good example is the literature on the green revolution worldwide. IARC social scientists who studied the effects of the green revolution were primarily concerned with documenting its spread and benefits. (An excellent recent example is the work of Herdt and Capule 1983.) Criticisms of its impacts had to come from outside the system, and these were quite stinging in their indictments (e.g., Griffin 1974; Hewitt de Alcántara 1976; Lappe and Collins 1979; Pearse 1980). For more than a decade, unproductive debate has centered on whether the green revolution was "good" or "bad." Evenhanded assessments that point out the very substantial positive benefits of the green revolution while also indicating some of its unintended negative effects are still difficult to find (see Lipton with Longhurst 1985 for the best attempt to date).

Thus, while much good work in the social science of agricultural research and development has been carried out both domestically (e.g. Busch 1980; Busch and Lacy 1983; Friedland, Barton, and Thomas 1981) and internationally (e.g., Griffin 1974; Hewitt de Alcántara 1976), it seems that most of this work will have to occur outside the agricultural establishment.

There is a very unfortunate lack of explicit recognition that socioeconomic and political issues within and among nations are the principal problems of developing countries. The attitude should not be that agricultural R&D cannot do anything about these issues. Such an attitude only perpetuates and promotes the present emphasis on a "technological fix" that will solve some problems in the absence of a better socioeconomic or political situation. Because it chooses to ignore social science *of* agriculture issues, the agricultural technology being created often exacerbates existing socioeconomic and political difficulties. Biological agricultural scientists must acknowledge that social science expertise can be useful in directing R&D programs, identifying appropriate organizational forms for research and extension systems, anticipating some of the potential problems arising from technological change, and assisting governments to design workable agricultural, food, and nutrition policies. Collaboration and teamwork among biological scientists and social scientists to reach their shared humanitarian goals is sorely needed.

Thus, I return to the title of this chapter. The social sciences are perhaps only halfway to making a real contribution to true agricultural development. Social researchers must be involved not only as service-oriented appendages of biological research programs, but also as leaders in identifying technologies and policies to implement positive programs and mitigate negative consequences of agricultural change. Such efforts can help engender the more just and equitable social systems envisioned in the New Directions legislation of the 1970s.

NOTES

This chapter results from a project I have been codirecting with David Barkin of the Centro de Ecodesarrolla in Mexico City. Portions of the research were sponsored by INTSORMIL through contract number AID/DSAN-G-0149, and through a grant from the United Nations University. The chapter is reprinted, with revisions, from *Human Organization* 47(4):343–353, copyright Society for Applied Anthropology 1988. I appreciate the helpful comments made by C. Milton Coughenour, Kathleen DeWalt, and Della McMillan.

1. When I refer to social sciences here, I am focusing principally on sociology and anthropology, though much of my argument also applies to agricultural economics.

2. Despite the progress that has been made, there are still relatively few social scientists among the large number of agricultural scientists. Van Dusseldorp has estimated that for every thousand scientists in agricultural research centers, only one is an anthropologist or sociologist (1977). More recently, Rhoades reported that of 736 senior scientists employed by the CGIAR system, only three are anthropologists (1985:50). To my knowledge, no sociologists are employed as senior scientists in any of the IARCs.

3. The large number of anthropologists who have conducted applied

social research in agricultural R&D settings has made a significant impact. There is now a recognized subdiscipline of agricultural anthropology, and an organization known as the Anthropological Study Group on Agrarian Systems publishes a bulletin titled *Culture and Agriculture.*

4. The *in* and *of* distinction is borrowed from Straus's (1957) discussions of sociology in and of medicine.

5. It is important to emphasize that the results of the OSS wheat-breeding program changed the face of world agriculture through what became known as the green revolution. However, it was largely left to social scientists and others outside the Rockefeller Foundation (and later the CGIAR structure) to question the socioeconomic effects of the green revolution. In recent years, social scientists associated with the CGIAR system have begun a couterattack with a new revisionist view of the green revolution. These individuals, justifiably, want to demonstrate results from the CGIAR system so as to assure continuing donor support (Buttel 1986). More evenhanded analyses of the positive and negative aspects of agricultural research are just now beginning to appear, some of which have been undertaken at the behest of the CGIAR system (de Janvry and Dethier 1985; Lipton with Longhurst 1985).

6. Wellhausen was one of the first agricultural scientists to recognize the disparities MAP was creating. He persuaded the Rockefeller Foundation to establish what has become known as the Puebla Project to try to deter- mine how new technologies could be spread to resource-poor farmers. In a 1986 personal communication, Wellhausen stated: "We urgently need to come up with some special strategies for gaining a more rapid adoption of adequate technologies by small- and medium-size farmers especially in the rainfed, more unfavorable agricultural areas. The International Centers are beginning to realize this and are emphasizing, more than ever before, the development of varieties of food crops with greater stability under conditions of drought and problem soils." He went on to indicate also that "your work is fundamental to getting on with Mexico's second step in agricultural development."

7. These data were collected as part of a collaborative project between INTSORMIL and the Universidad Autónoma Metropolitana-Xochimilco in 1984. Four sorghum-growing farming communities (*ejidos*) were selected in different ecological regions of the country. Farm families were interviewed concerning their work histories, farming practices, nutritional strategies, household characteristics, income sources, and other topics. A full analysis of these data in book form is in process. More details concerning sampling procedures and other data on the communities may be found in DeWalt and Barkin (1986) and in the case-studies report issued by the Universidad Autónoma Metropolitana Unidad Xochimilco (1986).

8. A few CIMMYT researchers have recently begun to conduct "farm-based policy research" (Martínez 1986). However, the starting point of their analysis is clearly the farm, so it does not (and probably cannot) stray far into more political kinds of analysis.

9. Some food-quality varieties that are adapted to high, arid valleys are now being bred in Mexico, by researchers from ICRISAT in collaboration with researchers in INIA. It is ironic that, although much of this research was carried out under the auspices of INTSORMIL, the findings and ideas have had little effect on INTSORMIL work in Mexico; but they have been quite influential with ICRISAT researchers (Guiragossian 1986:320–334).

REFERENCES

Austin, James, and Gustavo Esteva (eds.). 1987. *Food Policy in Mexico: The Search for Self-Sufficiency*. Ithaca: Cornell University Press.

Barkin, David. 1982. El uso de la tierra agrícola en México. *Problemas del Desarrollo* 47/48:59–85.

Barkin, David, and Blanca Suárez. 1983. *El fin del principio: las semillas y la seguridad alimentaria*. México: Océano.

———. 1986. *El fin de la autosuficiencia alimentaria*. México: Editorial Océano y Centro de Ecodesarrollo.

Barkin, David, and Billie R. DeWalt. 1985. La crisis alimentaria Mexicana y el sorgo. *Problemas del Desarrollo* 61:65–85.

Borlaug, Norman. 1983. Contributions of Conventional Plant Breeding to Production. *Science* 219:689–693.

Busch, Lawrence. 1980. Structure and Negotiation in the Agricultural Sciences. *Rural Sociology* 45:26–48.

———. 1986. La Construction Sociale du Milieu Naturel. In *Milieux et Paysages*. Yvon Chatelin and Georges Riou, eds., pp. 55–69. Paris: Masson.

Busch, Lawrence, and William Lacy. 1983. *Science, Agriculture, and the Politics of Research*. Boulder: Westview Press.

Buttel, Frederick H.. 1986. On Revisionism and Pendulum Swings: A Review Essay. *Rural Sociology* 51:229–234.

Byerlee, Derek, Michael Collinson et al. 1980. Planning Technologies Appropriate to Farmers—Concepts and Procedures. Mexico: CIMMYT.

Byerlee, Derek, L. Harrington, and D. L. Winkelmann. 1982. Farming Systems Research: Issues in Research Strategy and Technology Design. *American Journal of Agricultural Economics* 64:897–904.

Cernea, Michael M. (ed.). 1985. *Putting People First: Sociological Variables in Rural Development*. New York: Oxford University Press.

CGIAR. n.d.. International Agricultural Research Centers: Achievements and Potential Part IV (draft of August 31, 1985).

Chávez, Adolfo. 1982. Perspectivas de la nutrición en México. Publicación L-50. Tlalpan, México: Instituto Nacional de la Nutrición.

Collinson, Michael. 1983. *Farm Management in Peasant Agriculture* (2nd ed.). Boulder: Westview Press.

DGEA. 1981. Consumos aparentes de productos agrícolas 1925–1980. *Econotécnica Agrícola* 5(9).

———. 1982a. Boletín interno. Información Económica Nacional 9(1) August 11.

———. 1982b. Consumos aparentes de productos pecuarios (1972–1981). *Econotécnica Agrícola* 6(9)

———. 1983a. Producción de granos básicos en México. *Econotécnica Agrícola* 7(12).

———. 1983b. Información agropecuaria y forestal 1980. México: Secretaria de Agricultura y Recursos Hidráulicos.

de Janvry, Alain, and Jean-Jacques Dethier. 1985. Technological Innovation in Agriculture: The Political Economy of Its Rate and Bias. CGIAR Study Paper No. 1. Washington, DC: World Bank.

DeWalt, Billie R. 1983. Anthropology's Contribution to the International Sorghum/Millet Project. *Practicing Anthropology* 5(3):6,10.

———. 1985a. Mexico's Second Green Revolution: Food for Feed. *Mexican*

Studies/Estudios Mexicanos 1:29–60.

————. 1985b. Anthropology, Sociology and Farming Systems Research. *Human Organization* 44:106–114.

————. 1985c. Economic Assistance in Central America: Development or Impoverishment? *Cultural Survival* 10:14–18.

DeWalt, Billie R., and David Barkin. 1985. El sorgo y la crisis alimentaria Mexicana. In *El sorgo en sistemas de producción en América Latina.* Compton L. Paul and Billie R. DeWalt, eds., pp. 153–167. Mexico: CIMMYT and INTSORMIL.

————. 1986. Seeds of Change: The Effects of Hybrid Sorghum and Agricultural Modernization in Mexico. In *Technology and Social Change* (2nd ed.). H. Russell Bernard and Pertti J. Pelto, eds., pp. 137–165. Prospect Heights, IL: Waveland Press.

Foreign Assistance Act. 1979. Legislation on Foreign Relations through 1978: Current Legislation and Related Executive Orders (Vol. 1). Washington, DC: U.S. Senate and House of Representatives Joint Committee.

Friedland, William H., Amy Barton, and Robert Thomas. 1981. *Manufacturing Green Gold: Capital, Labor, and Technology in the Lettuce Industry.* Cambridge: Cambridge University Press.

García Sordo, Mario. 1985. Insuficiente producción para satisfacer la demanda de proteínas de origen animal. *UnoMasUno* January 9:8.

González Casanova, Pablo. 1980. The Economic Development of Mexico. *Scientific American* 243:192–204.

Griffin, Keith. 1974. *The Political Economy of Agrarian Change:An Essay on the Green Revolution.* Cambridge: Harvard University Press.

Guiragossian, Vartan. 1986. *Primera reunión nacional sobre sorgo: Memorias* (1984). Marín, NL: Universidad Autónoma de Nuevo León.

Herdt, R. W., and C. Capule. 1983. Adoption, Spread, and Production Impact of Modern Rice Varieties in Asia. Los Baños, Philippines: IRRI.

Hewitt de Alcántara, Cynthia. 1976. Modernizing Mexican Agriculture. Geneva: UN Research Institute for Social Development.

Hoben, Allan. 1980. Agricultural Decision Making in Foreign Assistance. In *Agricultural Decision Making: Anthropological Contributions to Rural Development.* Peggy F. Barlett, ed., pp. 337–369. New York: Academic Press.

Horton, Douglas E. 1984. Social Scientists in Agricultural Research: Lessons from the Mantaro Valley Project, Peru. Ottawa: IDRC.

IRRI. 1982. The Role of Anthropologists and Other Social Scientists in Interdisciplinary Teams Developing Food Production Technology. Los Baños, Philippines: IRRI.

Jennings, Bruce. n.d.. Political Science: A Study of International Agricultural Research (draft manuscript).

Lappé, Frances Moore, and Joseph Collins. 1979. *Food First: Beyond the Myth of Scarcity.* New York: Ballantine Books.

Lipton, Michael, with Richard Longhurst. 1985. Modern Varieties, International Agricultural Research, and the Poor. CGIAR Study Paper No. 2. Washington, DC: World Bank.

Martínez, Juan Carlos. 1986. Toward Farm-Based Policy Research: Learning from Experience. Paper presented at the Sixth Annual Farming Systems Research & Extension Symposium, Manhattan, KS.

Matlon, P., R. Cantrell, D. King, and M. Benoit Cattin (eds.). 1984. Coming

Full Circle: Farmers' Participation in the Development of Technology. Ottawa: IDRC.

Meissner, Frank. 1981. The Mexican Food System (SAM): A Strategy for Sowing Petroleum. *Food Policy* 6:219–230.

Montañez, Carlos, and Horacio Aburto. 1979. *Maíz, política institucional y crisis agrícola.* México: Editorial Nueva Imagen.

Netting, Robert. 1974. Agrarian Ecology. *Annual Review of Anthropology* 3:21–56.

Oasa, Edmund, and Bruce H. Jennings. 1982. Science and Authority in International Agricultural Research. *Bulletin of Concerned Asian Scholars* 14(4):30–45.

Paul, Compton L., and Billie R. DeWalt (eds.). 1985. *El sorgo en sistemas de producción en América Latina.* México: CIMMYT and INTSORMIL.

Pearse, Andrew. 1980. *Seeds of Plenty, Seeds of Want: Social and Economic Implications of the Green Revolution.* New York: Oxford University Press.

Pitner, John B., José Luís Lazo de la Vega, and Nicolás Sánchez Durón. 1954. El cultivo del sorgo. México: Programa Cooperativo de Agricultura y Ganadería de México y la Fundación Rockefeller.

Plucknett, Donald L., and Nigel J. H. Smith. 1982. Agricultural Research and Third World Food Production. *Science* 217:215–220.

Quinby, J. Roy. 1971. *A Triumph of Research: Sorghum in Texas.* College Station: Texas A&M University Press.

Redclift, Michael. 1981. Development Policy Making in Mexico: The Sistema Alimentario Mexicano (SAM). Working Paper in U.S. Mexican Studies No. 24. San Diego: University of San Diego.

Rhoades, Robert. 1985. *Breaking New Ground: Agricultural Anthropology.* Lima: CIP.

Rhoades, Robert, and Robert Booth. 1982. Farmer-Back-to-Farmer: A Model for Generating Acceptable Agricultural Technology. *Agricultural Administration* 11:127–137.

Rich, Bruce. 1986. Environmental Management and Multilateral Development Banks. *Cultural Survival* 10(1):14–18.

Rockefeller Foundation. 1957. Mexican Agricultural Program, 1956–1957: Director's Annual Report. New York: Rockefeller Foundation.

Ruttan, V. W. 1982. *Agricultural Research Policy.* Minneapolis: University of Minnesota Press.

Straus, Robert. 1957. The Nature and Status of Medical Sociology. *American Sociological Review* 22:200–204.

Universidad Autónoma Metropolitana Unidad Xochimilco. 1986. Los sistemas agroeconómicos del sorgo. México: Universidad Autónoma Metropolitana Unidad Xochimilco.

Van Dusseldorp, D. B. W. M. 1977. Some Thoughts on the Role of Social Sciences in the Agricultural Research Centres in Developing Countries. *Netherlands Journal of Agricultural Science* 25:213–228.

Wellhausen, Edwin J. 1976. The Agriculture of Mexico. *Scientific American* 235:128–150.

———. 1986. Personal communication, letter of 9 October 1986 to David Barkin and Billie R. DeWalt.

Whyte, William F. 1984. Personal communication cited in Rhoades 1985:3.

Yates, P. Lamartine. 1981. *Mexico's Agricultural Dilemma.* Tucson: University of Arizona Press.

3

Social Science in INTSORMIL's Attack on Hunger in Sudan

C. Milton Coughenour and Edward B. Reeves

In the International Sorghum/Millet CRSP's publication titled "Fighting Hunger With Research . . . A Team Effort" (1985:8), two purposes are outlined for INTSORMIL. The primary one is "to organize and mobilize financial and human resources necessary for mounting . . . a collaborative effort [to provide] the knowledge base [to alleviate] the principal constraints to improved production, marketing, and utilization of sorghum and pearl millet." The second is to "improve the capabilities of host country institutions to generate, adapt, and apply improved knowledge to social conditions." This chapter discusses the role of social science in fulfilling these objectives on INTSORMIL's Sudan project. The discussion is organized in three sections: (1) the context and record of INTSORMIL's Sudan work; (2) social science research goals and accomplishments; and (3) social science impacts on INTSORMIL's achievements.

THE CONTEXT AND RECORD OF INTSORMIL IN SUDAN

More than four-fifths of the Sudanese population works in agriculture, and sorghum and millet are the principal cereals. However, the rate of growth in cereal production is lower than the rate of population growth, and the annual change in cereal yield is declining (IADS 1981). Sudan is rated as a "food crisis" country, yet its potential for increased food production through improved technology seems high.

In 1980, INTSORMIL developed a working relationship with Sudan and its research institutions. The existence of a relatively well-developed agricultural research establishment in Sudan provided an important source of potential collaborators for INTSORMIL scientists—though this establishment unfortunately included no social scientists.

As enunciated in INTSORMIL's first objective, the principle of collaboration requires the mobilization of both U.S. and host country scientists. But, it was recognized from the beginning that a complete disciplinary match could not be attained in the Sudan project. Although this was not clearly and widely articulated, U.S. scientist resources in INTSORMIL were greater and more diverse than could be expected in any developing country. Thanks to flexibility in the "collaborative" model, INTSORMIL social scientists were nevertheless able to undertake research in Sudan despite their lack of counterparts. Ultimately, however, this lack had critical negative consequences for social science participation in this CRSP.

Also evident in INTSORMIL's first objective is the focus on sorghum and pearl millet. Although agronomic and biological scientists, and even agricultural economists, are often closely identified with particular commodities, sociologists and anthropologists usually have a broader orientation to agricultural and/or socioeconomic development. As will be seen, this difference in professional orientation can also have negative consequences for the role and contributions of social scientists.

Finally, biological scientists typically differ from social scientists, and especially sociologists, in their approach to institution-strengthening—INTSORMIL's second objective. While the former primarily define "strengthening" as training other scientists, the latter are likely to think that the institutions themselves need to be altered. This was the case among social scientists on the project in Sudan, and the consequences have been mixed.

The majority of INTSORMIL social sicentists have been associated with the University of Kentucky, which has received the bulk of program funds for social research. During the first six years of INTSORMIL's operation, the University of Kentucky played a prominent role in this CRSP's research program in general, and in Sudan in particular. Throughout, the Administrative Board—which makes all final budgetary and project policy decisions—included a Kentucky representative. A Kentucky team member also served continuously on the Technical Committee, which makes annual recommendations on projects and funding levels. In addition, team members participated in all program planning committees for the annual INTSORMIL workers' meetings.

As with most INTSORMIL projects, the general research objectives of the Kentucky project had to be specifically adapted to Sudanese conditions. The project's first objective was to understand the goals, resources, strategies, and constraints in the "sociocultural complex" of production, marketing, and consumption of grain sorghum and pearl millet. This came to be defined as the farming systems research (FSR) component of the Sudan project. The second project objective focused on the structure and process of, as well as constraints to, communication among agricultural scientists. When the Sudan research was begun, a broader "sociology of agriculture" research perspective was adopted. The third general focus was on the linkages between farmers and change agents and the constraints to diffusion and adoption, taking into account the conditions and priorities of agricultural administrators in Sudan.

There was some initial difficulty in identifying possible host countries. The CRSPs were unprecedented. USAID missions were accustomed to supervising projects that they had proposed, whereas the CRSPs were created by USAID/Washington. Moreover, CRSPs bore the additional onus of academia. However, in November 1980 an INTSORMIL team, which included a Kentucky social scientist, visited Sudan and developed a memorandum of understanding (MOU) with the Agricultural Research Corporation (ARC). A wider working relationship also was established that included the University of Khartoum and the Western Sudan Agricultural Research Project (WSARP), an arm of the ARC. Started in 1979, WSARP was funded for six years by the government of Sudan, USAID, and the World Bank. Since its principal mission was to establish four research stations in western Sudan, WSARP provided important logistical support to INTSORMIL research teams operating in North Kordofan.

These initial negotiations revealed that Sudanese government officials and agricultural scientists wanted to help the poorer farmer but had little understanding of the goals and constraints characteristic of limited- resource farming systems. One provision in the ARC-INTSORMIL MOU authorized Kentucky sociologists and anthropologists to begin field studies of farming systems in North Kordofan. These were conducted between 1981 and 1982. In June 1981, an amendment to the MOU provided for a study of the ARC research system (Lacy et al. this volume), as envisioned under the second objective of the Kentucky project.

In March 1983, plans were developed with officials of the Kordofan Regional Ministry of Agriculture, the USAID agricultural officer, and the WSARP director to study change in traditional agriculture and networks of agricultural communication. Fieldwork for this phase was carried out during 1984. Findings from the three phases of research have been published, but analysis and reporting of the results of all three field projects continues. Each of these social science research projects and their contributions are described below in greater detail.

SOCIAL SCIENCE RESEARCH GOALS AND ACCOMPLISHMENTS

The FSR Studies

The FSR method fit INTSORMIL's needs in the early years of the program. FSR is well suited to determining how limited-resource farmers cope with the social, economic, and ecological conditions under which they make a living (see Uquillas and Garret, this volume). With such information, INTSORMIL agricultural scientists are better able to direct their research to the problems of dryland, limited-resource farmers. The FSR method has additional advantages. First, it operationalizes the holistic perspective that economic anthropologists commonly use in field research. Second, it underscores a philosophy of agricultural development that emphasizes the importance of maintaining a dialogue between farmers and scientists in developing appropriate technology. Third, its core concepts are familiar to agricultural scientists; it therefore facilitates interdisciplinary work. Fourth, agricultural development agencies regarded the approach favorably at the time.

The FSR team was composed of two anthropologists. In selecting the target area and defining specific research objectives, the team worked with other INTSORMIL scientists and with officials in ARC, WSARP, ICRISAT, and especially the USAID mission in Khartoum. The FSR work was carried out in 18 villages around el-Obeid, the capital of Kordofan Region and the dominant marketing center in western Sudan. The investigation focused on the constraints faced by limited-resource farmers in two respects: the agricultural production system and household economy, stressing the knowledge system and decision strategies of farmers; and institutional aspects of land tenure and local market organization, stressing problems of access to and distribution of resources. Instead of isolating sorghum and millet production and distribution, a systems viewpoint contextualized these crops in a set of biotechnical, economic, and institutional relationships. The FSR team conducted in-depth interviews in the villages prior to surveying 166 limited-resource farmers and 58 village merchants and middlemen.

This fieldwork resulted in three technical reports (Reeves 1984; Reeves and Frankenberger 1981, 1982) and a number of papers and other publications. The reports describe a complex multicrop and livestock farming system coupled with local and migratory agricultural wage labor, merchandising, gum arabic collection, handicrafts, and numerous other income-generating activities. Almost all Kordofan farmers grow millet, and three-fourths raise some sorghum; all also raise one or more cash crops (sesame, groundnuts, and/or roselle). Most cultivate various vegetables, including watermelon, cucumber, okra, and cowpeas. Cattle, sheep, goats, and donkeys are the principal livestock, although a few households also own camels. Livestock are important as a mechanism of savings/investment and as a reserve in bad crop years.

Self-sufficiency is the basic strategy with respect to farm inputs. Farmers save their own seed, if possible, and provide their own labor. If their own resources are inadequate, kin are the first source of both these inputs; markets are the last resort. Most important are the strategies of mixed cropping, intercropping, and opportunistic replanting. These serve to optimize production, reduce labor and other input costs, and offset environmental and market risks. The availability of land is not a constraint *per se*, although the availability of good-quality land within commuting distance is limited. The system of land tenure tends to result in a family's having widely dispersed fields. However, this landholding pattern may be adaptive in view of the sporadic rainfall. To optimize the allocation of management and labor, mature family members of both sexes commonly have responsibility for the separate fields. Crop selection for near and distant fields is determined to some extent by the family's mix of market and subsistence production goals.

A complex system of village, district, and urban markets exists for cash crops, as well as for staple food crops. A number of market alternatives are available to farmers. These include local middlemen in the village; the government-administered village auction market, and outside agents and transporters. Crops can also be marketed in bulk at the large urban auction market, or directly (and often illegally) to wholesale buyers and warehousers in el-Obeid. As compared to smallholders, the larger producers more often take advantage of these external opportunities to obtain higher returns.

From INTSORMIL's standpoint, identification of production and marketing constraints and strategies was the most important contribution of the FSR studies (Reeves and Frankenberger 1985). Natural constraints identified include wind erosion, particular pests and diseases, low soil fertility, and inadequate rainfall. Labor and seeds, chemicals for controlling pests, and the availability of drinking water are also constraints. Most such constraints can be addressed through research, while credit and commodity auction procedures and pricing policies can be improved through institutional reforms.

Since this information was available early in the collaboration with Sudanese scientists, it had considerable influence in shaping subsequent research objectives. For example, the INTSORMIL agronomist stationed at el-Obeid in 1982 used the social science findings in developing his own research on drought tolerance; intercropping; early-maturing varieties of sorghum and pearl millet; labor-saving technologies for land preparation, planting, and weeding; control of *senta* (a major pest of millet); bird resistance; the fodder quality of sorghum stover; and the construction quality of millet stalks—all the while bearing in mind the extremely limited financial resources of Kordofan farmers.

The ARC Study

The ARC study identified constraints on research for the benefit of small, limited-resource farmers. An important assumption here is that successful R&D is closely linked with the capability of the research system as a whole.

The problems of the entire ARC thus had to be examined. A sociological perspective for understanding research systems had already been developed in Busch (1980) and Busch and Lacy (1983) for the United States. This framework was applied in Sudan, coupled with an earlier study of agricultural research capabilities there (Joint Team Report 1977).

The results of this study are summarized in Lacy and Busch 1985 and Lacy et al. 1983; details of the research are also discussed in Lacy et al. this volume. Briefly, however, the principal recommendations emerging from this work centered on increased financial and other support of ARC personnel and activities, the development of an overall agricultural research policy committee, concentration of personnel at fewer research stations, greater emphasis on FSR in the research program, and stronger linkages with extension.

Unfortunately, changes in governmental and ARC administrations and a further decline in the Sudanese economy have not been conducive to implementing the recommendations. Moreover, since opportunities to directly assess implementation of the recommendations have not been forthcoming, the impact of this study is largely unknown. However, with regard to a greater research emphasis on FSR, the visible success of INTSORMIL's FSR studies led to the sponsorship of two FSR training workshops for WSARP and ARC scientists, and to more active involvement in on-farm research by Sudanese scientists recruited for WSARP since 1984.

Studies on Communication and Change in Agriculture

The principal purposes of the 1984 studies on communication and change in North Kordofan were to determine the nature and extent of recent change in agricultural technology and to identify the channels through which new information flows to farmers, both men and women. Secondary objectives were to assess change in the villages since the 1982 FSR study, to measure the impact of a new farm program broadcast on el-Obeid radio, and to evaluate farmers' knowledge of different varieties of sorghum and millet.

Research was carried out in two phases. In the first, male and female farmers in 15 villages were interviewed regarding recent innovations in agriculture, farmers' sources of agricultural information, the basis of farmers' interests in new technology, general characteristics of the villages, and farmers' varietal knowledge of sorghum and millet. In the second phase, two villages were selected for intensive study of the communication networks for agricultural information and the diffusion of three innovations. The results of the first phase have been published in Coughenour and Nazhat 1985. A dissertation has been written on one of the two village studies (Nazhat 1986); analysis of the data from the second village and comparative analysis of both villages are still under way.

Primarily as a result of inflation and drought, living conditions had deteriorated between 1981 and 1984, and they became much worse after the 1984 season. In 1984, millet and sorghum were still the most important cereal crops. Roselle had increased and groundnuts had decreased in importance as cash crops. During the 1981–1984 period, farmers had done considerable experimenting with new seeds. In all, 24 new "varieties" were mentioned, along with several new kinds of implements. If a new variety is believed superior to existing ones, most village farmers (both men and women) begin using it within three years. Men obtain information about most new varieties first; women obtain information from men. Both groups believe that sorghum and millet varieties differ in their utility for various types of food, housing, and forage purposes. However, farmers are most interested in early-maturing, drought-resistant, and high-yielding varieties. Both men and women are willing to make some sacrifice to obtain such seed. Thus, the motivation to try new seeds is high, and substantial change is occurring in response to environmental pressures. Still, the farming system *per se* remains the same.

Most of the new seeds that people had experimented with were "farmers'" varieties, although a few had been developed by research scientists for use on large mechanized farms. Seed innovations had spread from their origin along kinship networks to villages in the el-Obeid area. Merchants are also important in the spread of new seeds. Kinship ties, which constitute the informal networks of communication, also structure information flows along tribal lines. Merchants had also been instrumental in spreading new seeds. The extension service had not been influential in any of the innovations studied. Moreover, since the radio signal from the el-Obeid station is too weak to be heard in any of the villages visited, newly instituted farm broadcasts had had no impact. The FSR/E agronomist was viewed favorably by villagers. However, relatively few villagers knew about new, research-generated seeds that were being tested, because of the suppression of information about these seeds on the part of the demonstrator farmers who were collaborating in on-farm trials.

These findings led to recommendations that more on-farm trials be attempted, extension workers make use of periodic market days to optimize farmer contacts, special institutional arrangements be made for farmers to exchange grain for hybrid seed, the linkages between research and extension be strengthened, and a seed distribution system be developed, including an education and training program for merchants so as to improve their reliability and trustworthiness. Although these recommendations were discussed in seminars with research, extension, and USAID personnel in Sudan, there has been no opportunity to assess their institutional acceptance.

SOCIAL SCIENCE IMPACTS

Because of the lack of information, it is impossible to make a full assessment of the impact of the work of INTSORMIL social scientists. It is apparent, however, that the unique organization of the project made their impact both more and less than it might have been—"more" in that, under the relatively decentralized management of INTSORMIL, social scientists were able to chart their own course and to capitalize on the available opportunities as they saw them; and "less" in that social science impacts depended almost entirely on the willingness of agronomic and social scientists to make use of each other's findings.

Nevertheless, a number of positive impacts can be identified. The FSR work definitely encouraged INTSORMIL and the Sudanese government to allocate more resources to projects to help limited-resource farmers. The social scientists' baseline information on farming systems was used in planning research at the new agricultural experiment station at el-Obeid. In fact, the INTSORMIL agronomist was posted to el-Obeid *because* of the success of the FSR group's diagnostic analysis. The agronomist arrived before the anthropologists had left the field, and he used their findings to design and develop his own research.

The FSR team influenced INTSORMIL priorities and directions by helping to organize conferences and workshops. It also bolstered the effort to get more overseas involvement among INTSORMIL's U.S. scientists. By establishing a research site and providing important baseline data, social scientists were also instrumental in convincing INTSORMIL to conduct field research, both in Sudan and other CRSP country sites.

The impact of the FSR team is evidenced in other ways, too. As a result of the information it developed, INTSORMIL collaborated with other organizations in Sudan to fund long-term breeding and agronomic research emphasizing alleviation of the constraints on limited-resource farmers. Two major goals of these collaborative efforts are improved intercropping and better stand establishment (i.e. successful germination and growth of the crop). The FSR team had found these were very important to farmers for assuring adequate yields with the least expenditure of labor. Also, the breeding of early-maturing and drought-resistant varieties was encouraged by the FSR work.

Although it is too early to demonstrate significant gains in sorghum and millet utilization as a result of the FSR and agronomic studies, the importance of on-site testing is now more widely recognized by Sudanese researchers. The el-Obeid agronomist field-tested early-maturing varieties of sorghum and millet, as well as the new hybrid sorghum developed under INTSORMIL, ICRISAT, and Sudanese government auspices. The field testing demonstrated the superiority of several new varieties in rainfed areas.

However, it is not known how well they may be accepted under ordinary farming conditions. This could be assessed in carefully designed farmer-managed trials.

Another way to assess the impact of social scientists is to ask how INTSORMIL might have been different without them. This question directs attention to some of the mistaken ideas that have been exploded. One is the notion that limited-resource farmers are irrational and homogeneous. In describing the many different types of cropping and livestock systems and farmers' finely tuned strategies to cope with variation in rainfall patterns and income opportunities, the field studies essentially destroyed this myth. The record of innovations considered by farmers during the past five years alone, plus their documented interest in new, early-maturing and higher-yielding varieties, also demolished the notion that traditional farmers are uninterested in agricultural innovations and that their technology is static or unchanging.

Similarly, many Sudanese officials and expatriate experts alike believed that the small farmers of western Sudan were poorly integrated into the market economy, and that, to the limited extent they did participate, they were being severely exploited by rural middlemen. Moreover, it was assumed that market infrastructure (e.g., transportation and storage) was primitive and inefficient. The evidence collected by social scientists working in the field, however, demonstrated that all these ideas are largely unfounded. Production of cash crops is virtually universal and is critical to farmers' livelihood. Rural middlemen are rarely able to exert monopoly power over farmers. Transportation and storage methods offer farmers a range of alternatives that are highly effective in view of the adversities of climate and geography. These findings argued all the more strongly for the importance of technical innovations and food-crop improvement as a means of enhancing both agricultural yields and the welfare of the rural population.

As the designers of the Kentucky project had hoped, the entire technological development process—from the laboratory, to production on-farm, then marketing and consumption—was studied. Constraints at all levels were identified. As is often the case, the findings have been most relevant to agricultural scientists, research planners, and extension administrators. Results have provided guidance for technical research. They also indicate that some institutional reform of both the research and extension systems is needed for more efficient technology to develop. Social scientists could be of great assistance in making these reforms.

Some of the primary clientele—limited-resource farmers—have directly benefited from the FSR team's assistance in local development projects in the field, and from on-farm trials of new seeds that the team encouraged. Limited-resource farmers have also benefited indirectly from the research, to the extent that improved sorghum and millet seeds have become available more quickly and with greater confidence in their relative advantage than would have been the case without INTSORMIL's social science studies. It is hoped that these indirect benefits will continue to multiply.

In addition to the positive impacts outlined here, several factors have limited the impact of social science in the Sorghum/Millet CRSP. The contributions of social research have been recognized by most INTSORMIL agricultural scientists, administrators, and program evaluators. However, it is our impression that all parts of the Kentucky project have not been seen as equally valuable. The importance of the FSR study was widely heralded, but the studies of the ARC and of changes in agricultural technology and the communication of agricultural information among farmers seem to have been much less used. Of course, many of the recommendations emanating from these studies are more difficult to implement. They require additional financing, restructuring, or the resolution of conflicting interests. Also, the studies identify constraints that INTSORMIL cannot deal with by itself. Sudanese officials must be the actors, and such action often is resisted by various groups.

A related problem has been the lack of social science collaborators within ARC, WSARP, or the Kordofan Regional Ministry of Agriculture. This has been critical in several respects. Without collaborators, U.S. social scientists had to start from zero, as it were, in each field investigation. After the field study, the team and its resources disbanded, leaving little in the way of accumulated expertise. This defect becomes more important, even critical, in implementing recommendations. No one was on hand to follow up in working with other scientists and/or local officials. The social scientists thus have been forced to "make their own waves"—a difficult task at best.

Another difficulty relates to the fact that INTSORMIL's structure is multidisciplinary, yet it lacks clear goals and firm program management. It is not surprising that biological scientists might be slow to recognize the importance of social science, but we discovered that social scientists themselves had to learn how their work might be relevant to the research decisions of biological scientists. Social scientists were slow to recognize the importance of their participation at all levels in the research planning process. Moreover, despite the presence of social scientists on the Technical Committee of INTSORMIL, interdisciplinary coordination for program development has been poor.

This problem has become especially acute under INTSORMIL's new organizational plan, which aims to overcome the earlier lack of a geographic research focus by establishing research coordinators for designated ecogeographical zones. For example, Sudan is the prime research site in INTSORMIL's East Africa Eco-Geographical Zone. Although social scientists are members of the zonal groups, they have been systematically excluded from the planning process. The rationale varies, but typically host countries argue that since they have no social science research directed toward agricultural development, social scientists should not attend the planning workshops. INTSORMIL's Management Entity has not insisted otherwise. Nevertheless, this is precisely where important social science input might best be made and the need for social research debated and planned.

Lack of collaborators and interdisciplinary coordination has had another deleterious consequence: INTSORMIL's failure to recognize the need for the iterative and/or monitoring aspects of FSR and social science research. The present feeling within INTSORMIL seems to be that, although FSR is important in providing baseline information, once this task is accomplished any problems arising in the course of future technical development will require only economic assessments at most. Issues of who adopts what technology, and why or why not, are largely ignored, as are the broad range of noneconomic impacts of technology development. Consequently, the failures associated with earlier programs of technological development are likely to be repeated. For example, initial reports indicate that the widely heralded hybrid sorghum mentioned above is not fully acceptable to consumers, but the reasons for its rejection are obscure.

Additional research on farming systems and on the acceptance of new seeds and agronomic practices has been planned. However, as part of a general budget readjustment necessitated by the Gramm-Rudman act, the Administrative Board of INTSORMIL did not fund Kentucky's research project in 1986-1987. A change of government in Sudan, armed rebellion in the south, and general reductions in USAID programs also have substantially increased the difficulty of collaborative research, and further work under the Kentucky project is problematic. Fortunately, other INTSORMIL projects, are conducting some limited social science research. For example, agricultural economists at Purdue University are developing a linear program model of farming systems and evaluating new technology.

One can only speculate how eliminating social research will impact INTSORMIL's program in Sudan and elsewhere. The program will probably be severely handicapped in evaluating its activities and in guiding the development and acceptance of new technology. Although economic analyses of the new sorghum varieties promise to fill part of the gap (Habash 1985), the broader assessments that an FSR-type of analysis would provide will not be forthcoming. INTSORMIL will need this input to avoid the kinds of adverse impacts that new agricultural technology has had in the past. In the absence of relevant "social intelligence," INTSORMIL is likely to have difficulty fulfilling its main mission: "fighting hunger with research."

REFERENCES

Busch, Lawrence. 1980. Structure and Negotiation in the Agricultural Sciences. *Rural Sociology* 45:26–48.

Busch, Lawrence, and William B. Lacy. 1983. *Science, Agriculture, and the Politics of Research.* Boulder: Westview Press.

Coughenour, C. Milton, and Saadi M. Nazhat. 1985. Recent Change in Villages and Rainfed Agriculture in Northern Central Kordofan: Communication Process and Constraints. Report No. 4. Lexington: Department of Sociology, University of Kentucky and INTSORMIL.

Habash, Mohammed K. 1986. Diffusion of New Sorghum and Millet Technologies: Evaluation of Alternative Cropping Systems in the Rainfed Area of North Kordofan, Sudan. Lafayette, IN: Department of Agricultural Economics, Purdue University (unpublished research paper).

IADS. 1977. Sudan Agricultural Research Capabilities. Joint Team Report. New York: IADS.

————. 1981. Agricultural Development Indicators. New York: IADS.

INTSORMIL. 1985. Fighting Hunger With Research . . . A Team Effort. Lincoln, NE: INTSORMIL.

Lacy, William B., and Lawrence Busch. 1985. Agricultural Research in Sudan. In INTSORMIL Fighting Hunger with Research: A Five-Year Technical Research Report of the Grain Sorghum/Pearl Millet Collaborative Research Support Program. Judy F. Winn, ed., pp. 178–184. Lincoln, NE: INTSORMIL.

Lacy, William B., Lawrence Busch, and Paul Marcotte. 1983. The Sudan Agricultural Research Corporation: Organization, Practices, and Policy Recommendations. Lexington: Department of Sociology, University of Kentucky and INTSORMIL.

Nazhat, Saadi M. 1986. Technology Diffusion for Agricultural Development and Desertification Control. Ph.D. dissertation, Department of Sociology, University of Kentucky.

Reeves, Edward B. 1984. An Indigenous Rural Marketing System in North Kordofan, Sudan. Report No. 3. Lexington: Department of Sociology, University of Kentucky and INTSORMIL.

Reeves, Edward B., and Timothy Frankenberger. 1981. Farming Systems Research in North Kordofan, Sudan. Report No. 1. Socioeconomic Constraints to the Production, Distribution and Consumption of Millet, Sorghum, and Cash Crops in North Kordofan, Sudan. Lexington: Department of Sociology, University of Kentucky and INTSORMIL.

————. 1982. Farming Systems Research in North Kordofan, Sudan. Report No. 2. Aspects of Agricultural Production, and Household Economy, and Marketing. Lexington: Department of Sociology, University of Kentucky and INTSORMIL.

————. 1985. Millet and Sorghum in a Sudan Farming and Marketing System. In Intsormil Fighting Hunger with Research: A Five-Year Technical Research Report of the Grain Sorghum/Pearl Millet Collaborative Research Support Program. Judy F. Winn, ed., pp. 171–177. Lincoln, NE: INTSORMIL.

4

Agricultural Research in Sudan: The Perspective of INTSORMIL Social Scientists

William B. Lacy, Lawrence Busch, and Paul L. Marcotte

The International Sorghum/Millet Collaborative Research Support Program (INTSORMIL) is devoted to improving the production, distribution, and consumption of these two cereals among small producers in less-developed countries. In addition, the program seeks to improve the institutional capacity of its host countries to generate and adapt new knowledge through training and collaboration with local scientists. The sociologists and anthropologists in this multidisciplinary project have focused on sociocultural constraints to production, distribution, and consumption of sorghum and millet in low-rainfall areas, such as the Sahel of Africa, where these crops are particularly important. INTSORMIL has addressed these constraints in the context of the various social structures involved in sorghum and millet production and distribution. Consequently, the research has focused on farming, marketing, extension, and research systems. This chapter highlights one such interrelated social system: the agricultural research system in Sudan.

Among the major constraints faced by agricultural development projects in sub-Saharan Africa is the basic infrastructure to support their efforts. The agricultural research system is an important and often essential part of that infrastructure and of the process of economic development. Indeed, Mellor (1986) states that "first and foremost" in a strategy for broad foreign assistance policy "is the investment in agricultural research and its support services." Furthermore, the agricultural research system is vital to the success of any program of collaborative research between scientists in developing and developed nations.

Despite these facts, the agriculture research system is either ignored in the work of natural and social scientists or taken as given. When attention is directed to the research system, it usually takes the form of briefly summarizing budgets, human resources, and organizational structures or of identifying research products to be disseminated to farmers. In contrast, our work in Sudan and elsewhere sought to place INTSORMIL's research in a broader sociology of agricultural science perspective (DeWalt this volume). The research reported here addressed the internal dynamics of Sudan's Agricultural Research Corporation (ARC), including its organization and practices, as well as the social, economic, and political situation in which it is embedded.

SUB-SAHARAN AFRICA AND SUDAN

Sub-Saharan Africa is a vast region encompassing 41 countries that are considered the poorest in the world's economy. While these nations' economies are dominated by the agricultural sector, in only 11 of 31 countries for which data are available did the average annual growth rate of agriculture exceed the population growth rate between 1973 and 1974. In addition, sub-Saharan Africa as a whole is the only area of the world where per capita food production has declined over the past two decades. In 1985, approximately 170 million of its 540 million people were fed entirely with imported grain. Africa is losing its ability to feed itself (Brown and Wolf 1986).

While there is no such thing as a typical African economy, Sudan exemplifies all the conditions described above. In the late 1970s, the UN identified it as one of the least developed countries in the world. Approximately 65% of Sudan's population works in the agricultural sector; agricultural products, especially cotton, made up over 70% of the country's exports in 1983 (Bank of Sudan 1983).

During the postcolonial period, agricultural development in Sudan has emphasized large-scale irrigation projects (such as the Gezira and Kenana schemes or the Rahad Project), which require substantial capital and often heavy commitments of public funds. But, the bulk of agricultural land and labor, particularly for food, is still devoted to small-scale farming and pastoral systems of livestock production. In addition, approximately 80% of all crops are grown in rainfed areas. In the 1970s, many policymakers, planners, and foreign donors shifted their attention to small-scale farming and small-scale projects. However, because of population increases caused by a growth rate of 2.8%, augmented by over a million recent refugees (Gurdon 1986), agricultural and food production per capita both declined considerably between 1973 and 1984(FAO 1985). This decline has been worsened by drought in the 1980s. Finally, a prolonged colonial experience and the current long and bloody civil war have made it extremely difficult to achieve political stability and economic development.

THE AGRICULTURAL RESEARCH CORPORATION

Despite the difficult social, economic, and political environment, the Sudan's agricultural research system has grown substantially since its modest beginning in 1902. Initially, research stations and laboratories were staffed by British scientists and were established to meet the demand of the Lancashire cotton industry. They focused almost exclusively on cotton, particularly in the proposed irrigation area between the two Niles that eventually became the Gezira Scheme. By the late 1940s, concern for nutritional deficiencies forced attention to food crops. Research in this area began in 1952, but the system included only about 50 scientists to conduct research on both export and food crops.

Fifteen years later, the semiautonomous Agriculture Research Corporation was created. In 1977, preexisting research functions in the areas of food processing, forestry, fisheries, range management, and wildlife were incorporated into the ARC. More recently, with the establishment of the Western Sudan Agriculture Research Project, progress has been made toward improving rainfed agriculture and livestock production in the west and integrating economic scientists into the organization.

Today, with approximately 175 scientists and 140 assistant scientists (including a large number who are abroad for training), the ARC accounts for approximately two-thirds of Sudan's agricultural research. Foreign scientists are a very small minority on the staff. In addition, there are roughly 600 technical assistants, 400 clerical and support staff, and nearly 4,000 laborers (ARC 1980). The ARC has achieved a critical mass of well-trained scientists, but it faces other human resource problems and serious economic constraints arising from deteriorating economic conditions in the Sudan generally.

Little information had been collected on this key agricultural research system. Indeed, we were unable to find any in-depth study of any African research system. Consequently, our research involved a variety of information sources, including reviews of historical materials; project reports and government documents; a series of 1982 on-site interviews of about two hours each with 62 ARC scientists; nine questionnaires returned from ARC scientists whose work sites were not visited; and approximately 20 interviews with research administrators and government officials. The number of respondents ($n = 71$) represented approximately 55% of the ARC on-site scientific staff in Sudan. Additionally, questionnaires were sent to approximately 50 Sudanese students enrolled in U.S. universities between September 1982 and May 1983. Twenty-five of these students were supported by the ARC, with the remainder being supported by other government or private organizations. Their response rate was approximately 50% ($n = 25$).

Human Resources

Since the rate of development of science, technology, and social institutions is determined in large part by human resources (e.g., scientists and staff), the backgrounds, professional training, and capacity of ARC scientists were examined. Although Sudan's agricultural scientific community has increased significantly during the last two decades, its size and growth are about average for developing countries in Africa. For example, the annual growth rate between 1970 and 1980 for selected nations was Nigeria 17.3%, Zambia 3.4%, Madagascar −.6% (Oram and Bindlish 1981). The ARC scientific community is well-trained; 65% hold PhDs, a figure that far exceeds the World Bank target of 20%. Among ARC scientists, most master's-level and nearly all PhD-level education was received at universities in Great Britain and the United States.

Despite this relatively large and well-trained scientific community, there are a number of human resource–related problems. During the early to mid-1980s, the research staff continued to be augmented by significant numbers of newly trained scientists returning from overseas. This has put pressure on an already overextended research system and has exacerbated the erosion of operating budgets. Furthermore, declining budgets threatened the system's ability to retain its scientists. At the same time, the increasing scale and complexity of the ARC and the intense competition for funds in the national budget have illustrated the need for personnel trained in research management. Inadequate budgets also made it extraordinarily difficult for the ARC to compete for farm labor during peak planting and harvesting periods. Many scientists reported that experimental plots were not harvested on time or at all, thereby wasting the work of trained scientific personnel. Finally, the development of human resources should be congruent with Sudan's overall needs and priorities. This requires a closer examination of the balance between scientists devoted to export and/or cash crops as opposed to those concentrating on food crops for national consumption, and to their disciplinary, institutional, and geographical distribution.

Research Resources

ARC scientists are strongly oriented toward applied research. They categorized their research over the last five years as 83% applied, 13% basic, and 4% development. Most of this work takes place in experiment-station fields (56%), and about a third is conducted in the laboratory. The low percentage of research in farmers' fields (3%) reflects the lack of adequate transportation and the relative weakness of institutional ties that would permit on-farm experiments.

Various resources are necessary to the research process. ARC scientists rated the adequacy and importance of the resources for their work on a scale of 1 (very adequate, very important) to 5 (very inadequate, very unimportant). Availability of experimental land was seen as the most adequate resource, followed by personal freedom to determine research problems. On the other hand, equipment and financial support were seen as the most inadequate.

Transportation, availability and quality of trained technical help, and opportunities for advanced education were also seen as inadequate (Table 4.1). While the perceived adequacy of resources differed significantly, scientists viewed most of these inputs as very important to their work. They saw financial support and operating supplies and materials as the two most critical, but they ranked all resources as important. Furthermore, the discrepancy between adequacy and importance is quite large for many of the resources.

Sudanese students enrolled in PhD programs in the United States likewise rated the resources available to them at their host institutions (Table 4.1). Scientific literature, personal freedom to incorporate new materials and techniques and to determine research problems, and transportation were the most adequate resources. While these four factors received the highest adequacy ratings, there was virtually no difference between this group of variables and the remaining resources. The range was 1.4–2.2; thus, all were considered adequate to very adequate. The only inadequate rating was given for availability and quality of labor. With regard to importance: scientific literature, equipment and tools, opportunities for advanced education, and personal freedom to incorporate new materials and techniques into research were considered the most important. While these were rated slightly higher, all resources were considered to be very important.

Not surprisingly, the Sudanese students (all of whom were enrolled in major U.S. land grant and agricultural schools) considered their institutional resources to be significantly more adequate than did the ARC scientists on site in Sudan. The students rated every resource, Except for experimental land, the students rated every resource as more adequate than did the Sudanese scientists.

These findings were generally consistent with those for Asian rice breeders (Hargrove 1978), U.S. scientists (Busch and Lacy 1983), and the international community of sorghum scientists (Marcotte, Busch, and Lacy 1983). Sudanese and other scientists from less developed countries agree with scientists from developed countries as to what is important with respect to resources, but the former labor under much less adequate research conditions. It is to the credit of ARC scientists that they have not used current fiscal problems as an excuse to abandon a meaningful research program. However, about a third of the Sudanese scientists expressed their intent to seek work in other countries with more adequate resources, support, and salaries if research conditions in Sudan did not improve.

Career Advancement

All organizations should have a reward system that provides a career ladder, offers employee incentives, and encourages support for the organization's

TABLE 4.1. RATINGS OF ADEQUACY AND IMPORTANCE OF RESOURCE FACILITIES

Resource Facilities	Scientists[a]		Students[b]	
	Adequacy	Importance	Adequacy	Importance
Operating supplies and materials	3.6	1.2	2.1	1.9
Experimental land	1.7	1.5	2.2	2.6
Research equipment and tools	4.0	1.3	1.8	1.7
Transportation	3.8	1.3	1.6	2.4
Trained help	3.7	1.4	2.2	1.9
Freedom to incorporate new materials and techniques into research	2.1	1.6	1.5	1.7
Freedom to determine research problems	1.9	1.6	1.6	1.9
Contact with other scientists	2.7	1.4	2.0	1.8
Opportunities for advanced education	3.7	1.5	1.9	1.7
Opportunities to gain scientific recognition	3.2	1.4	2.1	1.8
Opportunities for professional advancement	3.2	1.5	1.8	1.9
Training opportunities for people who work under you	3.7	1.5	2.2	2.3
Average Mean Score	3.3	1.4	2.0	1.9

[a]Mean ratings of 71 scientists in Sudan -- 1 = very adequate/important;
5 = very inadequate/unimportant.

[b]Mean Ratings of 25 Sudanese students in the U.S. -- 1 = very adequate/
important; 5 = very inadequate/unimportant.

goals. In research institutions, this system must also take into account the enormous diversity of research products, as well as the differing pace of production across disciplines. Finally, the reward system should consider the relevance of research products to the institution's clientele.

Scientists were asked what criteria they felt were important for advancement within the ARC. Publications were seen as the single most important criterion. Primarily, this meant writing annual reports, although several scientists also published in British and U.S. journals. Number of years of service was seen as the second most important criterion, while actual evaluation of research projects ranked third. Only one out of six scientists identified problem-solving or meaningful research as a criterion for promotion.

These responses indicate discontinuity between the goals of the ARC and the system used to reward its scientists. As with most scientists, there is little assurance that publications will benefit clients. Likewise, length of service with the ARC is likely to be unrelated to any client needs. Few ARC scientists viewed fieldwork or problem-solving as important in career advancement. Consequently, although the ARC does use objective criteria for promoting its scientists, such criteria may not encourage them to generate results useful to potential client groups. However, with little additional expenditure, it may be possible to change the reward system to better direct research toward the needs of farmers and other clients.

Scientific Communication

Because production of scientific knowledge is intimately bound to the ability to exchange information, systems of scientific communication in the ARC were assessed. With respect to formal communications, the major means by which ARC scientists (56%) keep abreast of current literature is regular scanning of journals. ARC scientists read approximately 2.5 journals regularly, e.g., *Agronomy Journal, Experimental Agriculture, Crop Science,* or *Food Science and Technology.* Travel (11% of scientists) and publications other than journals (5%) were considered to be of little importance. Unfortunately, relatively few scientific journals are available to ARC scientists because of budgetary constraints and foreign currency restrictions. Likewise, travel—which agricultural scientists from developed countries consider a major source of information—is not a principal channel of communication for ARC scientists because of insufficient funds for travel both within and outside Sudan. To compensate for this relatively weak formal communication network, ARC scientists have developed a strong informal network. Forty-five percent report that they converse daily with colleagues in their departments. This compares quite favorably to scientists in other countries. For example, U.S. agricultural scientists report that they talk about research with their departmental colleagues somewhat less than weekly (Lacy and Busch 1983).

In sum, scientific communication in the ARC is restricted in several significant ways. Access to journals is limited by the small numbers of titles in libraries and the lack of transportation to libraries. Access to fellow colleagues at other stations, institutions, or nations is also limited by restricted travel opportunities and minimal telephone services. Effective agricultural research policy must address the scientific communication system, its integral relationship with the goals and products of agriculture and agricultural R&D, and potential conflicts in the present system.

Research Goals and Beneficiaries

By definition, agricultural research is a goal-oriented activity. This is implicit in its strong mission orientation. However, the particular goals of research may differ markedly from program to program, discipline to discipline, and scientist to scientist. In addition, scientists' perceptions of research goals may differ significantly from those of administrators.

To assess the relative importance of various research goals to ARC scientists, a list of 10 common goals was utilized. Scientists ranked each of these 10 on a scale of 1 (no importance) to 5 (highest importance) in terms of their own research. Mean scores ranged from a high of 4.5 for increasing agricultural productivity and 4.3 for developing new knowledge, to a low of 2.6 for improving marketing efficiency. Significantly, only one goal ranked below the midpoint of 3 on the 5-point scale (Table 4.2). This suggests that, unlike their U.S. counterparts, ARC scientists take a broad view of research goals in their work. In fact, these scores may understate the differences, given the narrower range of disciplines in the ARC. The principal goal of ARC scientists is to increase agricultural productivity. It seems apparent that in order to pursue this mission, scientists must understand the circumstances of their clients. Moreover, one of the most important and difficult roles for the scientist as a change agent is to diagnose the needs of clients (Rogers and Shoemaker 1971). Perhaps even more difficult is to incorporate that perception into an ongoing applied program.

Given this requisite for understanding and diagnosing client needs, researchers were asked whom they perceived as the main audience for their research (Table 4.3). The largest group of perceived beneficiaries was farmers (50% of responses), followed by industry (24%) and extension/government (16%). This identification of farmers as the principal audience appears consistent with the goal of ARC scientists to increase agricultural productivity. However, it deviates somewhat from previous studies. For example, the most important perceived beneficiaries for U.S. agricultural scientists were large farmers and the general public, followed by other scientific disciplines, small farmers, and agribusiness, but with minimal differentiation among beneficiaries (Busch and Lacy 1983:167-168).

The data on perceived research goals and beneficiaries in Sudan suggest some potential and fundamental anomalies in the role of agricultural research there. First, although scientists see farmers as their research audience, they have limited or nonexistent communication links with these potential clients. When scientists were asked how their audiences received information about ARC research, the most popular answers were reports and publications. Ironically, however, adult literacy in Sudan is only 20% (World Bank 1980). Therefore, most farmers could not use such reports. ARC scientists' next most frequent answer to this query was information dissemination through extension. However, because of the country's serious economic difficulties,

TABLE 4.2.   GOALS OF AGRICULTURAL RESEARCH AMONG SUDANESE AGRICULTURAL
SCIENTISTS AND STUDENTS

| Goals | Total (n=71) | Scientists[a] | | | Students |
		1 (n=30)	2 (n=16)	3 (n=25)	(n=25)
Increase agricultural productivity	4.5[b]	4.6	5.0	3.9	4.7
Develop new knowledge or improved methodology	4.3	4.2	4.1	4.6	4.6
Decrease production costs of farm products	3.9	4.0	4.1	3.7	3.8
Improve level of rural living	3.6	3.3	3.1	4.2	4.6
Protection from insects, disease, and other hazards	3.6	3.4	3.7	3.8	4.3
Protect consumer health and improve nutrition	3.6	3.2	2.9	4.7	4.2
Promote community improvement	3.4	3.2	2.5	4.2	4.2
Expand demand by developing new products or enhancing product quality	3.4	3.0	2.9	4.3	3.9
Expand export markets	3.2	3.1	2.9	3.6	3.5
Improve marketing efficiency	2.6	2.4	2.2	3.2	3.5

[a]Group 1 agricultural scientists at Gezira and Shambat, Group 2 scientists at remote regional stations (Hudeiba, Kadugli, Kenaana, New Halfa, Rahad, Sennar, and Yambio), Group 3 scientists at the commodity stations and specialized centers (Food Research Center, Forestry Research Center, Gum Arabic Research Station, Fisheries Research Center, and Wildlife Research Section).

[b]Scale 1 to 5 -- 1 = of no importance; 5 = of highest importance.

the Sudanese extension service lacks both the staff and resources to disseminate information.

Another anomaly centers on research goals. Scientists see certain goals as significantly more important than others in the conduct of their research. In contrast to their counterparts in developed countries, Sudanese scientists view a wider range of goals as important. However, various subgroups differ in their perception of the most important goals. This would be relatively unproblematic if there were no link between the maximization of particular research goals and the flow of research benefits to certain groups; but this is not the case. For example, successful research to increase agricultural productivity is most likely to benefit literate farmers near experiment

TABLE 4.3.   SCIENTISTS' PERCEIVED BENEFICIARIES OF AGRICULTURAL RESEARCH

Beneficiaries	Scientists' Responses	
	N	%[a]
Farmers	29	46.8
Industry	15	24.
Extension/government	10	16.1
General public	4	6.5
Students/universities	3	4.8
Projects	1	1.6
Total	62	99.8

[a]Does not sum to 100 due to rounding.

stations, processing and marketing firms able to purchase agricultural commodities at lower prices, and perhaps consumers—although if food quality and nutritional goals are generally neglected, little or no benefit may accrue to consumers. Similarly, emphasis on research to expand export markets may benefit certain export-crop farmers while also raising consumer prices for food crops. The promotion of community improvement may also cost some groups and benefit others. For example, crops and livestock can be protected through the use of chemical sprays, but such chemicals may increase health hazards to farm workers, rural residents, and ultimately the general public.

Finally, the pursuit of any goal involves costs and benefits. It may appear that the solution is to develop a system that maximizes benefits and minimizes costs. However, this approach addresses only the issue of outcomes; it ignores questions concerning beneficiaries and those likely to incur costs. No simple economic cost/benefit analysis can resolve this fundamental problem. These complex issues highlight the need for a more informed, comprehensive agricultural research policy.

CONCLUSIONS AND SIGNIFICANCE OF THE STUDY

The current situation in the ARC combines opportunity with the frustration of inadequate resources. The staff, soon to be augmented by additional colleagues, is generally well-trained and highly committed to applied research in agriculture. However, the facilities, supplies, and other research resources are inadequate for even the present staff. Without adequate funding, the available human resource potentials will be underutilized and possibly even lost to the system.

In summary, it is not enough just to provide funds for training new scientists and technicians. Budgetary support for operational costs other than salaries is essential, yet it is often neglected. Training and staff development should be matched with the provision of recurrent funds and capital investment to support their research. Infusion of adequate funding and resources for current operations, as well as for institutional development in the ARC, should be a high priority of the Sudanese government and other agencies interested in agricultural development in Sudan.

In addition to analyzing the ARC research system and offering recommendations to ARC administrators and scientists, INTSORMIL sociologists' "research of research" provided an important and possibly unique social science contribution to agricultural development work in Sudan. First, it treated the ARC in more than the cursory style of many external reviews of research systems. The study included in-depth interviews with junior scientists as well as department heads and station directors, surveys of scientists in training, and site visits to over half the research stations in the system. This provided multiple perspectives from a representative sample, plus observations useful to both Sudanese policymakers and foreign assistance agencies interested in strengthening the research capacity.

Second, this investigation complemented the work of other INTSORMIL social scientists regarding farming systems, extension structures, and marketing networks. The study represented one of the few occasions in which all these essential social systems in the food chain were examined in the same project.

Third, analysis of the ARC system furnished U.S. biological scientists in INTSORMIL with insights into the research milieu of their potential Sudanese collaborators. As with the CRSP structure, international agricultural development increasingly stresses collaboration between scientists in developed and developing countries. Understanding agricultural research organizations is important for the success of collaborative efforts.

Fourth, international development analysts increasingly emphasize the role of national agricultural research for development. Investment in agricultural R&D and its support services is currently a major focus of foreign assistance policies. Therefore, well-designed studies of the research system take on added significance for guiding these investments.

Finally, studying the research system provides new insights into the interrelationships among research, extension, and producer clients. The focus on research requires the reformulation of traditional views of information flow between research and extension. In this model, the research system is no longer taken as a given that provides value-free knowledge. Instead, it is viewed in terms of its internal and external dynamics and its broader technical, social, economic, and political context.

NOTES

Portions of this chapter appeared in Lacy, Busch, and Marcotte 1983.

REFERENCES

ARC. 1980. List of Research Scientists and Senior Administrators. Khartoum: ARC.

Bank of Sudan. 1983. 24th Annual Report. Khartoum: Bank of Sudan.

Brown, L. R., and C. Wolf. 1986. Reversing Africa's Decline. In *State of the World: 1986*. L. R. Brown et al., eds., pp. 175–194. New York: Norton.

Busch, L., and W. B. Lacy. 1983. *Science, Agriculture, and the Politics of Research*. Boulder: Westview Press.

FAO. 1985. FAO Production Yearbook, 1984. Vol. 38. FAO Statistics Series No. 61, pp. 77, 79, 87, 89. Rome: FAO.

Gurdon, C. 1986. Sudan in Transition: A Political Risk Analysis. London: Economist Intelligence Center.

Hargrove, T. R. 1978. Rice Breeders in Asia: A 10-Country Survey. Manila: IRRI.

Lacy, W. B., and L. Busch. 1983. Informal Scientific Communication in the Agricultural Sciences. *Information Processing and Management* 19(4):193–202.

Lacy, W., L. Busch, and P. Marcotte. 1983. The Sudan Agricultural Research Corporation: Organization, Practices, and Policy Recommendations. Lexington: INTSORMIL and University of Kentucky Department of Sociology.

Marcotte, P., L. Busch, and W. B. Lacy. 1982. An Analysis of an International Agricultural Science Community: Case Study—Sorghum. Unpublished paper.

Mellor, J. W. 1986. The New Global Context for Agricultural Research: Implications for Policy. Food Policy Statement No. 6. Washington, DC: IFPRI.

Oram, P. A., and V. Bindlish. 1981. Resource Allocations to National Agricultural Research: Trends in the 1970s. The Hague: ISNAR.

Rogers, E. M., and L. F. Shoemaker. 1971. *Communication of Innovations: A Cross-Cultural Approach*. New York: Free Press.

World Bank. 1980. *Poverty and Human Development*. Oxford: Oxford University Press.

5

Social Science Approaches to Including Nutrition Research in the International Sorghum/Millet CRSP

Kathleen M. DeWalt and Billie R. DeWalt

Research in southern Honduras as part of the International Sorghum/Millet Project (INTSORMIL) began in 1981. The primary task of University of Kentucky social scientists was to outline the socioeconomic constraints on production, distribution, and consumption of sorghum—an important crop grown on the Pacific coast of Central America. Conducted entirely by anthropologists and sociologists, this research was originally designed as a diagnostic study within the farming systems research (FSR) framework (B. DeWalt 1985; Shaner et al. 1981).

In this INTSORMIL study, significant components of the FSR "diagnosis" included the role of sorghum within the food system of southern Honduras, ways in which agricultural research could improve its role, and potential nutritional consequences of agricultural change. As fieldwork progressed between 1982 and 1984 it became evident that most farming systems research focused too heavily on production aspects of the food system. FSR needs to be supplemented by what we call "nutrition systems research" (K. DeWalt 1981, 1983; Richards 1932; Tripp 1982, 1984).

FARMING SYSTEMS RESEARCH FINDINGS

Since, the results of INTSORMIL's FSR work in southern Honduras have been reported in detail elsewhere (B. DeWalt and Alexander 1983; DeWalt and DeWalt 1982; B. DeWalt and Duda 1985; Stonich 1986), the main findings are only briefly summarized here in order to provide a background for describing the most important nutrition systems research components and findings.

From 1981 to 1984, research focused on three agrarian-reform communities of the coastal plains and six communities in two ecological zones of the highlands. We found that sorghum is an extremely important part of intercropping schemes in both lowland and highland communities.

These cropping systems have evolved primarily in response to regional rainfall patterns. Southern Honduras is marked by distinct dry (December to April) and rainy (May to November) seasons. However, the approximately 1,600 mm average rainfall masks considerable variation in actual rainfall from year to year. Also, a very distinct dry period called the *canícula* often occurs during the rainy season. Usually falling in July, the *canícula* poses an additional risk to cropping.

Maize is the basic food staple in southern Honduras, but it is a very risky crop because of the rainfall patterns noted above. To minimize crop loss, a maize with a very short growing season is raised. The main crop is planted in late April or early May for harvest during the *canícula* in July. If the rains begin late, or if the *canícula* begins early, this crop may be lost. Another maize crop is sometimes planted in August to take advantage of the rains after the *canícula*, but this crop is even more likely to fail. To minimize risk and ensure some sort of harvest, farmers intercrop sorghum with the early planting of maize. This system might appear to make little sense from an agronomic perspective because the plants compete for the same nutrients, but sorghum's greater drought tolerance is a distinct advantage. Sorghum stays in the field long after the maize has been harvested. Because photoperiod sensitive varieties are employed, sorghum does not flower until October and is not harvested until December. Cowpeas are also sometimes added to the intercropping system.

Sorghum is used for three purposes in southern Honduras: as a grain for making tortillas, the basis of the household diet; as feed for domestic livestock, especially pigs and chickens; and as a cash crop, large quantities of which enter the national marketing system, usually as livestock feed.

In southern Honduras, land is increasingly being converted to pasture for cattle (B. DeWalt 1983, 1986), and sorghum is becoming important within the cattle production system. During the lengthy dry season, cattle graze the sorghum residues. Late in the rainy season, landowners sometimes plant dense stands of sorghum; this forage sorghum is pulled up, bound into hands, and stored for cattle fodder during the dry season.

In the highlands, sorghum and maize are planted as part of a shifting cultivation system. Secondary forest is cut, and after two or three years of cultivation, the land is allowed to return to forest or is turned into pasture for livestock. In addition to the increased conversion of cropland into pasture, there is growing evidence that fallowing cycles are being shortened (Boyer 1983, Durham 1979). Also, soil fertility is declining, and soil erosion is becoming an ever-greater ecological threat (DeWalt and Alexander 1983; Stonich 1986). As a result, yields of basic grains in the region are dropping. In 1982, for example, the average yield of sorghum per hectare was only 540 kg; the comparable figures for maize and beans were 550 kg and 270 kg respectively.

The more productive lowlands are farmed mostly by large landowners who plant cash crops (e.g., sugarcane, cotton, melons) and, increasingly, pasture for cattle. A few agrarian reform communities were created in the lowlands during the late 1970s and early 1980s. In these communities, farmers often produce the same cash crops on land that is worked collectively (Adelski 1983), but usually each family is also allocated one or two hectares for cultivating grains for household needs.

FSR research conducted by INTSORMIL social scientists in nine communities in the region identified a number of food-crop production and storage constraints. The most important constraints were the erratic rainfall patterns and the declining productivity (and erosion) of the soil. In approximate order of importance, other constraints included postharvest storage losses to granary weevils and in-field losses to birds, plant disease, and insect damage (DeWalt and DeWalt 1982). These are all problems being addressed by INTSORMIL agricultural scientists. However, in our view, more important than the FSR findings are the constraints and recommendations identified by the nutrition systems research.

NUTRITION SYSTEMS RESEARCH

It is increasingly evident that several decades of technological modernization and economic growth have not significantly improved the nutritional status of marginal, rural populations. Consequently, there have been calls for a reevaluation of the potential for agricultural R&D projects directly to address nutritional problems among rural populations (FAO 1982; Pinstrup-Anderson 1981; Swaminathan 1984; USAID 1982a, 1982b, 1984a, 1984b). Arguments for the explicit inclusion of nutritional goals in agricultural R&D have followed two related lines.

The first is based on the realization that present approaches to improving the nutritional status of economically marginal rural people have not had, and are not likely to have, a positive impact. Nutrition programs are probably best suited for solving specific nutritional problems in small target groups at special risk (Beaton and Ghassimi 1979; Kennedy and Pinstrup-Andersen 1983, Pinstrup-Andersen 1981). Overall economic growth, where it has occurred, has frequently bypassed rural areas. The notion that the benefits of development will eventually "trickle down" to the nutritionally at risk in rural areas has not been vindicated (Selowsky 1979).

A second, related argument is that past failures to explicitly include nutritional goals in, or to anticipate the nutritional impacts of, the development of agricultural technology may have led to the deterioration of nutritional status among rural populations, especially small farmers. For example, in a review of nutrition, consumption, and agricultural development, Fleuret and Fleuret (1980) conclude that few programs to improve the productivity of small farmers have had a positive impact on family nutritional status. Some may even have contributed to a decline in nutritional status. Several studies of the impact of Plan Chontalpa in Tabasco, Mexico, show similar results (Dewey 1980, 1981a, 1981b; Hernández et al. 1974). There, productivity improved dramatically, but only the urban population's nutritional status was improved. Postmortems such as these have led to a growing realization that, while agricultural technology is not nutritionally neutral, the ways in which development projects and changing agricultural technology affect nutritional status are not clearly understood (Lunven 1982).

To tackle these issues, four areas must be addressed in agricultural research programs aimed at improving farm-family nutrition. These are: (1) targeting agricultural programs to those at greatest nutritional risk; (2) understanding utilization of crops and the potential impact of new crops or new varieties on overall diet, and predicting the impact of new agricultural technology on food consumption; (3) recommending ways in which agricultural R&D programs can improve the nutritional situation of those most at risk; and (4) monitoring and evaluating program impacts on food consumption and nutritional status. Each of these has somewhat different data needs and requires a different approach to data collection and analysis. Below, we illustrate these needs and approaches with INTSORMIL social science research in southern Honduras.

Targeting Agricultural Programs

Targeting agricultural research to groups at risk or to the nutritionally neediest is a crucial first step in incorporating nutrition into agricultural projects. As Reutlinger (1983) and others have pointed out, agricultural and rural development projects often fail to reach the people whose nutritional needs are greatest. Information necessary for targeting research and projects to such groups is thus quite important. Several approaches to targeting are discussed in Campbell 1985, Frankenberger 1985, Mason 1983 and 1984, and Mason et al. 1985. Joy (1973) and others (e.g., Valverde et al. 1981) have suggested an approach that includes identifying "functional classes" (that is, groups that are at risk because they share common problems, ways of making a living, resource constraints, and other factors) for whom a set of recommendations can be made. The notion of functional classification in the nutrition literature parallels the "recommendation domains" (Byerlee et al. 1982; B. DeWalt 1985) of FSR approaches to agricultural R&D.

The process and outcomes of targeting include the identification of specific nutritional problems, either through surveys or the use of secondary data; the selection of specific at-risk groups, defined in terms of their unique nutritional needs and the constraints they face in meeting these needs; and an analysis of the etiology of malnutrition. Through such research, targeting can identify crops and cropping techniques that can address those needs through agricultural research.

In the work of INTSORMIL social scientists, targeting research to the needs of the rural poor began with the identification of sorghum and millet as important crops for investigation. Like most of the CRSP commodities, sorghum and millet have been relatively neglected in terms of research, even though they form the subsistence base in a number of regions of the world experiencing nutritional stress. Furthermore, these crops are most likely to be used by groups at greatest nutritional risk. Improved availability of such crops therefore should differentially benefit those most at risk.

In order to identify those households at greatest risk of malnutrition in southern Honduras and to document the pattern of sorghum use in relation to nutritional needs in the region, we collected data on household nutritional status and dietary adequacy, with an emphasis on the use of alternative grains. Estimates of household nutritional status were based on anthropometric measurements of children 60 months of age and under. Length was measured in centimeters using an infantometer for children unable to stand unaided. For children able to stand, height was measured with a board in which a metal meter tape had been imbedded. A sliding headboard was used to read the height. Weight was measured to the nearest 100 grams, using a spring-type Salter scale for children under 10 kg. Children over 10 kg were weighed using a dial-face spring scale. Children's weight for age, height for age, and weight for height were calculated as a percentage of standard using the World Health Organization standards (WHO/FAO 1979).

Of all the children measured in the nine research communities, 65% were less than 95% of standard height for age (that is, stunted), but only 13% were under 90% of standard weight for their height (wasted). This pattern suggests that two-thirds of these children experienced undernutrition at some time in their first five years of life, but that acute undernutrition, as measured by low weight for current height, is less of a problem at any one time.

Dietary adequacy for all families was analyzed using estimates of food intake from 24-hour recalls of family meals, plus a food-use interview that focused on the week before the interview date. Amounts of energy and protein available to the household were calculated and expressed as a percentage of household needs. Protein and energy needs were calculated using WHO estimates of the requirements for individuals of the same age and sex as household members. These figures were then summed for the household.

On the average, families met 110% of their energy needs and 200% of their protein needs. However, these findings mask considerable variation, because 49% of the families did not meet their estimated energy requirement. In contrast, only 1% of families failed to meet their need for protein, thus indicating that calories are a much more significant limitation than is protein.

Although nutritionists in the Ministry of Health in Tegucigalpa and at INCAP (Institute for Nutrition for Central America and Panama) had reported that sorghum was not an important food for direct human consumption in the region, we found that this was not the case. Overall, basic grains, either maize or sorghum, provided 75% of the energy and 64% of the protein available to families. However, use patterns for the different grains varied among families, especially in the highland communities. Families in the poorest households—those of tenant farmers and sharecroppers and those headed by women—were much more likely than were landowners to use sorghum rather than maize, to use sorghum a greater percentage of the year, and to purchase sorghum for food (Thompson et al. 1985). They were also the families at greatest nutritional risk. Thus, improved availability of sorghum would more likely benefit the most nutritionally at-risk segments of the highland communities.

In the lowland agrarian-reform communities surveyed, the most interesting variation in sorghum use occurred between years. When lowland communities were originally surveyed in the summer of 1982, less than 3% of the families reported using sorghum. But a year-long drought began with the second planting season in 1982, and the second maize crop of 1982 and the first crop of 1983 failed. Resurvey of the lowland communities in 1983 showed that 25% of the families were using sorghum. While this was much less than the 68% of highland families using sorghum at the same time, it is a dramatic increase from 1982. The conclusion is that, for lowland communities, sorghum is most crucial in times of economic hardship.

Two specific questions regarding the nutritional problems of poor Central American communities had been raised by biological scientists. One was whether there was a need in the region for "quality protein" sorghum, i.e., sorghum high in lysine. The second question related to the finding by some INTSORMIL biological scientists that sorghum-based diets increase ascorbic acid requirements (Klopfenstein et al. 1981, 1983). This could be a critical limiting factor because some research has suggested that ascorbic acid may be a limiting nutrient in Central American diets (Futrell et al. 1982; INCAP 1969).

With regard to the first question, although the diets of communities in southern Honduras are poor, the limiting factor appears to be energy rather than protein. The need for high-quality protein is, of course, greater among small children than adults. We therefore surveyed children's diets separately and found that children are differentially fed high-protein foods, such as milk and eggs. Our conclusion is that, while quality protein sorghum might benefit groups with a *severely* limited diet, sufficient protein sources are available in southern Honduras and used so that the limiting factor contributing to protein-calorie malnutrition is energy.

Dietary data for ascorbic acid are not yet analyzed, but we have documented the wide availability and use of fruits and vegetables with high ascorbic acid content. Qualitative data on the seasonal availability of fruits and vegetables suggest that wild or cultivated fruits are available almost year-round. During April, mangos and a wild fruit called *tiguilote* are available. In April and May 1983, highland households were also consuming approximately 200 wild plums (*jocote*) per week. The harvest of acerola (*nance*), a wild fruit with one of the highest-known ascorbic acid contents, occurs from May to the end of June. A second harvest of mango begins in August. These second-season mangos are of inferior quality and are often wormy; since they are not suitable for sale, they are more likely to be consumed within the household. Throughout the fall, a series of wild fruits is available until the rains end. During the dry season, some local citrus are available. At this time, too, households have more cash, and they appear to buy more of the staple vegetables, such as cabbage and potatoes. Most families eat cabbage several times a week, either cooked or raw in a salad. Market-basket surveys show that potatoes are purchased at least once a week by almost all families. At the end of the dry season, in February and March, cashew fruits ripen and constitute a favored snack food.

Our information on the availability and use of ascorbic acid-containing fruits and vegetables differs somewhat from other studies. We are tempted to conclude that because many of these foods are gathered from the wild and consumed casually, their use has been poorly reported in dietary surveys. The incorporation of ethnographic methods into our survey research allowed us to document the use of these foods. Whatever the final conclusions concerning the effect of sorghum consumption on ascorbic acid requirements, from our surveys there appear to be abundant sources of ascorbic acid available to families in southern Honduras. Thus, improving the production and availability of sorghum for human consumption need not focus on increased ascorbic acid requirements.

Understanding and Predicting Potential Impacts

The second area of investigation in the nutritional systems research framework is the utilization of crops or other foods that are to be introduced, improved, or made more available through agricultural research. For example, the introduction of new, more productive varieties of food crops would have little impact on local diets if such varieties lack the characteristics that make them acceptable foodstuffs or if they are nutritionally inferior. Acceptability is closely tied to methods of food preparation and the kinds of products that result. For example, the grain quality characteristics that produce an acceptable porridge may be different from those for an acceptable flatbread or fermented beverage.

Preparation techniques may, in themselves, influence the nutritional quality of food. The relationship between niacin availability and the alkaline treatment of maize has been recognized for some time (Katz et al. 1974). Where such relationships between indigenous preparation techniques and the nutritional quality of a food are unknown, introducing new food crops without anticipating the effects of preparation may impair dietary adequacy. An analysis of the acceptability and important organoleptic properties of food crops must also include an understanding of food beliefs and preparation practices relating to the crops.

Sorghum has probably been a part of southern Honduran diets for about 100 years. The *criollo* (landrace) grains used have been selected for their appropriateness as a food as well as for their agronomic qualities. A wide variety of products are made from sorghum, many of which are sorghum equivalents of foods also prepared from maize.

For example, sorghum tortillas are prepared using essentially the same method as for maize tortillas. The grain is "nixtamalized" by heating in an alkaline solution of ashes or lime. The hot mixture is then allowed to sit for several hours or overnight. In the highlands, ashes are preferred in preparing sorghum tortillas because the pericarp of sorghum reportedly peels more easily than when lime is used. In the coastal lowlands, the available firewood leaves a salty ash that is said to be unsuitable for preparing tortillas; here, lime is always used. Cooking time for sorghum is roughly one-third the time for maize, or only about 10 minutes versus 30. Some women say the shorter the cooking time, the better and whiter the appearance of sorghum tortillas. It is also claimed that sorghum tortillas equal maize tortillas in quality if the sorghum is not overcooked. Overcooking is said to produce a less acceptable, darker tortilla. After cooking and soaking, the grain is washed and the pericarp removed. The grain is then ground in a hand mill and reground on a stone quern. The resulting *masa* is formed into flat rounds and baked for several minutes on a griddle. When some maize is available, it is preferable to prepare tortillas using half maize and half sorghum to stretch the maize.

While the tortilla is the most common and important product made from sorghum, a number of other foods are also prepared. *Rosquillas* and *rosquetes*, hard cookie-like products, are made from either maize or sorghum masa to which ground fresh cheese, sugar, and other ingredients are added. During the winter months, popped sorghum is formed into balls using honey, to make *albarotes*. A soft drink, *agua fresca*, is made from ground sorghum mixed with water and sugar. Sorghum masa cooked in water or milk produces an *atole*, or thin porridge. In the past, a coffee substitute was prepared by roasting sorghum that is first soaked to prevent popping and then ground to a coffee-like consistency. This could be used alone or mixed half-and-half with coffee beans.

All the products mentioned above were recognized in all the communities surveyed. In all areas, maize was preferred over sorghum for tortillas and most other products. When we began our research, the extent of the use of sorghum as a food was unclear. Consumption studies carried out by INCAP (1969) did not mention sorghum, and the staff of the national nutrition planning commission reported that it was an insignificant part of Honduran diets. These omissions and misconceptions probably arose from people's reluctance to admit to consuming sorghum, and from poor probing by interviewers unaware of the extent of sorghum use. Such findings reflect the generally low prestige of sorghum.

However, the perceived acceptability of sorghum as a maize replacement differs from area to area and from time to time. In general, sorghum is more acceptable in highland communities, where it serves as an insurance crop in the subsistence farming system. In the lowlands, commercialized agriculture results in a diet that is more likely to be purchased; when funds permit, maize is preferred. In INTSORMIL's first survey of lowland communities, few households reported making tortillas from sorghum. Women generally stated that, during the two or three weeks of the year when maize was un-available, they would use sorghum. They claimed that the "hill people" were sorghum users, not they. The second survey followed two cropping cycles of drought. During the drought, resources were much more limited in the lowlands than in the highlands. Because it was cheaper than maize, sorghum was purchased far more frequently in the lowland communities; responses concerning its acceptability as a human food became much less negative.

In sum, the most important grain-quality characteristics of sorghum are those contributing to high-quality tortillas. The most acceptable sorghums are those that produce the lightest colored tortillas. Shorter cooking time and ease of pericarp removal are also important. These desirable food-quality characteristics, however, need to be balanced against other important aspects of sorghum production. Postharvest storage loss to granary weevils is a significant constraint on sorghum availability. However, the most weevil-resistant sorghums may not be the best food-quality ones. Several of the "improved" varieties of sorghum previously released in the region are more susceptible to weevils than are the criollo varieties. While this does not affect the desirability of the grain when it is grown as a cash crop for sale immediately following the harvest, many people felt that the "improved" varieties were not suitable for home storage and consumption.

A second area of sorghum acceptability has to do with a very different "quality." In Latin American food classification systems, foods (as well as illnesses and medicines) are classified as having an essential quality that can range from hot to cold. Sorghum is ranked as "cooler" than maize, which is considered neutral. Although not everyone still follows the traditional hot/cold food classification system, some people report that nursing mothers should not eat sorghum tortillas because the coolness could sicken their infants. Some nursing women will therefore prepare sorghum tortillas for their families and maize tortillas for themselves. For children, however, all sorghum-based foods are considered appropriate.

Even when they are considered appropriate and acceptable, sorghum tortillas are believed to be less filling than are maize tortillas. A frequently reported formula holds that five sorghum tortillas are as filling as four maize tortillas. This observation may relate to the controversy surrounding the digestibility of sorghum protein and its effect on human nutrition. Studies of children recovering from malnutrition show poor digestibility of sorghum protein in a product made from whole ground sorghum (McLean et al. 1981). However, digestibility appears to be affected by processing methods. Sorghum that has been decorticated and heat-extruded has been found significantly more digestible (McLean et al. 1981). To date, however, there has been little testing of sorghum prepared in traditional dishes, in contrast to the well-known finding that the preparation of maize for tortillas alters the availability of a number of nutrients, including niacin and several amino acids.

Since our research in Honduras, several INTSORMIL technical scientists have begun to investigate the digestibility of sorghum products prepared by indigenous techniques. For example, in experiments with young pigs, Serna-Saldívar et al. (n.d.) have demonstrated that protein digestibility of pearled sorghum cooked in a lime solution is roughly equivalent to that of similarly prepared maize. The digestibility of protein in several African dishes where sorghum is cooked in an acid medium is similar to other staple grains (Kirleis n.d.). Further testing of sorghum products prepared with traditional techniques such as nixtamalization would be an important addition to understanding potential nutritional problems in sorghum-based diets.

Recommending Ways Agricultural
Research Can Improve Nutrition

A set of tentative recommendations emerged from our farming systems and nutrition systems research. These were discussed formally and informally with biological scientists, especially the plant breeder who has led INTSORMIL's efforts in southern Honduras since late 1981. Input from both social and biological scientists resulted in a set of goals that have guided further sorghum R&D in the region.

First, it was decided that a sorghum improvement program in the region would be valuable because sorghum is differentially utilized by the poorest members of the population. The most resource-poor farmers grow the crop, and the most resource-poor families include it more frequently in their diet. Thus, improved sorghum production, especially by small farmers, would likely improve nutrition for those most at risk.

Second, it was determined that the photoperiod sensitive varieties of sorghum grown in the region are uniquely adapted to the ecological circumstances. Early-maturing hybrids are suitable only for commercial farmers in the lowlands. Targeting research results to those most in need would be better achieved if local varieties were improved. Furthermore, double-cropping sorghum in the lowlands could greatly increase pest problems because a suitable habitat for these pests (especially the sorghum midge) would be present for a much longer period of the year. Therefore, breeding goals have focused on improving criollo sorghum varieties in southern Honduras. Some work on hybrids will be carried out, but only as a secondary goal.

Third, improved varieties resulting from the breeding program should fit within existing cropping systems and the Honduran government's relatively resource-poor seed distribution and extension programs. Unlike hybrids, varieties do not require an elaborate extension infrastructure because they can be passed on from farmer to farmer. Farmers already engage in such trading of germplasm. In addition, landrace varieties are already fairly high-yielding given the conditions under which they are grown. The greatest hope for improved yields may lie in a dwarfing gene to reduce the height of current varieties, thus allowing the plants to put more energy into seed production and less into the stalk. Furthermore, reduction of height likely could be accomplished without reducing the value of sorghum for livestock. The tall sorghum stalks are so woody that they are not very palatable for cattle. Reducing the height while keeping leaf biomass high is the goal.

A fourth advantage of working primarily with local varieties is that they already have several important grain-quality characteristics. For example, their hard pericarp provides some protection against granary weevils. The "best" existing varieties (in terms of their acceptability as a human food) were identified, and breeding goals centered on enhancing these food-quality characteristics.

Fifth and finally, it was determined that there was no real need to build a quality-protein component into the breeding program. The limiting factor in the region is calories, so improved yields and grain quality are more important goals for biological research.

Monitoring and Evaluating Program Impacts

As research continues and improved varieties are created, we feel strongly that their acceptability to farm families in the region must be assessed. The data we collected were useful not only for project planning, but also for social science monitoring and evaluation of the effects of INTSORMIL R&D. We hoped that during the course of the project we could continue to collect anthropometric and household economic data to determine whether the benefits of INTSORMIL research were in fact reaching and assisting those for whom they were most intended, but the social science component of INTSORMIL has since been eliminated. Consequently, further monitoring under program auspices will not be possible. Nevertheless, we hope eventually to use the baseline information that we gathered to conduct a meaningful evaluation of the impact of this CRSP research program on communities in southern Honduras.

SUMMARY AND CONCLUSIONS

The inclusion of a nutrition systems approach in farming systems research in southern Honduras allowed us to directly address a series of questions important for guiding and implementing biological agricultural research in the INTSORMIL CRSP. Information generated by social scientists has had an impact on the research priorities of sorghum breeders and other scientists working on issues of grain quality and utilization.

We have argued strongly for targeting research to meet the constraints of small farmers, especially those who rent land. At the same time, consumption data suggest that much of the sorghum eaten by such families in southern Honduras is purchased. Hence, an increase in sorghum availability in local markets with a decrease in price is likely to differentially benefit those at greatest nutritional risk.

Information on sorghum acceptability and utilization has highlighted the need to investigate indigenous methods of preparation, both to understand the grain-quality characteristics necessary to produce acceptable foods and to evaluate the nutritional significance of processing techniques. Finally, an understanding of the place of a single commodity such as sorghum in the diet as a whole is necessary in order to evaluate the importance of the nutritional characteristics of alternative varieties in establishing breeding priorities.

REFERENCES

Adelski, M. Elizabeth. 1983. The Role of Cotton in the Agricultural System of Southern Honduras. *Practicing Anthropology* 5(3):14, 18.

Beaton, George, and Hossein Ghassemi. 1979. *Supplementary Feeding Programs for Young Children in Developing Countries.* New York: UN Children's Fund.

Boyer, Jefferson. 1983. Agrarian Capitalism and Peasant Praxis in Southern

Honduras. Ph.D. dissertation, Anthropology, University of South Carolina.

Byerlee, Derek, L. Harrington, and D. L. Winkelmann. 1982. Farming Systems Research: Issues in Research Strategy and Technology Design. *American Journal of Agricultural Economics* 64:897–904.

Campbell, Carolyn. 1985. Rationale and Methodology for Including Nutritional and Dietary Assessment in Farming Systems Research/Extension. Bean/Cowpea CRSP Working Paper 85.3E. Cornell University: Bean/Cowpea CRSP. Mimeo.

DeWalt, Billie R. 1983. The Cattle Are Eating the Forest. *Bulletin of the Atomic Scientists* 39:18–23.

―――. 1985. Anthropology, Sociology and Farming Systems Research. *Human Organization* 44:106–114.

―――. 1986. Economic Assistance in Central America: Development or Impoverishment? *Cultural Survival Quarterly* 10:14–18.

DeWalt, Billie R., and Sara Alexander. 1983. The Dynamics of Cropping Systems in Pespire, Southern Honduras. *Practicing Anthropology* 5(3):11, 13.

DeWalt, Billie, and K. M. DeWalt. 1982. Socioeconomic Constraints to the Production, Distribution and Consumption of Sorghum in Southern Honduras. INTSORMIL Farming Systems Research in Southern Honduras Report No. 1. Lexington: University of Kentucky College of Agriculture.

DeWalt, Billie R., and Susan Duda. 1985. Farming Systems Research in Southern Honduras. In Fighting Hunger with Research. Judy F. Winn, ed., pp. 184–192. University of Nebraska: INTSORMIL.

DeWalt, K. M. 1981. Diet as Adaptation: The Search for Nutritional Strategies. Federation Proceedings 40:2606–2610.

―――. 1983. *Nutritional Strategies and Agricultural Change.* Ann Arbor: University of Michigan Research Press.

Dewey, Kathryn G. 1980. The Impact of Agricultural Development on Child Nutrition in Tabasco, Mexico. *Medical Anthropology* 4(1):21–54.

―――. 1981a. Nutritional Consequences of the Transformation from Subsistence to Commercial Agriculture in Tabasco, Mexico. *Human Ecology* 9(2):151–187.

―――. 1981b. Agricultural Development, Diet and Nutrition. *Ecology of Food and Nutrition* 8:265–273.

Durham, William. 1979. *Scarcity and Survival in Central America: The Ecological Origins of the Soccer War.* Stanford: Stanford University Press.

FAO. 1982. *Integrating Nutrition into Agricultural and Rural Development Projects: A Manual.* Nutrition in Agriculture No. 1. Rome: FAO.

Fleuret, P., and Ann Fleuret. 1980. Nutrition, Consumption and Agricultural Change. *Human Organization* 39:259–260.

Frankenberger, Timothy R. 1985. *Adding a Food Consumption Perspective to Farming Systems Research.* Washington, DC: USDA, Nutrition Economics Group, Technical Assistance Division, Office of International Cooperation and Development; and USAID, Bureau for Science and Technology, Office of Nutrition.

Futrell, Mary, Robert Jones, Louis Blum, and Eunice McCulloch. 1982. Socioeconomic and Nutritional Factors Relating to Grain Sorghum Production and Consumption in Southern Honduras: Preliminary Summary of 1981 Field Research. Starkville: Mississippi State University. Mimeo.

Hernández, M., C. P. Hidalgo, J. R. Hernández, H. Madrigal, and A. Chávez.

1974. Effect of Economic Growth on Nutrition in a Tropical Community. *Ecology of Food and Nutrition* 3:283–291.

INCAP . 1969. *Evaluación nutricional de la población de Centroamérica y Panamá: Honduras*. Guatemala City: INCAP.

Joy, Leonard. 1973. Food and Nutrition Planning. *Journal of Agricultural Economics* 24:165–192.

Katz, S. H., M. L. Hediger, and L. A. Valleroy. 1974. Traditional Maize Processing Techniques in the New World. *Science* 184:765–774.

Kennedy, Eileen, and Per Pinstrup-Andersen. 1983. Nutrition-Related Policies and Programs: Past Performances and Research Needs. Washington, DC: IFPRI.

Kirleis, Allan. n.d. Personal communication to Kathleen DeWalt.

Klopfenstein, Carol, Elizabeth Varriano-Marston, and Carl Hoseney. 1981. Effects of Ascorbic Acid in Casein vs. Sorghum Grain Diets in Guinea Pigs. *Nutrition Reports International* 24:1017–1028.

Klopfenstein, Carol, Carl Hoseney, and Elizabeth Varriano-Marston. 1983. Effects of Ascorbic Acid in Sorghum-, High Leucine-, and Casein-fed Guinea Pigs. *Nutrition Reports International* 27:121–129.

Lunven, Paul. 1982. The Nutritional Consequences of Agricultural Development and Rural Development Projects. *Food and Nutrition Bulletin* 4(3):17–22.

Mason, John. 1983. Minimum Data Needs for Assessing the Nutritional Effects of Agriculture on Rural Development Projects. In Nutritional Impact of Agricultural Projects, Papers and Proceedings of a Workshop Held by the United Nations Inter-Agency Subcommittee on Nutrition. J. Muscat, ed., pp. 24–40. Rome: IFAD.

———. 1984. Data Needs for Assessing the Nutritional Effects of Agricultural and Rural Development Projects: A Paper for Project Planners. Nutrition in Agriculture No. 4. Rome: FAO.

Mason, John, Marito García, Janice Mitchell, Karen Test, Clarence Henderson, and Hamid Tabatabai. 1985. Nutritional Considerations in Project Planning: A Case Study of Assessment Methods. *Food Policy*, May:109–122.

McLean, W. C., et al. 1981. Protein Quality and Digestibility of Sorghum in Preschool Children: Balance Studies and Plasma Free Amino Acids. *Journal of Nutrition* 111:1928–1936.

Pinstrup-Andersen, Per. 1981. Nutritional Consequences of Agricultural Projects: Conceptual Relationships and Assessment Approaches. World Bank Staff Working Paper No. 456. Washington, DC: World Bank.

Reutlinger, Shlomo. 1983. Nutritional Impact of Agricultural Projects: Conceptual Framework. In Nutritional Impact of Agricultural Projects, Papers and Proceedings of a Workshop Held by the United Nations ACC Subcommittee on Nutrition. J. Muscat, ed., pp. 1–16. Washington, DC: IFAD.

Richards, Audrey. 1932. *Hunger and Work in a Savage Tribe*. London: G. Routledge and Sons.

Selowsky, Marcelo. 1979. Balancing Trickle Down and Basic Needs Strategies: Income Distribution Issues in Large Middle-Income Countries with Special Reference to Latin America. World Bank Staff Working Paper No. 335. Washington, DC: World Bank.

Serna-Saldívar, S. O., et al. n.d. Nutritional Value of Sorghum and Maize Tortillas. College Station: Texas A&M University. Mimeo.

Shaner, W. W., P. F. Philipp, and W. R. Schmehl. 1982. *Farming Systems Research and Development: Guidelines for Developing Countries*. Boulder: Westview Press.

Stonich, Susan. 1986. Development and Destruction: Interrelated Ecological, Socioeconomic, and Nutritional Change in Southern Honduras. Ph.D. dissertation, Anthropology, University of Kentucky.

Swaminathan, M.S. 1984. Nutrition and Agricultural Development: New Frontiers. *Food and Nutrition* 10(1):33–41.

Thompson, Karen S., Kathleen M. DeWalt, and Billie R. DeWalt. 1985. Household Food Use in Three Rural Communities in Southern Honduras. INTSORMIL Farming Systems Research in Southern Honduras Report No. 2. Lexington, KY: University of Kentucky Experiment Station.

Tripp, Robert. 1982. Including Dietary Concerns in On-Farm Research: An Example from Imbabura, Ecuador. CIMMYT Working Paper. El Batán, Mexico: CIMMYT.

———. 1984. On Farm Research and Applied Nutrition: Some Suggestions for Collaboration Between National Institutes of Nutrition and Agricultural Research. *Food and Nutrition Bulletin* 6(3):49–57.

USAID (United States Agency for International Development). 1982a. AID Policy Paper: Nutrition. Washington, DC: USAID.

———. 1982b. AID Policy Paper: Food and Agricultural Development. Washington, DC: USAID.

———. 1984a. Nutrition Sector Strategy. Washington, DC: USAID.

———. 1984b. Africa Bureau: Nutrition Guidelines for Agriculture and Rural Development. Washington, DC: USAID.

Valverde, Victor, William Vargas, Philip Payne, and Anne Thompson. 1981. Data Requirements and Use in Nutrition Planning in Costa Rica. Food Policy Feb:19–26.

WHO/FAO. 1979. Measurement of Nutritional Impact. WHO/FAO 79.1. Geneva: WHO.

PART 2

Nutrition CRSP

6

The Program and the Field: Social Science in the Nutrition CRSP

Dorothy J. Cattle

Over the last decade, social scientists have actively promoted perspectives that are both theoretically and practically complementary to other fields investigating human nutrition (e.g., Cattle and Schwerin 1985; Fitzgerald 1976; Fleuret and Fleuret 1980; Greene 1977; Greene and Johnston 1980). Nutrition as a discipline spans conceptual-theoretical, methodological, and empirical aspects of a broad range of interests, concerns, and academic fields. It can be approached from a variety of perspectives focusing on questions of production and consumption. Nutrition research increasingly involves collaboration among many disciplines, posing the familiar problems of achieving communication and common understandings. Experts from different disciplines have very different points of view, as well as differing scientific techniques and tools to apply to nutrition problems.

There cannot be a single optimum approach to explaining malnutrition; the ability to detect and respond to effects of inequities or inefficiencies in food acquisition, production, and consumption is imperative. A systems approach or a holistic perspective has often been offered to counter the narrow perspectives commonly applied to nutrition problems. However, these holistic approaches have not been consistently effective in organizing our knowledge or in manipulating our data on both the sociocultural and biomedical aspects of nutritional phenomena. Individual scientists and, more recently, multidisciplinary teams have attempted to combine the meaning and importance of both aspects. The Nutrition CRSP represents one such effort.

The results of such a complex research endeavor emerge from an interaction among scientific, sociocultural, and project contexts and not merely from a research design *per se*. Even when social scientists are less involved than are biological scientists in research design, they may nevertheless substantially influence adaptation of the design to the sociocultural and project contexts of a field study (e.g., Uquillas and Garrett this volume). These design adaptations are not a simple compromise, but an ongoing process in field situations. An important part of the field situation is the project itself, a newly created context that CRSP anthropologists addressed through design and operational recommendations. Although in the late 1980s, analysis of Nutrition CRSP field data is just beginning, prior program phases illustrate the types of scientific integration that can be achieved and the range of social science contributions to those efforts.

Because the Nutrition CRSP is structured differently than the agricultural commodity CRSPs, I first describe the planning and program organization process. During the planning phase of the Nutrition CRSP, social scientists from a variety of disciplines (anthropology, sociology, political science, psychology, and economics) participated in a series of workshops to identify specific research issues; coauthored research proposals and the final planning report; reviewed proposals for individual projects under the Nutrition CRSP; and served in administrative roles. These programmatic and scientific activities were essential to the integration of biological and sociocultural aspects within the Nutrition CRSP and to the formulation of the initial program structure. A discussion of these activities follows the two descriptive sections on the Nutrition CRSP's development.

Next, a sampling of initial in-field social science contributions from one of the three Nutrition CRSP projects, the Kenya project, is presented. Field implementation of the Nutrition CRSP in Kenya involved a range of contributions from social scientists. However, here I limit discussion to social scientists' participation in site selection and their collaboration on most phases of in-field design and operations. These contributions brought the field situation into closer correspondence with the scientific context.

The conclusion discusses broader applications of the Nutrition CRSP social science experience to other situations and opportunities, including: research integration of multiple disciplines; organizational integration of a project within already extant structures; community preparation and participation; types and uses of results; and the constraints and responsibilities of basing a large, complex research study within a rural area. Additional social science contributions will become evident only through post–field data and policy analysis.

THE PROGRAM:
DEVELOPING AND DEFINING THE NUTRITION CRSP

The Nutrition CRSP grew out of a 1974 presidential request to the National Academy of Sciences (NAS) for recommendations "on how [U.S.] research and development capabilities can best be applied" to major worldwide hunger and malnutrition issues (Gerald Ford, cited in NAS 1977a:iii). NAS Study Team Nine was impanelled to define research priorities for human nutrition; it recommended determination of both energy needs and the effects of substandard energy intakes as a priority (NAS 1977b). The team pointed out that the most widespread type of malnutrition appears to be inadequate food intake resulting in inadequate energy intake. The NAS ranked the relationship between food intake and human functioning first among the 22 priority areas documented by all 12 study teams. The Academy's steering committee review emphasized:

> Nutrition is fundamental to human life, performance, and well-being. Levels of nutritional well-being both influence and reflect social and economic development in every country. . . . Presently, nutritional deprivation is doing immense damage to human lives and societies throughout the world. For a nation, widespread malnutrition can mean impaired physical and mental growth and development of its children, reduced working capacity and income of its adults, increased costs from disease and health care, and high death rates. The intangible costs of reduced human vitality may be even greater (NAS 1977a:59, 64).

With USAID support, in 1977 the Committee on International Nutrition Programs of the Food and Nutrition Board of the National Research Council held a workshop on potential research leading to a functional definition of nutritional status. Five major functional areas were identified: disease response, reproductive competence, work output, cognitive function, and social and behavioral function (Food and Nutrition Board, National Research Council 1978). To further define such areas and establish a research program, the University of California–Berkeley was awarded a planning grant by USAID in 1978.

Planning the Program and Guidelines for Research

To determine what was known about the ways varied levels of marginal food-energy intake affect an individual's functioning in society, a multidisciplinary workshop on each of the five functional areas was held. Another purpose of these meetings was to develop an international and interdisciplinary multiproject research program. The workshops included about 80 scientific investigators from developing and developed countries, representing a range of disciplines. Two background papers were commissioned for each workshop, one from a social science viewpoint and one from a biological perspective. Both were to present state-of-the-art knowledge and to suggest research approaches.

The participant structure of these workshops encouraged consideration of social science research strategies and results. The various workshop recommendations attempted to clarify the nutritional research design and some of its sociocultural contexts. The research approach that emerged differed from most previous human nutrition field studies in three ways: (1) nutritional status was replaced by food-energy intake as the independent variable; (2) the functional consequences of marginal (mild-to-moderate) malnutrition, contributing to the perpetuation of deficient intake, were incorporated into the research design; and (3) behavioral as well as environmental aspects and interrelationships within household units were considered integral parts of the study, as dependent rather than confounding variables.

Recommendations from the five functional workshops were reviewed with regard to feasibility, acceptability, importance, and relevance of such studies to developing countries (DCs) at a sixth workshop attended by experienced foreign investigators and staff from the World Health Organization (WHO) and the Food and Agriculture Organization (FAO) of the United Nations. Their report, "Précis: Collaborative Research Support Program on Intake and Function," emphasized DC perspectives (Calloway et al. 1980:5–6) and enunciated eleven important points: (1) the unit of study is the household; (2) the mother–child dyad is the logical focal point; (3) food intake is represented by energy (calorie) intake consisting of a range of habitual mildly-to-moderately restricted energy intakes; (4) resulting data are generalizable to nutrition problems in developing countries, and are not country-specific; (5) certain core research determinants are necessarily common to all Nutrition CRSP country projects; (6) food intake is the major independent variable; (7) nutritional status measurement is an explanatory intermediate variable; (8) selected study communities are to be politically and socially stable with low migration rates; (9) specific research topics are expected to have potential policy and program applications; (10) U.S. standards for human research are to be followed, including obtaining the informed consent of participants; and (11) beneficial services provided during the studies are to be maintained upon conclusion of the projects. Additionally, for scientific and ethical reasons, the précis strongly stated that the preferred CRSP research approach should be naturalistic rather than interventionist. In nutrition studies, the latter is an experimental, case control, or supplementation design.

The précis served as the guideline for all research proposals submitted to the Nutrition CRSP for review. In 1979, grant applications were sent to four peer reviewers representing epidemiology or statistics, nutrition with a medical orientation, nutrition with a biological sciences orientation, and social science or psychology. Next, the proposed projects were prioritized by a scientific advisory group. The resulting integrated collaborative research program plan gained USAID approval in mid-1980. Funding and administrative start-up occurred in September 1981. Central management responsibility rested with the Institute of International Studies at the University of California–Berkeley. The Nutrition CRSP hired its own senior administrative staff independently of the institute, with daily central management handled mainly by various social scientists. This association with an international-oriented institute likely provided the Nutrition CRSP with an appropriately broader context than it would have had if situated within a medical or biological entity.

The program design incorporated three geographically defined research projects—Egypt, Kenya, and Mexico. Each addressed the same critical questions regarding relationships between levels of food intake and human physiological, behavioral, and societal functions. All shared common design elements or an initial core information base. Screening and community selection required that baseline surveys combine nutritional and socioeconomic indicators to estimate ranges of the major variables, plus anticipated rates of biological occurrences (such as births) and social occurrences (such as attrition). Other aspects of the core involved scheduling and coordinating observations, measurements, and other protocols for data collection. Some of these routines needed to be matched to biological and sociocultural events at the community, as well as the individual, level. Additional information such as the nature of family dynamics in relation to the major nutrition variables, was also required. This eventually called for the operational integration of clinical, biomedical, nutritional, and social science data routines.

Early consideration also was given to specifying collaborative formats to be utilized across projects prior to, during, and after fieldwork to ensure continued interaction of ideas, hypotheses, analyses, and other research outcomes. The promotion of collaboration was an important part of prefield deliberations. Although research findings from the Nutrition CRSP were expected to have scientific value, an equally important goal was to utilize overall program and specific project findings to develop policies and potential programs to lessen deprivation in the three host countries and elsewhere in the world.

During almost a decade of prefield development of the Nutrition CRSP, interest in the research priority regarding relationships between mild to moderate malnutrition and human functioning increased, partly through the awareness generated by involving a broad range of professionals in the CRSP. The narrowness and limitations of previous approaches, such as conventional anthropometic measures of human nutritional needs, were recognized. Elements of the research design were also linked to broader DC concerns, as well as to those of other policymakers and planners.

Social Science Participation in Program Planning

Throughout the development of the Nutrition CRSP, anthropologists, sociologists, political scientists, psychologists, and economists made significant planning and scientific contributions. Additionally, a number of socially relevant issues were introduced by CRSP biological and medical scientists.

Programmatic and administrative contributions. The planning process continually involved many social science disciplines in areas such as initial scientific recommendations to the NAS; CRSP development workshops, meetings, and consultations; and in review, advisory, and administrative positions. Social scientists were coinvestigators on many of the proposed projects, and the research proposals submitted reflected their influence. The three projects selected all had social scientists as principal investigators (PIs) or senior researchers.

Even prior to fieldwork, CRSP social scientists learned about the strengths, weaknesses, interests, and orientations of their fellow investigators and made use of such information in numerous meetings and discussions. As the CRSP was implemented, project investigators became adept at handling scientific and programmatic negotiations across disciplines. Indeed, all CRSP scientists learned valuable cross-disciplinary communication skills. But social scientists perhaps absorbed relatively more new information, having come from a social perspective into the center of a biomedical and nutritional program where, from the outset, biological scientists were more focused and knowledgeable on central nutritional issues. As social scientists gain more skill in these situations, they in turn can better educate their collaborating colleagues about social factors having nutritional consequences. This interplay not only sharpens social science contributions to biological research, but also points such research in socially meaningful directions.

During program development, several different viewpoints—epidemiological, anthropological, and analytical—were introduced. CRSP participants with an epidemiological perspective viewed thematic data collection as a primary research operation, whereas anthropologists expected a more flexible, field-informed design. Investigators with an analytical viewpoint emphasized early and close linking of data collection with analytical models and procedures. Negotiating these broad differences was an important process in CRSP development, especially since a PI from each project serves as a rotating member of a scientific coordination board. Additionally, successful coordination across the Nutrition CRSP's three projects required reaching consensus and a common understanding about the research program.

CRSP social scientists made a concerted effort to integrate social and biological perspectives during the planning phase. This was largely accomplished through substantial investments of time, early and continual interaction with biomedical scientists, social scientists' uniform and evident presence in research decisionmaking, and other responsibilities, such as peer review.

The DC perspective. Investigators from developing countries and international agencies also established the place of social science in the program. They stressed the social context by specifying the types of communities to be involved and the household as the relevant unit of analysis. Their firm recommendation for a naturalistic study also strengthened the position of field-experienced social scientists in the research program. By adopting U.S. human research guidelines, especially informed consent, their review raised another issue for social scientists. Anthropologists, for example, are experts on problems of informed consent in field studies and how to gain such consent in varied and complex cultural, educational, and other circumstances.

DC professionals also raised scientific and ethical considerations regarding the use of research results and the maintenance of community services that might be initiated during research. The use of nutritional research for application and policy purposes requires interpreting results for politicians, economists, a variety of social scientists, and biotechnical and medical personnel. Often these same professionals must be approached to continue community services established by projects. Therefore, biomedical and social scientists need to be able to interrelate their information and to foresee the implications of ongoing project operations. This can be effected only if social scientists are involved at a level commensurate with their other scientific colleagues.

Contributions to research design. The CRSP emphasizes nutritional research from a biomedical perspective, including traditional measures of nutritional status. This emphasis affected the role of social sciences within the program's scientific framework. Selection of the household as the major study unit exemplifies the evolution of the common design. Originally, the nutrition research was thought of as household-based, that is, as embedded in the dynamics of that social unit. The choice of which household members to study then arose since there was a biomedical requirement to focus on the food intake of specific individuals in relation to particular functional outcomes—e.g., mothers and their infants in relation to reproductive success and growth and development. Additionally, the choice of households evolved from efficiency considerations at a research and a field level. Finally, the household became important for the types of individuals it contained and for operational and logistical concerns. Thus, a biomedical focus and questions of research efficiency, rather than a social dynamics emphasis, shaped the Nutrition CRSP's use of the household.

Although both anthropology and medicine (including some fields of nutrition) are person-oriented, they examine people within very different contexts. Anthropologically, the person is viewed as a social entity with attendant roles, statuses, and responsibilities, who inhabits an environmental, organizational, and institutional milieu. Medically, the person is viewed much more individualistically, often both as patient and problem (Cattle 1981). Units commonly are framed biologically, e.g., as a reproductively active adult pair or as a nursing female. Another aspect of viewing the person medically is that each individual accumulates a corpus of data, an empirical history of attributes. The milieu is absent, as are sociocultural processes.

Social scientists thus have a difficult task. There are usually few opportunities to insert social theory into a scientific framework already considered adequate to accommodate nutritional research. In the Nutrition CRSP, however, the biomedical research came to be seen as so daunting that sociocultural complexities were added to the scientific discourse in certain, somewhat expectable, ways. For example, social scientists provided necessary predictions about the phasing, sequencing, and rate of the research that affected study design. Not surprisingly, part of their work was to furnish background data, too. However, CRSP social scientists also were able to build ongoing social data collection into the research design in conjunction with the biomedical procedures. Because most of the original CRSP social scientists had training or research experience in nutrition, they were more influential in integrating methods and issues in social research with the variety of nutritional techniques required by the design. Another familiar role for social scientists is facilitating implementation of the R&D design. In the Nutrition CRSP, this contribution was made more challenging and anthropologically interesting because social scientists had been brought in at the program's inception.

The research design derived mainly from scientific and policy concerns for specific areas of nutrition. Although many scientists involved during the planning and design phases acknowledged the importance of the complexity of human society, that complexity was not the basic theoretical framework for the nutritional investigations. However, even with its strong emphasis on a nonsocial framework, in its long evolution the Nutrition CRSP involved social scientists early on, in several capacities, operationally integrating them into the research process across the life of the program.

THE FIELD: THE KENYA PROJECT

In February 1982, the Kenya project began host country operations. This section describes some of the substantive social science contributions to field implementation of the Nutrition CRSP in Kenya.

Site Selection

Kenyan and U.S. colleagues together defined site selection in terms of both a study population and a spatial area, thus incorporating a range of social and practical concerns into the criteria specified by the research design. This definition in part derived from the field experiences of host country scientists and the U.S. anthropologist. Besides design requirements, site selection had to take into account governmental recommendations, present and potential logistic problems, overall convenience, and the likelihood of scientific and operational success. Also, selection had to be conducted relatively quickly and efficiently. This meant it had to use basic information and be done right the first time. For a project as large and complicated as the Nutrition CRSP, early field mistakes could be very costly in time, money, and data. There were also broader social ramifications if the project were later re-sited: disruption of local commitments; relocation of employees; and the creation of uncertainty among officials, staff, and potential participants.

CRSP investigators involved in site selection usually represented three viewpoints—anthropology, community health, and nutrition. Site selection was mainly based on a three-way evaluation of social interaction and interpretation, Kenyan field experience, and nutritional assessment in relation to design needs. Under these circumstances, selection was first of all a social process, among the participating colleagues as well as between them and the people visited in potential field sites. Precise nutritional and other criteria were important but not dominant because the data necessary to ensure the scientific suitability of the selected sites would not be available until well into the main study phase of the project. Judgment therefore relied more on what was seen, heard, and discussed, and less on what was measured. The selection teams understood this process, thus reflecting their appreciation of a broad scientific perspective and their willingness to base decisions more on social information. The team anthropologist presented and evaluated this information and linked Kenyan field expertise and social information to the nutritional data.

Embu District in Eastern Province was the favored administrative unit for the Kenya project. Several one- or two-day surveys were made in various parts of the district. These visits emphasized different activities and a range of individuals occupying different socioeconomic roles. Although provincial and district officials sometimes accompanied the selection team, at other times the team met with local officials and residents without attracting undue attention. Therefore, at least some visits were "naturalistic," as opposed to "formal," for both the CRSP investigators and the local population. This allowed the anthropologist to evaluate potential sites based on factors more closely resembling an actual field situation.

A key information area was people's perception of the project and their willingness to participate. The site selection team had to develop an explanation of the project that was understandable both to potential participants and local officials. With a grasp of the intended project, chiefs and other leaders were better able to evaluate it from the standpoint of their levels of responsibility, potential sociopolitical risks, and possible benefits. They could also assess how the project would or would not fit in their area, e.g., with regard to the availability of the required household types and the potentials for local household support and participation. The anthropologist refined the "CRSP explanation" in accord with officials' reactions and questions plus Kenyan investigators' interpretations. Through repeated explanations of the proposed project, the selection team also became aware of the local inhabitants' concerns and expectations. In the process of creating a useful explanation responsive to these expectations, an important anthropological contribution was to build in local understandings of the CRSP. This was crucial to initiating and sustaining participation by a range of individuals, as stipulated in the research framework.

The selection process itself consisted of a two-way evaluation, including local leaders' views of the selection team as representatives of the project, and the team's assessment of local leadership and other criteria in relation to research and project requirements. The anthropological part of this evaluation went beyond specific quantitative criteria to consider feasibility from the viewpoint of both local populations and individual CRSP researchers. Additionally, anthropological knowledge of local infrastructure and interpersonal relationships established during site visits influenced the eventual operational design of study-area censuses.

In-field Design and Operation

Although the Nutrition CRSP research design was developed for use across Egypt, Kenya, and Mexico, the Kenya project design had to be created *de novo* socially, spatially, and structurally, for it to be appropriate to its context. Congruence among these dimensions, the program design, and the different CRSP disciplines had to be achieved. This was not a linear or immediate process. Other field actions concerned bringing CRSP research expectations into the reality of a population more familiar with applied activities. A clear distinction between research versus applied projects had to be drawn without raising inappropriate expectations or creating unnecessarily negative reactions.

Social scientists contributed to in-field design and operations in a variety of ways. Anthropological responsibility was especially broad during early field phases. It spanned personnel matters; operational design, scheduling, and mapping; initial field interviewing; designating and designing a pilot area for field-testing; pretesting research protocols; and selecting the study households. Thus, the anthropologist created and supervised a variety of

CRSP activities requiring the attention and understanding of local officials. Here, three specific examples of anthropological contributions to in-field design and operations are presented, drawing upon the realms of communications, spatial units, and disciplinary structures.

Communications. One outgrowth of site selection was a sensitivity to local patterns of communication. These patterns were assessed from a social science perspective and then incorporated into all field operations. For example, village chiefs customarily call and officiate at community meetings. The project therefore adopted this forum to disseminate information about its activities, providing the chief and his counselors with a description of the entire scope of the CRSP. Continual anthropological involvement ensured that these individuals received complete social and nutritional explanations and information.

Along with local residents and staff, the most senior project personnel attended these community meetings. As noted, a major initial purpose of the meetings was to introduce and explain the project and request the support and permission of the local population to start field operations. At these meetings, local officials spoke of the relationships between their specific responsibilities and CRSP activities, noting political, social, and economic concerns. Other local groups also contributed to these initial meetings. For example, a theater troupe presented an original play about malnutrition. A women's organization or church group might also add to the meeting. Project staff usually were unaware of these events ahead of time and had no control over their content. In addition to comments and speeches by residents, there was always a question-and-answer period. Senior field staff answered for functional areas, while the anthropologist covered community infrastructure and environmental information, household and individual levels for child development and social functions, and specific activities related to other functions and project operations (e.g., training field personnel, setting policies on confidentiality, piloting questionnaires and other research methods, and selecting households for inclusion in the study sample).

When either the residents or the project personnel perceived that a meeting was needed, the chief and his elders would ascertain its purpose and arrange a time. Later meetings included public explanation of new procedures that were not well understood or accepted by participants (skinfold measurements and drawing blood are two examples), introduction of additional local staff, and expression of project commitment to the local area. Meetings were thus held for explanatory, expressive, and problem-solving purposes at different points (introduction, transition, etc.) throughout the project. These meetings served the population and the project well. In part, they derived from the early experiences of the anthropologist on the site selection team.

Another major communication effort was creation of a liaison role for a Kenyan field staff member experienced in government surveys. This liaison and ombudsman position evolved out of this individual's work with the anthropologist during early field operations. His tasks included monitoring local fieldworkers' relationships within the project and the local area, identifying communication problems between senior staff and local staff, reporting community dissatisfactions with any aspect of the project, and generally helping to resolve any relationship problems. The project succeeded in large part thanks to the skills and knowledge of this liaison agent and to the continual heavy investment of project time and attention in local communication in all its forms. The project's relationship to the local area was a continuing issue for CRSP social scientists, who emphasized its importance throughout the design of field operations. There was always a way for any individual on the project or in the community to get the attention of those in charge. Thus, the project was never distanced from the community.

Spatial units. The spatial design of the project gave it a manageable identity for both residents and staff. Study households were dispersed over 60 km^2 of rural landscape. The anthropologist suggested that this expanse be divided into four operational clusters, with each cluster containing approximately the same number of households (about 70), a field office, and the required complement of field teams. Whether participating in the CRSP or not, residents in each cluster could thus become familiar with local staff and project facilities. Since most staff lived in their assigned clusters, they developed social, as well as work-related, persona. They thus became visible in familiar community contexts as well as in their research roles. By breaking the spatial design into clusters, field teams were able to establish closer working relationships among themselves and to view the project "as a whole" on a small scale. Based on the anthropologist's initial in-field design suggestions, this large research project was operationally and spatially scaled down with no loss of scientific intent.

Disciplinary structures. The project devised a team approach to data collection. Kenyan fieldworkers were divided into teams related to the major areas of data collection on the Nutrition CRSP—namely, food intake, and the functional areas of reproduction, growth (anthropometry), development (cognition), activity (social development and child care), morbidity, and household social and economic characteristics. Senior staff worked almost daily with one or more teams in their areas of expertise. This structure gave senior staff in all disciplines (from pediatrics and nutrition to psychology and anthropology) a field awareness of each functional area. At the same time, fieldworkers were better able to relate to their fellows assigned to very different tasks who nonetheless shared similar experiences in coping with tight schedules and research-related events. The result was close integration of the diverse disciplines involved in the Nutrition CRSP. It was not perfect, but when it did not work, it was fairly easy to identify the problem spot and the reason for its existence.

In developing these in-field design and operation strategies, social scientists were structurally and scientifically in contact with other disciplines. Project success depended on anthropological experience and expertise as related to other specialties and the research framework, not for any singular social science contributions. The more pervasively anthropology was integrated throughout research operations, the more it contributed to project success. Within the Kenya project's team framework, social scientists developed procedures, designs, and information that were then used or refined by other scientists, and vice versa. For example, the anthropologist provided field orientation and training in interviewing techniques to the original staff; and subsequent specialized training incorporated parts of this program; also, periodic retraining developed from this early anthropological experience. Biomedical concerns about data quality control then were fit into a well-established orientation to staff performance. The essence of teamwork includes such embedding of contributions in the research endeavor. The internal and external social structure of the Kenya project worked to the advantage of both participants and researchers.

APPLICATIONS OF THE NUTRITION CRSP EXPERIENCE

Social scientists have had varied roles and responsibilities during the long emergence of the Nutrition CRSP program and the fielding of the Egypt, Kenya, and Mexico projects. From a disciplinary viewpoint, there were both opportunities and constraints to this involvement. Several are discussed below and are then related to possible applications of the CRSP experience to future international agricultural R&D projects. However, these and other aspects of social scientists' involvement in the Nutrition CRSP deserve fuller evaluation by scientists from all three projects. Indeed, such an extensive evaluation would be a useful social science contribution to our CRSP.

Opportunities and Constraints

As noted in previous sections, several senior social scientists joined the Nutrition CRSP at its inception. Social scientists were also situated at various other places in the program structure. This early and wide-ranging involvement provided not only a disciplinary voice, but also a disciplinary contact point for other social scientists more distant from the program and its development. Through the prominent use of social information and anthropological field expertise by the original senior staff, the Kenya project followed the social science concept of a "naturalistic" and community-based field study in almost all respects. This initial social perspective was successfully maintained by all subsequent disciplines, and it guided them into the field and made their entry smoother.

The Kenya project maximized and emphasized its localness, despite the fact that it formed part of a highly visible international program. Again, this was partially due to fitting project operations consciously into a field context and to recognizing explicitly the complexity of the research. The project was integrated at the local field level, with most important activities and both junior and senior staff involvement occurring mainly at that level. Host country and U.S. universities were connected directly to field operations and the project's administrative structure. The cluster structure made the project compatible with local infrastructure (road systems, health facilities, schools, etc.) and other conditions.

As a biomedical endeavor, the Kenya project could have been based in the local medical infrastructure, but this would have been unnecessarily limiting. Contextualizing the project within communities won more active support from local government, village leaders, and residents. Although this placed more responsibility for project success upon local actors, it also meant greater recognition for them. The project was incorporated into and visible across the social landscape, in full view and under broad obligations; an important part of individuals' participation in the project was the satisfaction of contributing to something larger than one's usual situation. This seemed to be true for both local residents and project staff.

Despite the successful integration of social perspectives into the project, anthropologists on the Nutrition CRSP felt some constraints. The program emphasized postulated relationships between and among biomedical, nutritional, and behavioral variables. People were viewed as biological, not social, entities, and data collection was timed to a biomedical rather than a social framework. This made it more difficult for CRSP social scientists to collect and interpret their information in a manner that would effectively inform project research procedures. For example, although Kenyan and U.S. social scientists conducted case studies on household dynamics to be used in refining research protocols, the studies were scheduled too late in the preliminary project phase to be completed and analyzed for this purpose. Similarly, the collection of quantitative data on climate, agriculture, and activity patterns was delayed, scaled down, or scheduled so as not to impinge on biomedical protocols and project resources. Anthropologists also felt somewhat constrained by having to work within a fixed research framework that had not been developed out of the social and field contexts of the particular culture. By concentrating on biomedical and nutrition issues, this framework placed secondary emphasis on social relationships and typical anthropological approaches and information.

In addition, the research framework stressed abstract biomedical research concepts and needs rather than readily comprehensible, local needs. There was therefore some tension between this "blueprint" approach and the more field-oriented "learning" or "processual" design model (e.g., Berg et al. 1973; Cernea 1985; Korten 1980; Thomas 1985; Winikoff 1978) with which social scientists are more comfortable. The "blueprint," or preset design, also limited the collection of social information. Because of the nature of the primary information to be gathered, data collection schedules had to be rigidly adhered to, with biological needs and goals taking precedence. Such constraints are not unexpected by social scientists on bionutritional projects. However, a closer examination of these limitations may prove fruitful for later phases of the Nutrition CRSP's analytical work, for application of CRSP data to policy questions, and for future planning of multidisciplinary projects.

Applications

The Nutrition CRSP experience as described here applies to several different areas; one is participation. In a field situation, it is obviously necessary to bring together several sets of participants who may have very different roles and perspectives. For example, one individual may be serving as a local subject of the inquiry, another as a local inquirer, and a third as an expatriate scientist. What is the significance to the local community of such varied participation? A project's impact is channeled partly through the ways people participate in and thus experience the project. That is, there is both a personal and social impact on participants that affects the community. Although biomedical research projects usually characterize participation by numbers of subjects or rates of attrition, much less attention is given to other, sociocultural aspects of participation. The latter differ from one field situation to another and can provide important information about project sustainability and success.

Nutrition CRSP findings are important to research issues in several disciplines, but the program's outcomes can have applications beyond scientific interests—for training, community development, project design, institutional coordination, and policymaking. The latter has always been an explicit goal of the Nutrition CRSP. Other, tentative steps toward broadening the importance of this CRSP's results will be taken, but attention and financial support for making them widely available for a variety of purposes is limited.

In general, programs have begun to make their information more accessible to colleagues in developing countries. The collaborative format of the CRSPs ensures this practice. However, such efforts must go beyond just leaving a data set behind. Results have to be available in-country to others with different purposes and areas of expertise. For example, clear documentation is important, especially when computer data bases are very complex. Similarly, scientists should describe all their protocols in a manner that makes them potentially replicable. Another consideration is the reporting of results. Programs such as the CRSP typically produce government-style reports and academic papers, which may not be enough to make project information more broadly accessible and applicable. The dissemination and impact of project information is an area that could benefit from closer social science scrutiny.

The experience of the Nutrition CRSP in integrating multiple disciplines across different phases of program development may serve as a model for future R&D, to be examined for its processes and structures and reworked for other circumstances. Disciplinary integration in the initial phases of fieldwork was accomplished in several ways. For one, because local explanations of the CRSP were needed, field staff found it necessary to conceptualize and enunciate all project activities and aspects as a coherent, understandable whole. For another, the organization of field teams by functional areas and the daily contact among them meant that disciplines could not become isolated from each other. Frequent interaction between and among senior personnel and fieldworkers also increased disciplinary integration. Moreover, since research in some functional areas required input from two or more disciplines or specialists, this prompted recognition of the need to solve problems by appealing to a variety of expertise. Early recognition that social information could have major effects on project functioning—e.g., through guiding operational design or enhancing the project's community reputation—increased respect for and integration of the social sciences involved in the field research. The employment of a full-time liaison person with the prerogative to move across research areas with inquiries and solutions to operational problems also kept the project operationally integrated across disciplines.

Organizational integration within the physical and social dimensions of the rural study area also contributed to smoother operations. Organizationally, the Kenya project was reminded of its community base. The project seemed to be regarded as a large, somewhat unusual local entity, but a part of the study area nevertheless. The many households not directly involved in the daily research activities recognized the project's presence by raising community concerns regarding it and its staff. The project promptly responded to all such inquiries and perceptions. This kind of community interaction was an ongoing project responsibility, and staff time was always available to handle it.

Partly because of its size, but also because of its base within the broader community, the project was not relegated to an obscure, impersonal corner of rural activity. This was important for a research effort that had to overcome the area's unfamiliarity with nonapplied activities and earn public acceptance. It may also be a measure of the Kenya project's success in translating abstract research goals into something organizationally and operationally meaningful to the community.

Nutrition CRSP social scientists, along with their colleagues in other disciplines, contributed to these efforts through an understanding of the local area and of the research program on food intake and human functioning. Over the decade of the Nutrition CRSP's development, anthropologists helped clarify a new model of community nutrition and a different set of questions about the nutritional vulnerability of populations (Paolisso and Baksh this volume). Early involvement of anthropologists shaped the scientific guidelines for fieldwork. Functioning as senior team members, anthropologists brought the scientific and the operational, the biomedical and the sociocultural needs of the CRSP into closer correspondence.

NOTES

The Nutrition CRSP/Kenya Project is supported by USAID Grant No. DAN 1309-G-SS-1070-00. The author, an anthropologist, was a senior investigator on the project from 1981 to 1985, and was involved in program planning from December 1978. Kenyan sociologists Benjamin Nyaga and Duncan Ngare paricipated in the field study beginning in late 1983. Other social scientists in the Nutrition CRSP made substantial contributions to the issues discussed here. Collaboration with Eric Carter, the field director during most of the early project fieldwork and the main study, and with PIs Nimrod Bwibo and Charlotte Neumann is gratefully acknowledged.

REFERENCES

Berg, Alan, Nevin S. Scrimshaw, and David L. Call (eds.). 1973. *Nutrition, National Development, and Planning*. Cambridge: MIT Press.
Calloway, Doris H., Christina Wood, Robin D. Beall, and Dorothy J. Cattle. 1980. Final Report to U.S. Agency for International Development on Contract No. AID/DSAN-C-0002, Collaborative Research Support Program on Intake and Function. Berkeley: Department of Nutritional Sciences, University of California.
Cattle, Dorothy J. 1981. The Paradox of Targeting Nutrition Programs. Paper presented at the 12th International Congress of Nutrition, San Diego.
Cattle, Dorothy J., and Karl H. Schwerin (eds.). 1985. *Food Energy in Tropical Ecosystems*. New York: Gordon and Breach Science Publishers.
Cernea, Michael M. (ed.). 1985. *Putting People First. Sociological Variables in Rural Development*. New York: Oxford Univerisity Press.

Fitzgerald, Thomas K. (ed.). 1976. *Nutrition and Anthropology in Action.* Assen, Netherlands: Van Gorcum.

Fleuret, Patrick, and Anne Fleuret. 1980. Nutrition, Consumption, and Agricultural Change. *Human Organization* 39(3):250–260.

Food and Nutrition Board, National Research Council. 1978. Report of a Workshop on the Need for Research and Nutrition and Function, July 18–21, 1977. Committee on International Nutrition Program. Washington, DC: NAS.

Greene, Lawrence S. (ed.). 1977. *Malnutrition, Behavior, and Social Organization.* New York: Academic Press.

Greene, Lawrence S., and Francis E. Johnston (eds.). 1980. *Social and Biological Predictors of Nutritional Status, Physical Growth, and Neurological Development.* New York: Academic Press.

Korten, David C. 1980. Community Organization and Rural Development: A Learning Process Approach. *Public Administration Review* 40(September–October):480–511.

NAS. 1977a. World Food and Nutrition Study. The Potential Contributions of Research. Washington, DC: NAS.

———. 1977b. Supporting Papers: World Food and Nutrition Study. Volume IV, Study Team 9, Nutrition. Washington, DC: NAS.

Thomas, Theodore. 1985. Reorienting Bureaucratic Performance: A Social Learning Approach to Development Action. In *Public Participation in Development Planning and Management: Cases from Africa and Asia.* Jean-Claude Garcia-Zamor, ed., pp. 13–30. Boulder: Westview Press.

Winikoff, Beverly (ed.). 1978. *Nutrition and National Policy.* Cambridge: MIT Press.

7

Anthropological Contributions to the Study of Malnutrition: The Nutrition CRSP Kenya Project

Michael Paolisso and Michael G. Baksh

Few people need to be reminded of the debilitating consequences of malnutrition. Throughout the developing world, lack of adequate food is a constant threat to individual health and societal well-being. Yet, the causes and consequences of insufficient nutrient intake are not well understood. Herein lies a major challenge for researchers from both biological and social sciences. Two disciplines, nutrition and anthropology, have obviously important roles to play, and they have recently joined efforts in the study of malnutrition and its consequences.

Because the history of joint research efforts between anthropologists and nutritionists is short, we are only now beginning to realize the rich possibilities for combining their respective research focuses (Jerome et al. 1980). Using the Kenya project as an example, this chapter discusses specific areas wherein sociocultural anthropology and nutrition research complement each other. First, we examine similarities and differences between anthropological and nutritional approaches to the study of chronic mild-to-moderate malnutrition. Anthropological contributions to the Nutrition CRSP's study of the functional consequences of such malnutrition are then outlined. In particular, we review the Kenya study's major anthropological data components and detail two research methodologies that place the project's core nutrition hypotheses in a broader social and economic context.

ANTHROPOLOGISTS AND NUTRITIONISTS

Anthropologists and nutritionists employ complementary approaches to the study of malnutrition. Historically, the former have looked first at the sociocultural context of food, primarily employing observational techniques; the latter have focused on the biological dimensions of nutrition, taking more experimental approaches (Harrison and Rittenbaugh 1981). However, these differences are becoming less pronounced with the growing recognition of the importance of studying dietary intake in a behavioral context. Today, anthropologists and nutritionists share a more holistic perspective, conceptualizing nutrition as a result of complex social and biological interactions.

As evidenced by the CRSP project discussed here, nutrition researchers have abandoned single measures of nutritional adequacy in favor of a broader functional definition. While they still conduct quantitative nutrient analyses, they are expanding the range of variables hypothesized as causally related to varying levels of food intake. Changes in individual growth, reproduction, illness, and physical work are seen as functional outcomes of the quantity and quality of nutrient intake. To establish the causal linkages between food intake and functional outcomes, analysis must acknowledge that the functional relationships exist in a sociocultural context; hence human beliefs and behavior must be integrated as intervening variables.

Integration requires input from social scientists trained in the investigation of the behavioral and cultural components of growth, reproduction, illness, and work. The anthropologist's role is to articulate the outcome measures of interest to nutritionists with other components of the sociocultural system. This task calls for the systematic collection of a broad range of sociocultural data that can be integrated into the functional outcome models generated by nutritionists.

FUNCTIONAL CONSEQUENCES OF
MILD-TO-MODERATE MALNUTRITION

As Cattle (this volume) points out, chronic mild-to-moderate malnutrition is a health and social problem warranting increased research by nutrition scientists. No precise estimate of the number of individuals suffering from chronic malnutrition is available. Its symptoms and consequences are not well understood, and it is therefore difficult to define and measure. Agreement is unanimous, however, that the problem is rampant throughout the developing world (Behar 1981).

The little information that is available suggests that while 1%–3% of children worldwide show signs of severe protein-energy malnutrition, at least 10 times as many children have symptoms of less severe malnutrition (Bengoa and Donoso 1974). Also, there are many claims that in developing countries 50%–60% of children under 5 years of age suffer from chronic moderate malnutrition (Behar 1981:237). In Kenya, for example, an estimated 30% of the children studied in the Kenyan National Nutrition Survey are subject to chronic mild-to-moderate protein energy malnutrition (Government of Kenya 1977, 1978/79, 1982). Another study concluded that 25% of

Kenyan children under age 5 are moderately malnourished, defined as 60%–75% or 70%–80% reference weight for height (FAO 1977).

The Nutrition CRSP began research on the consequences of mild-to-moderate malnutrition in a global context. The comparative research model employed resulted from the combined efforts of the three Nutrition CRSP projects in Egypt, Kenya, and Mexico. The program did not completely discount malnutrition indices derived from nutrient requirements measurements, usually expressed in calories/day—e.g., 2,700 cals/day/70-kg male (NAS 1974)—or from anthropometry (e.g., height-for-weight, weight-for-age) or biochemical analyses. However, it aimed to explore more comprehensive explanations of malnutrition. Specifically, the CRSP conceptualized malnutrition within a functional framework that sought to correlate food intake with individual performance in several critical functional areas, defining malnutrition as

> a state in which the physical function of an individual is impaired to the point where she or he can no longer maintain adequate performance in such processes as growth, pregnancy, lactation, physical work, or resisting and recovering from disease (Pacey and Payne 1985:24).

The program stressed investigation of five categories of functional outcome of moderate malnutrition (the independent variable): (1) cognitive/psychomotor skills development; (2) physical growth and nutritional status; (3) severity and frequency of illness episodes; (4) level of resting metabolism and activity expenditure; and (5) cultural practices of health and socioeconomic importance.

These five categories are interrelated and subsume more specific interactions. The model is therefore primarily a heuristic device for organizing research and suggesting more specific hypotheses. Six major research hypotheses were formulated (Table 7.1). They constitute the research core of the Nutrition CRSP. The hypotheses are explicit and overlapping, requiring a wealth of detailed social and biological data. The field research teams faced three major challenges in developing the necessary data collection methodologies: (1) each specialist needed to adjust collection procedures to the ethnographic setting; (2) the measures had to be applicable to the research interests of different specialists; and (3) the methodologies needed to be synchronized so that information was collected at intervals relevant to the various research interests.

The Kenya project, undertaken by the University of California–Los Angeles (UCLA) in collaboration with the University of Nairobi, involved nutritionists, physicians, psychologists, epidemiologists, and anthropologists. The project investigated the biological and social consequences of chronic mild-to-moderate malnutrition among the Embu people of central

TABLE 7.1. MAJOR RESEARCH HYPOTHESES TESTED BY NUTRITION CRSP

H_{1a}	Maternal food intake during pregnancy and lactation influences the infant's endowment at birth and its development during the first six months of breast-feeding.
H_{1b}	Maternal intake during pregnancy and lactation influences maternal child care and sanitation practices in relation to the infant.
H_{2a}	Food intake of the toddler during the period from 18-30 months affects the toddler's morbidity, body weight, and psychological development.
H_{2b}	Maternal intake during this period affects maternal child care and sanitation practices in relation to the toddler.
H_{3a}	Food intake of the 7-9-year-old child affects her/his morbidity and behavior, including school performance.
H_{3b}	Food intake of the mother and father influences their behavior toward the child and hence the morbidity and behavior of the child.
H_{4a}	Food intake of adults influences their morbidity, social-emotional responsiveness, and performance of usual responsibilities.
H_{4b}	These impact upon other members of the household (as stipulated in previous hypotheses).
H_5	In adults, a reduction of resting metabolic rates provides a major path of adaptation to restore energy equilibrium.
H_6	Household food intake affects household morbidity.

Kenya. The Embu are a Bantu-speaking group, occupying the southeastern slopes of Mount Kenya. Numbering 180,400 or 1.2% of Kenya's total population, the Embu are one of the country's smaller ethnic groups (Government of Kenya 1979). They are small-scale farmers who cultivate maize, beans, sorghum, and millet as food crops, and coffee, cotton, or tobacco for market sale. Households also maintain a few head of livestock and engage in casual or permanent wage labor to varying degrees.

Based on preliminary surveys, feasibility studies, and information from the Ministry of Health and the Department of Community Health at the University of Nairobi, three sublocations within the Kyeni South Location of Embu District were selected as study sites. These sublocations are inhabited by 11,810 individuals, residing in 2,059 households, and averaging 5.7 individuals per household (Government of Kenya 1979). The CRSP study population consisted of all sublocation households that included either a lead female who had been pregnant for less than three months or a toddler who could be observed during his or her 18–30-month growth period. The lead male and any school children aged 7-9 were also classified as target individuals. The project conducted data collection from January 1984 through March 1986. A total of 247 households were studied for a minimum of one year.

ANTHROPOLOGICAL CONTRIBUTIONS
TO THE KENYA PROJECT

From the outset, project anthropologists were encouraged that CRSP nutritionists viewed food intake as systematically related to a series of functional outcomes. Moreover, anthropologists saw exciting methodological challenges to incorporating a more holistic understanding of mild-to-moderate malnutrition into project hypothesis testing and analysis. For example, in addition to the Nutrition CRSP's primary focus on the functional consequences of varying levels of food consumption, a secondary focus on the Kenya study population's agricultural system was deemed imperative, particularly from an anthropological perspective. Of special importance was documenting the production outcomes of Embu farmers' cropping strategies.

During field research in Embu District, anthropological contributions took many different forms. A number of research components were designed and implemented primarily by anthropologists. We describe six of these components briefly, and then discuss two others in detail—the agricultural production and the time allocation studies. The goal of the latter two research strategies was to examine which combinations of agricultural practices provided the best level of nutritional intake.

Census update. Information on household and community demographics is mandatory baseline data for any sociocultural or nutritional investigation. The explanation of many household interactions of nutritional importance requires an understanding of the age, gender, status, or social position of the individuals involved. To collect such data, each enrolled household was censused every three months and its current composition compared with the previous record. Information collected on each individual included name, sex, birth date, marital status, social position, education, and amount of time away from location. Details of any deaths were also recorded.

Socioeconomic status. The nutritional characteristics of a household are closely related to its social position and economic well-being. Generally, higher social position and greater economic wealth translate into better nutrition. However, this relationship is not straightforward because of myriad socioeconomic factors both within and between households. To record such factors, a socioeconomic questionnaire was administered every third month. Social status questions addressed issues of education, leadership qualities, community participation, and noneconomic skills; economic questions focused on the household's agricultural and animal husbandry practices, material possessions, and income.

Sanitation and hygiene. Hypotheses 1 and 2 in Table 7.1 investigate whether maternal food intake influences the target mothers' sanitation and hygiene practices in relation to infants and toddlers. To provide data on this issue, as well as on general household cleanliness, every third month a questionnaire was administered regarding personal hygiene for the lead female, infant, toddler, and school child. Other questions sought information on the cleanliness of the kitchen, sleeping quarters, and compound. Additional information was collected on the location and type of latrine.

Household economics. In order to place food consumption within a broader economic context, project anthropologists developed a questionnaire on production of agricultural commodities. This instrument investigated the availability and utilization of crop land. Information collected was based either on receipts for crops sold (coffee, cotton, tobacco) or on informant recall. Data on marketing strategies were also collected. To complement the emphasis on production, the questionnaire also asked for information on household educational expenses.

Energy expenditure. The functional approach to defining malnutrition investigates whether individuals experiencing a particular level of nutrient intake are able to perform the physical work necessary to secure a livelihood. One useful measure of work is the number of calories expended in production activities. To determine the caloric price tag for each activity, both the amount of time the average individual spends in a given activity and the amount of energy expended per unit of activity-time must be calculated. The energy expended in a representative range of daily activities (work and nonwork) was measured with a Max-Plank respirometer. Heart-rate monitors supplemented this method of indirect calorimetry. Fourteen individuals participated in this study, and over 200 tests were completed. These energy expenditure data complemented the project's laboratory testing of resting metabolic rate (physiological change outcome function).

Child care. The quality of care given to infants and toddlers was hypothesized to be functionally related to a mother's nutritional status and her general activity pattern. Infants were observed at ages 2, 4, and 6 months, and toddlers were followed bimonthly during the 18–30-month stage. Each observation period lasted two hours, during which time the field enumerator recorded the type and quality of care received by the target child. Particular attention was given to coding who cared for the child (mother, sibling, grandparent, etc.), how the care was administered (holding, touching, calming, cleaning, watching, and so forth), and circumstances in which no care was given in situations of obvious need. Besides coding the observed responses and interactions, enumerators wrote qualitative comments on what they perceived as particularly typical or atypical instances of care or noncare. (Most enumerators were mothers themselves.) In addition, anthropologists periodically interviewed the field enumerators and a selected group of mothers about Embu perceptions of good versus bad care. A small sample of oral texts used to calm children was also collected.

Agricultural Production Studies

The Household Agricultural Crop Study (AG CROP). Administered monthly, this survey relied on recall to record agricultural activity. It was designed to complement the project's socioeconomic study on cash crops with detailed agricultural data on the major food crops that were harvested, stored, sold, purchased, or planted during the previous month. AG CROP addressed the three food crops that each enrolled household identified as "most important" in terms of production, consumption, and/or distribution. As expected, households consistently reported maize and beans as two of the three most important crops. Other responses included bananas, cassava, arrowroot, potatoes, millet, and sorghum.

The information recorded for each crop included whether the crop was planted during the long rains (mid-March through June) or short rains (October through November) or whether it was a perennial (such as bananas), the year it was planted (1983–1985), and the household's reasons for considering this particular crop important. If during the past month, the crop was planted, harvested, sold (to a government marketing board, locally in open markets, or to middlemen), or given to relatives, then the amount in kilograms was recorded, as were the earnings in Kenyan shillings, where appropriate. The quantity of the crop in storage was also noted, along with any purchases of the crop during the past month.

AG CROP responses provided a wealth of basic information on Embu agricultural production. Because data were collected on a monthly basis, they capture seasonal fluctuations in food availability; these can in turn be related to observed trends in household food consumption and nutritional well-being over time.

The Household Agricultural Production Study (HAPS). Started in March 1985, HAPS measured the actual production inputs and outputs for a sample of household agricultural land-use systems. Prior to that time, agricultural data were gathered through farmer interviews. Depending on the informant's recall or her/his understanding of the questionnaire's units of measure, this technique left open to question the reliability of such key information as the household's garden area and crop yields. To collect more accurate data on agricultural production, project anthropologists decided to actually measure a sample of gardens and weigh crop yields. Additional information on land tenure, agricultural inputs, cropping practices, and previous land use was also obtained.

HAPS consisted of a 25% subsample of households randomly selected from the 169 households still enrolled in the CRSP study as of March 1985. This yielded a sample of 42 households distributed evenly throughout the study area. Both subsistence and cash crop production was measured across an entire year in order to account for seasonal variation; the data are considered representative of the study area for the agricultural cycle of March 1985 to February 1986.

The investigation of garden production began soon after the new season's crops were planted. The first visit to each of the 42 households was devoted to explaining the study to participants, obtaining their consent and cooperation, and administering a miniquestionnaire focusing on agricultural inputs and practices (fertilizer, seed types, crop rotation, and other factors). Household gardens were also visually inspected, and appointments were scheduled for mapping.

When field staff returned as scheduled, a household adult accompanied them to the garden to identify its exact boundaries and any subdivisions. Actual mapping began once field staff were confident of the boundaries. With a starting point designated as Coordinate A, the team leader held her/his position while an assistant walked along the first "side" of the boundary carrying one end of a tape measure. The assistant staked the spot where the side ended (i.e., where the boundary took a turn), and that point was designated Coordinate B. The distance between the two coordinates was recorded, and the team leader determined the azimuth reading with a Brunton pocket transit by sighting on the stake at B. The team leader then moved to B, and the assistant proceeded to the end of the next "side," i.e., Coordinate C. This procedure continued around the boundary until the starting point was reached. The same technique was used to measure any distinct subplots of crop assemblages within the garden's boundaries (e.g., "maize only," "maize intercropped with beans") as well as any fallow areas.

Next, a map of the garden was drawn to scale using a protractor and rule. Scales of 1:500 and 1:1,000 were used for gardens of <4 and >4 acres, respectively. All coordinates, crop assemblages, and other important information were labeled on the map. Finally, a planimeter was used to calculate the area of all gardens and subplots from the scaled maps.

With completed maps in hand, HAPS teams returned to the gardens for a second visual inspection. These repeat inspections had two purposes: first, the map was compared with the now semimature garden, and any discrepancies were resolved; second, selected crop assemblages were ranked according to their anticipated level of production along four parameters— high, medium high, medium, low. Only "maize," "beans," "maize with beans," and "beans with maize" assemblages were ranked since these are the dietary staples of Embu households. This made for a possible total of 16 production/assemblage categories.

With the area of every maize and/or bean plot measured, and with every plot ranked according to anticipated production, the final task was to weigh crop yields from a sample of plots. After determining the total area of each of the four crop assemblages by the four ranks ("maize only—high," "maize only—medium high," etc.), plots were randomly selected until a 20% area had been reached within each category. Thus, for example, after determining the total area of "maize only—high," individual household plots were selected until their combined area equaled 20% of the total for maize ranked high.

The harvest of each plot within the 20% subsample was then weighed. For plots containing beans, the entire harvest was weighed immediately after threshing. For maize plots, the ears harvested from every fifth row were set aside and weighed after they had dried. Field staff assisted household members in harvesting and threshing in return for their cooperation.

The maize and bean weights obtained from the sample plots provide an excellent idea of a given household's level of food production. When compared with agricultural recall data for the same household, this information is invaluable. Taken together, the AG CROP and HAPS research strategies and their resulting data sets (one based on recall and the other on observation and infield measurement) reinforce each other and represent significant methodological and substantive contributions to holistic functional analyses of the causes and consequences of malnutrition.

Time Allocation

The immediate goal of the time allocation study was to provide behavioral data on activities directly and indirectly related to the research hypotheses. For example, testing of many of the hypothesized outcomes of chronic mild-to-moderate malnutrition required behavioral data for the lead female exclusively (hypotheses 1B, 2B), the lead male and female combined (3B, 4A), school-age children (3A), or other target children (3B, 4B). The necessary data were obtained through the application of a technique increasingly utilized by anthropologists and commonly referred to as "spot observation." This technique involves visiting households at random times of day to record the activities being performed by individuals.

In adapting the spot observation technique to any research setting, it is critical that the final protocol meet at least three conditions: (1) household members should be informed that they will be visited unannounced, but, to avoid observer's paradox phenomena, they should not know the exact time and date of each visit; (2) the time and day of the visit must be randomly selected; and (3) all hours and days under study (e.g., "daylight" hours on "weekdays") must be equally represented (Johnson 1975). Two additional factors unique to the Kenya project had to be taken into account in applying this technique: the need to keep personnel assigned to the study to a minimum because of limited financial resources; a desire to guarantee equal coverage of all households.

To meet all these conditions, project anthropologists devised a unique approach. The time of visit for any specific household was not selected using a random numbers table. The study area was simply too large (60 km^2) and the sample too dispersed for the field staff regularly and within a reasonably short lenth of time to visit households located far apart. Instead, with maps indicating the exact location of each enrolled household and with fieldworkers' knowledge of the local terrain, a fixed route was established that minimized interhousehold travel time while still leaving visiting times unspecified. This process thus provided a randomizing element. The weather, length of visit, terrain, puncture of a bicycle tire, and other elements combined to vary arrivals at each household during each completion of the route.

The procedure can be summarized as follow: on the first day of the study, the first household on the circuit was visited at 7:00 A.M. by the fieldworker scheduled for that day's morning shift, who then proceeded by bicycle to each subsequent household along the route. She/he was replaced at approximately 12:30 P.M. by the fieldworker assigned to the afternoon shift. Rendezvous was facilitated by the use of inexpensive walkie-talkies. The afternoon fieldworker continued along the route and made the final visit of the day at 6:00 P.M. The next household on the circuit was then visited the following day at 7:00 A.M. Upon reaching the end of the route, the fieldworker returned to the first household, and the procedure began anew.

The spot observation technique requires the fieldworker to quickly note the various activities of household members before they respond to her/his arrival. These are the activities that are recorded and eventually coded. For instance, a fieldworker arrives at compound "X" at 7:00 A.M. Using a prepared form listing the names of each household member, the enumerator quickly identifies each individual and notes the activity she/he is performing. At this hour of the morning, examples of activities might include the lead female heating maize and beans for the morning meal; an infant being held by the lead female's mother, who resides in the household; a toddler sitting near the lead female and playing with eating utensils; school-age children washing and dressing in school uniform; and the lead male sorting maize seeds.

Because the Kenya project enumerators were from the local area and had worked with the households for over a year, they knew most of the sample members by sight. This facilitated rapid spot observation of activity and identification of member absences or, conversely, of new arrivals and visitors. If someone was absent, other family members were asked about her/his activity and location. If the absentee was within five minutes' walk, the enumerator would visit the location and verify the activity. If the individual was far away, the activity was recorded as a report by family members. Activities were initially recorded in short, descriptive phrases (e.g., "lead male planting maize," "lead female washing infant"). These were then translated into activity codes, which in turn were keypunched and made computer-ready (Baksh and Paolisso 1987).

The time allocation study began in March 1985 and concluded in February 1986. A sample of 169 households, all enrolled as of March 1985, was visited from Monday through Friday between 7:00 A.M. and 6:00 P.M. and on Saturdays between 7:00 A.M. and 12:30 P.M. A few Sunday and evening visits were also made. During the course of the study, the route was completed 59 times, and each household was visited an average of 1.1 times per week. Moreover, data analysis shows that a balanced distribution of visits for each household and for all hours of the day was achieved. The hard work of the field enumerators enabled the Kenya project to collect approximately 86,000 observations of individual activity, making the Nutrition CRSP data base the largest time allocation study for a rural Third World population.

All data are now computer-entered and ready for analysis. Project staff at UCLA are undertaking preliminary analyses of a range of subjects. For example, CRSP anthropologists are asking questions about gender differences in time allocation, the role of siblings in providing child care, the amount of time households dedicate to various economic activities, and the effects of seasonality on household activities. Project nutritionists are looking at activities surrounding food preparation and consumption in order to identify patterns that help explain individual variation in dietary intake. Physicians are studying the illness data and behavioral responses to health problems in the family (e.g., what care is provided and by whom). In conjunction with anthropologists, physiologists are combining the energy-expenditure-in-activity measurements with the time allocation data to arrive at energy budgets for households, particularly during periods of intense activity and/or food shortage.

The foregoing represent only a few of the many possible uses for the data derived from the CRSP anthropologists' holistic time allocation study. The potential of such studies is immense. On the Kenya project, for example, the time allocation research produced data on *all* aspects of household life. This is evidenced in the major categories of activities used for coding observations: eating and drinking, food preparation, care of self and others, household labor, food production, cash labor, inactive, out of location, education, recreation, social, and other. Within each of these general activity categories, more specific codings of behavior can also be made (Baksh and Paolisso 1987).

As it was designed to do, the time allocation study provided invaluable information regarding the relationship among the relevant variables embodied in the CRSP's initial hypotheses. Furthermore, as field research progressed, it generated important supplementary hypotheses. For example, do adults and children who consume relatively low amounts of food spend more time engaged in low-level energy expenditure activities? Do households that spend more time producing both food and cash crops enjoy better diets than those producing food crops only? Do households of relatively high socioeconomic status spend more time "working" than do other households, or do they instead engage in more leisure, recreation, and social activities?

In sum, the Kenya project's time allocation study is an excellent example of how social science strengthens biological or technical science research, and of how a holistic approach facilitates focused hypothesis testing by providing data on both primary and intervening variables. Spot observations are efficient and feasible, and they generate large amounts of high-quality data. This in turn enhances the anthropologist's ability to speak to specific questions of interest to both social and non-social-science colleagues.

CONCLUSIONS

Anthropologists unquestionably can contribute much to multidisciplinary projects. On the Nutrition CRSP in Kenya, anthropologists filled a variety of roles, ranging from providing basic ethnographic description to designing and implementing research components that generated data critical to testing the proposed hypotheses. For example, findings from the census update, socioeconomic status, and sanitation and hygiene components all address core research concerns of the Nutrition CRSP. Project colleagues saw anthropologists' collection of such data as a well-defined, comprehensible, and valuable contribution.

Sometimes, however, the roles of social scientists require clarification vis-à-vis the nature of the cross-disciplinary research. On the Kenya project, for example, anthropologists also contributed research priorities and methods that, at least at first, were unfamiliar to the other scientists. This was the case with anthropological interest in contextualizing food consumption within the broader economic system by focusing on agricultural production. However, this focus made it possible to relate particular food- and cash-crop production strategies to the project's detailed food-intake data—an exercise of obvious relevance to the work of nutrition scientists. Equally relevant for the work of social scientists in international agricultural development are the methods used to collect production data and the benefits of combining measured production with the recall data of such instruments as AG CROP.

No other Nutrition CRSP research component better illustrates the value of anthropological input than the Kenya project's time allocation study. It not only provided data for testing proposed hypotheses, but it generated new hypotheses, along with the data needed to test them. Moreover, this research embodied the essential holism of the anthropological perspective. The time allocation study did not a priori define what activities would be important; rather, it recorded what was observed and then used these observations to construct an ethnographically appropriate coding framework. Working within their disciplinary norm of holism, anthropologists obtained the quantitative behavioral data that their nutrition-scientist colleagues required for focused hypothesis testing.

This work also had payoffs for anthropology as a discipline. Time allocation has only recently received wide recognition as an important research topic. Its methodology offers a number of advantages over more traditional recall, diary, and continuous observations techniques: it is a highly efficient way to gather information; it does not influence the behavior of the target individual; and it records data in a format that is easily computerized. Perhaps more importantly, when employed by well-trained and supervised field staff, it yields highly reliable results since in most cases the results are based on actual observation. However, anthropological work in this realm is still in an early stage of development, and researchers are experimenting with various methodologies for collecting time-use data (Gross 1984). Anthropologists on the Kenya project have made some significant refinements and additions to applying the technique under "real world" field conditions.

To conclude, the major contribution of anthropologists on the Kenya project was to place the nutrition sciences' target individuals (mothers, infants, toddlers, etc.) as actors within a larger sociocultural context so as to address the CRSP hypotheses' focus on the complex interrelations between biological and social environments. The task of the anthropologist on such interdisciplinary projects is systematically to record the proximate sociocultural variables interacting with the nutritional and health status of target individuals. To do so, the anthropologist uses questionnaires and quantitative measurement techniques; equally important, she/he participates, observes, and learns from the people in the study. Nutrition CRSP anthropologists' application of their disciplinary tools and skills resulted in a wealth of information on the socioeconomic context of chronic mild-to-moderate malnutrition in Kenya. As analysis progresses, this information will help researchers better understand the causes and consequences of such malnutrition, and generate workable responses to this debilitating malady in the Third World.

NOTES

The Kenya project was funded through USAID Contract Grant No. DAN 1309-G-SS-1070. The authors would like to thank Charlotte Neumann and Nimrod

Bwibo, the Kenya project PIs, for their confidence and support, plus all the CRSP research and administrative staff who helped us during fieldwork. Particular thanks go to William Martin, project administrator, and Duncan Ngare, project sociologist, for their assistance throughout the collection of agricultural and time allocation data. Finally, we cannot thank enough the Social Performance and Environment field staff for their friendship and hard work.

REFERENCES

Baksh, M., and M. Paolisso. 1987. Methods for the Collection of Time Allocation Data. Manuscript prepared for final report of the Nutrition CRSP Kenya Project.

Behar, M. 1981. What is Marginal Malnutrition? In *Nutrition in Health and Disease and International Development*. Symposium from the 12th International Congress of Nutrition. A. Harper and G. Davis, eds., pp. 237–246. New York: Alan R. Liss.

Bengoa, J. M., and G. Donoso. 1974. Prevalence of Protein-Calorie Malnutrition (1963–73). *PAG Bulletin* 4(1):3.

FAO. 1977. *The Fourth World Food Survey*. Rome: FAO.

Government of Kenya. 1977. Ministry of Economic Planning and Development, National Nutrition Survey. Central Bureau of Statistics. Nairobi: Government Printing Office.

———. 1978/1979. Ministry of Economic Planning and Development,. National Nutrition Survey. Central Bureau of Statistics. Nairobi: Government Printing Office.

———. 1979. Ministry of Economic Planning and Development, Population Census. Central Bureau of Statistics. Nairobi: Government Printing Office.

———. 1982. Ministry of Economic Planning and Development, National Nutrition Survey. Central Bureau of Statistics. Nairobi: Government Printing Office.

Gross, D. 1984. Time Allocation: A Tool for the Study of Cultural Behavior. *Annual Review of Anthropology* 13:519–558.

Harrison, G. G., and C. Rittenbaugh. 1981. Anthropology and Nutrition: A Perspective on Two Scientific Subcultures. Proceedings of the Federation of American Societies for Experimental Biology 40:2595–2600.

Jerome, N., R. Kandel, and G. Pelto (eds.). 1980. *Nutritional Anthropology: Contemporary Approaches to Diet and Culture*. Pleasantville, NY: Redgrave Publishing.

Johnson, A. 1975. Time Allocation in a Machiguenga Community. *Ethnology* 14:301–310.

Kaplan, D., and R. Manners. 1972. *Culture Theory*. Englewood Cliffs, NJ: Prentice-Hall.

NAS. 1974. *Recommended Dietary Allowances*. Washington, DC: National Academy of Sciences.

Pacey, A., and P. Payne (eds.). 1985. *Agricultural Development and Nutrition*. Boulder: Westview Press.

PART 3

Bean/Cowpea CRSP

8

Social Science Contributions to Bean/Cowpea CRSP Research: Profits and Potentials

Anne E. Ferguson

Each CRSP has a different organizational history and structure that has shaped the goals and strategies of its overall program and its social science component. This chapter describes the policy context in which the Bean/Cowpea CRSP was initiated, and how this context led to a strong social science focus on women in development (WID). The structure of the socioeconomics component and its research and training accomplishments to date are then highlighted. Finally, relationships among different kinds of socioeconomic research on this CRSP are explored.

POLICY CONTEXT AT THE PLANNING STAGE

The planning stage of the Bean/Cowpea CRSP took place during 1978 and 1979, at the height of the New Directions or basic human needs approach to U.S. foreign aid (DeWalt this volume). This orientation to development was an outgrowth of the 1973 Foreign Assistance Act, which targeted the needs of the poor in developing countries. The act specified that U.S. bilateral economic aid should support host country government undertakings directly aimed at improving the lives of the country's poorest citizens. The legislation thus emphasized microlevel projects that focused on small-farm labor-intensive agriculture and equity in income distribution, rather than macroeconomic instrumentalities and planning.

A key component of the new legislation was the 1973 Percy amendment, which directed that U.S. bilateral assistance "be administered so as to give particular attention to those programs, projects and activities which tend to integrate women into the national economies of foreign countries, thus improving their status and assisting the total development effort" (USAID 1982:2). Title XII of the International Development and Food Assistance Act ("Famine Prevention and Freedom from Hunger"), under which the CRSPs were initiated, reflects the channeling of development efforts toward poor, small-scale farmers and women in developing countries.

Development initiatives for these groups found a receptive audience at Michigan State University (MSU), the planning entity of the Bean/Cowpea CRSP.[1] In the late 1970s, MSU's Office of Women in International Development had established an active Project Advisement Task Force (PATF) to encourage women's participation in development and to provide input on gender issues to university personnel involved in project design and implementation. This task force was composed of researchers and students from the social sciences, liberal arts, natural sciences, human ecology, and nutrition. Encouraged by the WID policy, the biological scientists responsible for the planning grant included three PATF members in program planning—a psychologist, a rural sociologist, and a home economist. One of the PATF members became the first deputy director of the CRSP; in 1983, she was appointed director.[2]

Thus, in the policy sphere, the macrolevel parameters guiding the design of the Bean/Cowpea CRSP were set by the New Directions mandate, the Title XII legislation, and the Percy amendment. At the local level, MSU's Office of Women in International Development, through the PATF, was in a position to collaborate with the biological scientists responsible for program planning and to give the CRSP a strong WID focus. Implicit in this focus was the recognition that attaining the CRSP goal of reducing hunger by increasing the production and utilization of beans and cowpeas required research and technology development directed at women, since they are the principal producers of legumes in many DCs. The WID focus has also stimulated the active and sustained involvement of both U.S. and host country women in CRSP research and training program.

STRUCTURE OF SOCIAL SCIENCE IN THE BEAN/COWPEA CRSP

The socioeconomic component of the Bean/Cowpea CRSP is a small but nonetheless influential part of the program. As of 1987, three of 13 existing projects included social science or agricultural economics research. The majority of the 13 projects focus on limitations to bean and cowpea production imposed by insects, diseases, the physical environment, plant responses, or constraints in the areas of nutrition, food preparation, and storage. The three projects involving socioeconomic research are briefly described below.

1. "Breeding Beans for Disease, Insect, and Stress Resistance, and Determination of the Socioeconomic Impact on Smallholder Farm Families

in Tanzania." Washington State University and Sokoine University of Agriculture in Tanzania are collaborating in this multifaceted project; it incorporates a wide range of factors into its bean breeding program.[3] Among these are insect and disease resistance, high nitrogen-fixing capacity, ease of cooking, and nutritional criteria. Under the direction of an agricultural economist, the socioeconomic component has played an important role in establishing the research agenda. For example, it has brought to the attention of plant breeders factors such as regional variation in types of bean cultivars preferred for consumption and sale. Two primary research focuses are monitoring the impact of project innovations on smallholders and crop marketing. Studies are also under way on seed production and distribution networks. Throughout, particular attention is accorded to women, since they are the major producers, processors, and marketers of beans in Tanzania.

2. "Genetic, Agronomic, and Sociocultural Analysis of Diversity Among Bean Landraces in Malawi." This project is directed by MSU in collaboration with Bunda College of Agriculture.[4] It combines cross-disciplinary investigations of the generation, maintenance, and utilization of bean landraces in Malawi. Issues addressed include genetic and sociocultural factors affecting the generation and preservation or loss of genetic diversity, acceptance criteria for introducing improved bean cultivars, and the relative benefits to farmers growing pure lines versus mixtures. A primary focus of the socioeconomic research has been women's roles in the generation and maintenance of landraces.

3. "Appropriate Technology for Cowpea Preservation and Processing and a Study of its Socioeconomic Impact on Rural Populations in Nigeria." This food technology and nutrition project is directed by the University of Georgia in collaboration with the University of Nigeria, Nsukka.[5] The goal is to increase the utilization of cowpeas by developing new technologies (including storage methods and processing equipment) and by improving the nutritional value and safety of cowpea products. A major research thrust has been the design of a village-level processing mill to produce cowpea meal. Survey researchers and social scientists at the University of Nigeria have participated in the research process and are expected to play an important role in evaluating the success of the new technology.

During the initial 5-year grant period (1980–1985) of the Bean/Cowpea CRSP, there were two additional social-science-related projects. One consisted of an FSR component on a plant-breeding project in Guatemala. Unfortunately, this was never fully initiated because of human rights abuses and safety concerns about researchers in highland Guatemala. The other was an FSR project in Ecuador that had a strong social science orientation (Uquillas and Garrett this volume). Essentially, then, over the life of the program there have been five projects with socioeconomic focuses, three of which are ongoing as of the late 1980s.

Social scientists have also participated at the program, as well as the project, level. Since its inception, the Bean/Cowpea CRSP ME has employed a WID specialist to provide project investigators with information on the social organization of agriculture in the host countries for use in setting research agendas;[6] suggest potential consequences of technological changes introduced by the CRSP; foster research linkages between social and nonsocial (biological, food technology, and nutrition) scientists; establish ties between project researchers and host country women's groups and organizations; and encourage the inclusion of women and of gender issues in the Bean/Cowpea CRSP's student training program.

Both the WID specialist[7] and the Bean/Cowpea CRSP director are social scientists. Positioning social scientists at the management office and directorship levels has had a significant impact on the program as a whole. Their presence has made socioeconomic research contributions more visible and comprehensible than might otherwise have been the case. It also has encouraged CRSP biological research to address the needs of smallholders and women more directly. Attention to these groups has been further reinforced by the External Evaluation Panel, two of whose members from 1980 through 1986 were agricultural economists. Thus, although the socioeconomics component is small in comparison to the research efforts and resources devoted to the production disciplines, it has nonetheless played an important role in orienting overall research agendas.

TYPES OF SOCIAL SCIENCE AND
AGRICULTURAL ECONOMICS RESEARCH

As indicated above, there are no freestanding social science or agricultural economics projects on the Bean/Cowpea CRSP. All social scientists and agricultural economists on this CRSP have worked in close collaboration with biological scientists, food technologists, or nutritionists. The multidisciplinary and applied intertwining of these disciplines has implications for the nature of the research conducted.

Specifically, socioeconomic researchers have made two types of contributions as part of agricultural R&D teams. The first—which DeWalt (this volume) terms the social science *of* agricultural development—provides new knowledge and understanding in its own right about farming systems and agricultural transformations. It examines how changes in, e.g., land-tenure practices, labor patterns, and agricultural credit and pricing policies can lead to increased stratification among smallholders, and what the implications of this differentiation are for food crop production and agricultural development.

The second contribution—what DeWalt calls social science *in* agricultural development—provides data on the social and economic organization of agriculture that have immediate implications for the development of new or improved agricultural technologies. Here, research parameters and activities usually center on variables identified by the participating scientists as constraints on increasing or stabilizing production and utilization of food crops.

In both cases, the purpose is to generate and use scientific knowledge in a specific problem-solving context. In this sense, these contributions are forms of applied research. Although the work of Bean/Cowpea CRSP social scientists and agricultural economists is often informed by basic disciplinary research, this CRSP has provided little opportunity for them to conduct fundamental studies, the principal aim of which is to test and advance theoretical propositions and generalizations in particular fields of knowledge (Brush 1986).

Socioeconomic researchers were initially recruited into the Bean/Cowpea CRSP because they possessed specific skills that biological scientists recognized as useful for achieving project and program goals. Such skills included experience in collecting baseline data to permit the measurement of project impact, and knowledge of cultural or emic perspectives that could affect the adoption of project innovations. While this service-oriented role was the entry point for socioeconomic researchers on the CRSP, the collaborative nature of the work increased all CRSP scientists' understanding of the richness and potential contributions of one another's disciplines. This in turn allowed some expansion of socioeconomic research agendas. While these usually still have an applied orientation, they have nevertheless gone beyond the confines of baseline data collection and impact monitoring to incorporate the study of socioeconomic and cultural variables shaping the agricultural sector and hence influencing project goals.[8]

RESEARCH ACHIEVEMENTS

Social science and agricultural economics research results for the initial five-year grant period are outgrowths of primary field investigations in Malawi, Tanzania, Ecuador, and Nigeria and of secondary literature searches on these, countries plus Botswana, Cameroon, and Guatemala.[9] Two principal types of findings and contributions are discussed: first, studies of socioeconomic and cultural variables that influence the production and utilization of beans and cowpeas, including land-tenure patterns and size of land holdings, labor issues, and agricultural pricing policies, marketing structures, and foreign-exchange considerations; second, baseline studies and social science and agricultural economics contributions to agricultural research on plant breeding, crop management and economics, and technology development.

Studies of Socioeconomic and Cultural Constraints to Production

Land-tenure patterns and size of holdings. Size of land holding is an important consideration in farm production and management practices. In all the countries studied, small-scale farmers, especially women, produce a major portion of the food crops, including beans and cowpeas. However, in many of these areas, the land holdings needed for this production have been declining in size. In the mountainous northern region of Malawi, for example, where population pressure is high and cash-cropping of coffee is prevalent, the average amount of land per person has decreased by almost 25% between 1968 and 1980 (Barnes-McConnell 1986). Such changes have implications for the quantity of food crops grown and for human nutritional status; hence they are significant constraints to bean and cowpea production in their own right.

   Work in Ecuador on land tenure arrangements and size of land holdings has highlighted the need to differentiate among categories of smallholders in designing new or improved agricultural technologies. Project investigators have developed a microcomputer program to measure the degree of inequality in land holdings (Garrett, Golden, and Francis 1986). In one of the Ecuadorian study sites, for example, researchers found that many smallholders were nearly landless. These farmers received most of their income not from agriculture, but from off-farm employment. Other rural residents in this area were entirely dependent on wage work. This stratification within the small-farm category has many implications for the development of agricultural innovations; it must therefore be taken into account from the outset of research. For example, new labor-saving technologies that displace workers are often harmful to landless or land-poor families, even though these same technologies may benefit those who hire workers (Garrett 1986a,b,c). Thus, the impact of new or improved technologies or varieties is likely to vary by smallholder strata.

Labor considerations. Small farming households in many developing countries are directly caught up in and respond to events in the national and international economies. We have emphasized such micro/macrolevel relationships in studies of labor utilization patterns on small farms. For example, an extensive literature review of the small-farm sector in Botswana indicated that out-migration of men to work in the mines and cities of South Africa has resulted in a high percentage of female-headed households (Horn and Nkambule-Kanyima 1984). Male out-migration is also significant in other Bean/Cowpea CRSP countries, especially Malawi (Barnes-McConnell 1986) and northern Cameroon (Ferguson and Horn 1985). This trend can impact farming strategies, sometimes leading to a reduction in the area cultivated or a change in crop mix (Horn and Nkambule-Kanyima 1984;

Ferguson and Horn 1984). The feminization of farming also has implications for the development of new bean and cowpea varieties and technologies.

Most of the CRSP's socioeconomic studies of labor utilization have examined regional and local levels with regard to two interrelated concerns: variations in labor demands by season, and inter- and intrahousehold dynamics. The WID orientation of the participating researchers has stimulated a particular interest in the intrahousehold division of labor. Extensive data on this topic have been gathered in Malawi, Tanzania, and Ecuador; secondary data searches have been undertaken for Guatemala, Cameroon, and Botswana (Due, White, and Rocke 1985; Ferguson and Horn 1985). Researchers have called attention to the need to move beyond popular general conceptualizations of "the farm family" in the agricultural sciences and to focus instead on intrahousehold dynamics. For example, in constructing a farming systems methodology, project investigators in Ecuador incorporated the basic social science insight that the division of labor by gender and age within households varies by social stratum, ethnic group, and region.

Agricultural pricing policies, marketing structures, and foreign exchange. Food-pricing policies and marketing structures have a direct impact on the production of beans, cowpeas, and other food crops. In Tanzania, research indicates that policies designed to placate vocal urban consumers by keeping food prices low resulted in less food for the market. Per capita agricultural production is therefore falling (Due 1986). In contrast, the government in Malawi significantly raised producer prices for maize in 1981–1982, with the result that smallholders produced a record harvest, and the country became a net food exporter (Barnes-McConnell 1986).

In Ecuador, regional investigations supplied information on the legume marketing structure that was useful in setting the project's research agenda. In one region, farming systems research revealed that increased production and a stable supply of green legumes throughout the agricultural cycle would be a viable, income-generating strategy for smallholders. In contrast, in a second region, researchers found that no purpose would be served by extending legume production across the year because the market was monopolistic, with only a few large landowners and merchants controlling the marketing channels (Barsky 1983; Garrett and Goldstein 1984; Uquillas and Garrett this volume).

The effects of foreign exchange shortages and balance of payment problems on agricultural development were also investigated. In many of the host countries, such shortages limit the importation of fertilizers, chemicals, machinery, vehicles, and fuel. Taken together with land-tenure issues, these shortages also influenced agricultural credit policies. In some contexts, agricultural development banks gave priority to owners of medium or large farms producing crops for export rather than for domestic consumption. This meant that small-scale producers were unable to acquire needed production inputs or were forced to rely on credit from local money lenders (Due 1986; Ferguson and Flores 1987; Uquillas and Garrett this volume).

The issues addressed in such studies represent significant constraints to agricultural development, often impeding the production and utilization of legumes and other food crops. There is a growing recognition within the Bean/Cowpea CRSP that such problems require attention in their own right if hunger and malnutrition are to be overcome.

Studies of Other Constraint Areas

Baseline studies. Social scientists and agricultural economists have also contributed to the varietal research and technology design work of CRSP technical scientists through the collection of baseline data. In Tanzania, agricultural economists have gathered extensive FSR data on the types of crops produced on small farms; systems of mono and intercropping; the percentage of crop production consumed and sold; family income sources and living expenses; the division of labor by crop and by farming activity; the contribution of beans to family incomes; and consumption patterns and nutritional status (Due, White, and Rocke 1985). This information will permit monitoring of the effects of the new high-yielding bean cultivars being bred and tested by CRSP plant geneticists, pathologists, agronomists, and others. Similarly, in collaboration with nutritionists and food technologists, socioeconomic investigators at the University of Nigeria have conducted surveys of food preferences, infant-feeding practices, and nutritional status in two rural areas. This information will be useful in assessing the impacts of the new cowpea meal processing technology that CRSP technical scientists are developing (McWatters 1985).

Contributions to plant breeding. Socioeconomic research has highlighted the fact that improved varieties of beans and cowpeas must be compatible with local resources, needs, food preferences, and labor utilization and allocation patterns. Investigations in Cameroon (Ferguson and Horn 1984; Ta'Ama 1985), Botswana (DeMooy and DeMooy 1985; Horn and Nkambule-Kanyima 1984), and Malawi (Barnes-McConnell 1986) indicate that stability of yield is more important than quantity of yield to many small-scale farmers. For example, farmers in Malawi and Cameroon usually plant a mixture of varieties of beans or cowpeas. Various landraces within the mixture perform differently in response to environmental stresses. Thus, mixtures may increase the availability of legumes and other plant products (e.g., stovers, straws, leaves, and fodder) while simultaneously reducing the risk of crop failure. Social scientists have therefore emphasized the need for increased technical science research on varietal mixes when new and improved varieties are created, and on the maintenance of new varieties when these are introduced into mixtures.

In Ecuador, social science members of an FSR team gathered data that directly benefited the legume breeding program. For example, in one case, the efforts of a national agricultural program to develop a pole bean that would grow well with a newly introduced early-maturing maize variety were discontinued when CRSP researchers discovered that farmers in the region monocropped the new corn variety and followed it with a relay crop of beans or peas.

Social scientists have investigated the relative importance to breeding programs of still other social, cultural, and economic factors—seed color, size and taste preferences, cooking characteristics, nutritional features, and the use of plant residues for fuel or animal fodder. A synopsis of these factors was drawn up and distributed to CRSP plant breeders (Ferguson and Horn 1985).

Crop management and economics. The study of indigenous practices has led to changes in recommended plant-spacing patterns and other crop management practices. For example, farmers in Ecuador were spacing bean plants much farther apart than agronomists recommended. Further research by project social scientists demonstrated that the manual weed control practiced by the farmers required the spacing distances actually being used, a finding that led agronomists·to reconsider their recommendations (Garrett 1986c).

Socioeconomic studies in Tanzania (Due 1984) and Malawi (Barnes-McConnell 1986) indicate that new crop varieties and agronomic practices compatible with existing farming systems and cropping calendars stand a much better chance of acceptance and success. These studies also show how, without adequate socioeconomic research beforehand, the introduction of new varieties can have unforeseen consequences. A case from Malawi is illustrative: a new longer-season variety of maize was developed and introduced, but production of the new maize conflicted with labor requirements during the heaviest bean-growing season. Adoption of this new high-yielding maize resulted in delayed bean harvests, increased insect damage to beans in the field, and reduced bean yields (Barnes-McConnell 1986).

Technology development and adaptation. Careful research into farming systems has identified and addressed key production and utilization constraints to technology development and adoption. For example, in Botswana, research conducted under Bean/Cowpea CRSP and other auspices revealed that many farm households were headed by women who lacked access to adequate draft power for field preparation (Horn and Nkambule-Kanyima 1984). This information was used to design a minimum tillage ridger/planter that relies for traction power not on oxen but on donkeys—animals that women can more easily obtain and handle (DeMooy 1985). In Nigeria, social science investigations have also assisted in the design of new cowpea processing technologies. Research on food preferences and on family labor and consumption patterns has been used in the development of a village-level mill to produce a cowpea meal acceptable for preparing *akkara* and other popular dishes. It is anticipated that this and other new processing and storage technologies will significantly reduce women's work burdens and improve family nutrition (McWatters 1984).

STUDENT TRAINING

The social sciences have had an impact not only on research agendas, but also on student training programs in the Bean/Cowpea CRSP. Between 1980 and 1985, 57 students received MS and PhD degrees under CRSP auspices, and another 86 students were enrolled in graduate degree programs.[10] Approximately 15% of these 143 students were enrolled in social science or agricultural economics disciplines; 35% were in food technology and nutrition; and 50% were in agriculture. Reflecting WID efforts to integrate women into the program, 60 (42%) of the 143 were female.

Students attend a variety of U.S. and host country universities; many come together for the summer workshops annually sponsored by the Bean/Cowpea CRSP. Workshops on biological nitrogen fixation, MSTAT (a computer program for the agricultural sciences), and food-quality concerns have been held, with social science inputs to the last. Beyond these program-wide workshops, some projects sponsor additional workshops with a social science or agricultural economics component. For example, since its inception, the Tanzania project has held yearly regional bean meetings that have brought together students and researchers from a wide range of disciplines—both social and technical—to discuss progress in their fields. Through such interchanges, the valuable lessons learned from the sorts of socioeconomic research described throughout this chapter are shared and reinforced.

CONCLUSION

In long-term research-oriented programs like the CRSPs, although contributions from a social science *of* and social science *in* agricultural R&D are often contrasted (Brush 1986; DeWalt 1985 and this volume), the two do not necessarily exclude each other. In fact, a firm grounding in the social science *of* agricultural issues is imperative to conducting successful social science research *in* agriculture. This is so because the practices of small-scale farmers undergo continual modification and adaptation in response to factors associated with the household, the community, and the broader political economy. Traditional farming methods persist not by chance, but as the result of an ongoing process of selection (Brush 1985). Thus, static accounts of farming practices, food processing and consumption patterns, and so forth may ultimately be less useful in designing appropriate interventions than is the elucidation of larger processes and directions of change in the agricultural sector. Ideally, therefore, social scientists and agricultural economists on multidisciplinary agricultural R&D programs should bring to these ventures the same kinds of critical perspectives and disciplinarily grounded knowledge and skills as do their counterparts in the biological and technical sciences.

NOTES

1. M. W. Adams of the MSU Department of Crop and Soil Sciences directed the Bean/Cowpea CRSP planning grant with the collaboration of D. Wallace, on sabbatical from the Department of Vegetable Crops at Cornell University.

2. The director is Patricia Barnes-McConnell.

3. The U.S. principal investigator (PI) is Matt Silbernagel, a plant breeder from the USDA and Washington State University; the co-PI is Jean Due, an agricultural economist from the University of Illinois; and the host country PI is James M. Teri.

4. The U.S. PI is M. Wayne Adams, an MSU plant breeder. Between 1980 and 1986, the co-PI was Pat Barnes-McConnell, the CRSP director, As an anthropologist, I took over as co-PI in 1987. From 1980 to 1985, the host country PI was Todo Edje; Wilson Msuku now holds that post.

5. The U.S. PI is Kay McWatters, a food technologist at the University of Georgia. A number of survey researchers from the University of Nigeria have participated in the project. The host country PI is Dickson O. Nnanyelugo.

6. Toward this end, a series of Women in Agriculture Resource Guides has been compiled. The series reviews social science and agricultural economics literature on the small-farm sector and women's roles in agricultural production in the host countries. The guides examine the implications of this literature for project goals and also provide information on women's groups in the host countries.

7. Nancy Axinn was WID specialist with the Bean/Cowpea CRSP from the program's inception through 1983, when I assumed that responsibility.

8. At the same time that researchers have become aware of each other's potential contributions, CRSP funding levels have been reduced. Budget cuts have made it somewhat more difficult to act on these increased understandings through developing more inclusive or innovative research agendas that integrate additional scientists (of any sort) or through initiating a socioeconomic research project in its own right.

9. Jean Due was responsible for the agricultural economics research in Tanzania; Pat Barnes-McConnell directed the Malawi social science research team; Patricia Garrett coordinated the sociology component of the farming

systems project in Ecuador; and Kay McWatters oversaw the survey research in Nigeria. Nancy Horn and I carried out secondary data searches on the small-farm sector and women's roles in agriculture in Botswana, Cameroon, and Guatemala.

10. Eighty-seven of these 143 students were from host countries or other developing countries; the remainder were from the United States.

REFERENCES

Barnes-McConnel, P. 1986. 1985 Annual Report from the Social Science Component. Bean/Cowpea CRSP Malawi Project. East Lansing: Bean/Cowpea CRSP ME, Michigan State University.

Barsky, O. 1983. Información estadística sobre la producción de leguminosas y de frejol en Ecuador. CEPLAES Working Paper 83.4S. Quito: Proyecto INIAP/Cornell.

Brush, S. B. 1985. Diversity and Change in Andean Agriculture. Paper presented to the conference, "Lands at Risk in the Third World: Local Level Perspectives." Institute of Development Anthropology, Binghamton, New York, October 10–12.

———. 1986. Farming Systems Research. *Human Organization* 43(3):220–228.

DeMooy, C. J. 1985. Improving Cultural Practices and Agricultural Implements for Cowpea Production in Semiarid Botswana. Bean/Cowpea CRSP Research Highlights 2(4).

DeMooy, C. J., and B. DeMooy. 1985. Search for More Suitable Cowpea Varieties for Semiarid Conditions in Botswana. Bean/Cowpea CRSP Research Highlights 2(11).

DeWalt, B. R. 1985. Farming Systems Research. *Human Organization* 44(2):106–114.

Due, J. 1986. Agricultural Policy in Tropical Africa: Is a Turn-Around Possible? *Agricultural Economics* 1(1):19–34.

Due, J., and P. Anandajayasekeram. 1984. Contrasting Farming Systems in Morogoro, Tanzania. *Canadian Journal of African Studies* 18(3):583–591.

Due, J., M. White, and T. Rocke. 1985. Beans in the Farming Systems of Two Regions in Tanzania, 1980–82. Technical Report No. 4. Department of Rural Economy, Sokoine University of Agriculture, Morogoro, Tanzania, and Department of Agricultural Economics, University of Illinois at Urbana-Champaign, aAE-4602, August.

Ferguson, A. E., and N. Horn. 1984. Cameroon Women in Agriculture Resource Guide. East Lansing: Bean/Cowpea CRSP Management Office, Michigan State University.

———. 1985. Situating Agricultural Research in a Class and Gender Context: The Bean/Cowpea Collaborative Research Support Program. *Culture and Agriculture* 26(Spring):1–10.

Ferguson, A., and M. Flores. 1987. Guatemala Women in Agriculture Resource Guide. East Lansing: Bean/Cowpea CRSP ME, Michigan State University.

Garrett, P. 1986a. Social Stratification and Multiple Enterprises: Some Implications for Farming Systems Research. *Journal of Rural Studies* 2(3):209–220.

————. 1986b. Viable Objectives for Small Holder Programs: Variation by Social Strata. *Agricultural Administration* 22(2):39–55.

————. 1986c. Agronomic, Sociological and Genetic Aspects of Bean and Cowpea Yield and Adaptation. Bean/Cowpea CRSP-Cornell University/INIAP Ecuador Fiscal Year 1981/85 Report. Ithaca, NY: Cornell University.

Garrett, P., and D. Goldstein. 1984. Some Methodological Issues in Preintervention Farming Systems Research: Selecting Appropriate Techniques for Data Collection. Project Working Paper 84.4E. Ithaca, NY: INIAP Cornell Bean/Cowpea CRSP.

Garrett, P., D. Golden, and J. Francis. 1986. The Measurement and Analysis of Inequality Using Microcomputers. *Social Science Microcomputer Review* 4(2):194–206.

Horn, N., and B. Nkambule-Kanyima. 1984. Botswana Women in Agriculture Resource Guide. East Lansing: Bean/Cowpea CRSP ME, Michigan State University.

McWatters, K. 1984. Improving Food Accessibility Through Village-Level Production of Cowpea Meal. Bean/Cowpea CRSP Research Highlights 1(4).

————. 1985. 1986 Technical Summary. Appropriate Technology for Cowpea Preservation and Processing and a Study of its Socio-Economic Impact on Rural Populations in Nigeria. East Lansing: Bean/Cowpea CRSP ME, Michigan State University

Ta'Ama, M. E. 1985. A New Look at the Importance of Cultivars in Cowpea Research: Evidence from Northern Cameroon. Bean/Cowpea CRSP Research Highlights 2(5).

USAID. 1982. Women in Development. USAID Policy Paper, Bureau for Program and Policy Coordination. Washington, DC: USAID.

9

Regional Analysis, Farming Systems, and Social Science: Bean/Cowpea CRSP Experiences in Manabí, Ecuador

Jorge F. Uquillas and Patricia Garrett

This chapter illustrates how basic principles of social scientific methodology were adapted to farming systems research (FSR) and utilized by a multidisciplinary team in which agronomic scientists predominated. The rationale of the research design is described, the principal results of fieldwork in the Portoviejo River valley of Manabí, Ecuador are reported, and recommendations for future research are made. This chapter reflects the collaboration of scientists at the Instituto Nacional de Investigaciones Agropecuarias (INIAP) and Cornell University on the Bean/Cowpea CRSP.

The farming systems approach to research and extension provides a user-oriented perspective on agricultural research and development. In most Third World countries, attention has focused on export commodities. Recently, however, basic foodstuffs have assumed more importance as many countries define food self-sufficiency as a desirable objective. These efforts have been supported by multilateral and bilateral programs, including the International Agricultural Research Centers (IARCs) and the Collaborative Research Support Projects (CRSPs).

National efforts to increase the domestic production of basic foodstuffs address the needs of smallholders, who are the primary producers in many DCs, and the urban poor, who are the principal consumers. In Ecuador, the decision to accord these groups higher priority had implications for the nation's major agricultural research institution, INIAP. Scientists began to adopt a more comprehensive analysis of agricultural production in order to develop technologies appropriate to smallholders.

Conventional approaches that overemphasize experiment station research at the expense of trials under actual farming conditions have often produced technological innovations that are adopted by medium- and large-scale producers but rejected as inappropriate by smallholders (Shaner et al. 1982). Accordingly, the Consultative Group on International Agricultural Research (CGIAR 1978) recommended a farming systems perspective to improve problem identification, suggest new and/or enhanced production systems, and orient research toward potentially important innovations. These recommendations were heeded in several sites where INIAP was working with small-scale producers of basic grains. Consequently, FSR, which is actually scale-neutral, focused on the needs of smallholders for improved production practices in Ecuador.

THE DIAGNOSTIC PHASE OF
FARMING SYSTEMS RESEARCH

FSR can be conceptualized as a process of technological innovation that has successive phases, beginning with problem identification and ending with technology transfer.[1] Although collaboration is essential throughout the process, social scientific methodologies are particularly important during initial phases, which rely heavily on library research and the analysis of secondary data. The analysis of some data (e.g., soils maps) requires agronomic expertise, but many sources are better analyzed by social scientists. During the problem identification phase, experimental research may also be relevant. Some kinds of on-station experimentation can be conceptualized as a way of "interviewing the plants," permitting scientists to focus subsequent interviews with farmers on problems that they suspect exist because of their prior observations of trials. The benefits of using both experimental and library research is well illustrated by the case of Manabí.

Preparation for diagnostic fieldwork includes the analysis of available agronomic and socioeconomic data and the preparation of a preliminary report. This suggests focuses for field research and provides materials for training interviewers and orienting them to the study site. The analysis of secondary data is particularly useful to those unfamiliar with a zone, because it provides a contrast to the known. Quantitative data also allow regional scientists to "true" their perceptions, potentially challenging the data and/or their assumptions.

Preliminary research means scientists can build on existing information to focus interviews. Adequate preparation for fieldwork allows the team to select informants who are broadly representative of the major ecological and socioeconomic conditions in a region. Structured interviews focus on practices common to the zone. Library research and fieldwork interact to permit rapid problem identification.

There are several outputs from diagnostic field research, including preliminary subregional reports and an integrated regional analysis. Collectively, these documents describe the principal characteristics of crop and livestock production as they vary by subregion and social group, and they identify opportunities for subsequent research and extension activities. The unit of analysis for preliminary or diagnostic research is the subregion; this is why the Bean/Cowpea CRSP adopted the term "regional analysis."

Our thesis is that regional analysis provides valuable insights into ecological and socioeconomic variations in farming systems. Although it is important to describe existing farming systems, the fundamental purpose of diagnostic research is to identify priorities for subsequent agronomic and socioeconomic research. Structured interviewing with informants is the data-collection technique of choice. Like any methodology, however, it has inherent limitations and should be supplemented by survey research using probabilistic samples in zones where development activities will concentrate. Appropriately designed survey research permits the measurement of variation at the individual/household level. This is essential for the evaluation of certain agronomic, socioeconomic, and nutritional impacts of technological innovations (Campbell 1985; Garrett and Goldstein 1984).

THE ECUADORIAN CONTEXT

Ecuador experiences agricultural problems characteristic of many Third World countries. As in most of Latin America, productive resources are distributed unequally. Farms with fewer than 5 ha represent 67% of all units, though they occupy only 7% of the land. By contrast, large farms with more than 100 ha constitute 2% of all units, yet they occupy fully 48% of the land. Measured inequality is high. The Gini Index of Concentration, which ranges from a low of zero for perfect equality to a high of unity for perfect inequality, is 0.81 (Garrett et al. 1986).

Agriculture in Ecuador is oriented to both international and domestic markets. Historically, agricultural exports have been important; currently, they earn approximately 35% of the country's foreign exchange. Research and extension have traditionally focused on four major export crops (bananas, cocoa, coffee, and sugar), which are produced on large farms along the Pacific coast (Milford 1983).

Dietary staples in Ecuador have generally not benefited from agricultural research and extension. Gross agricultural production kept pace with population growth, increasing at approximately 3% per year during the 1970s. This reflects both increases in lands under cultivation and the improved productivity of a few crops, notably banana, African palm oil, soy beans, and hard corn. Nevertheless, yields of basic food crops (notably potatoes, rice, and soft corn) did not improve. Consequently, Ecuador was forced to import basic grains, and food imports increased at an annual rate of 13% (Milford 1983).

Confronting stagnant yields in basic grains and rising prices for imported food, Ecuador began to assign more importance to smallholder production.

INIAP needed to reconsider how it could achieve its basic institutional objective, the development of technological alternatives that increased agricultural production and productivity for the benefit of both producers and consumers. At this critical juncture, the institution's budget from both national and international sources was increased, thereby permitting better staffing and more on-farm research.

INIAP received substantial support from the Centro Internacional de Mejoramiento de Maíz y Trigo (CIMMYT), the Agency for International Development (USAID/EC), and the Instituto Interamericano de Cooperación para la Agricultura (IICA/OEA). With foreign assistance, INIAP's work on behalf of smallholders began seriously in 1976 and was subsequently institutionalized in the Department of Agricultural Economics, Program of Investigation in Production, or PIP (Moscardi et al. 1983). The Bean/Cowpea CRSP provided additional support during the early 1980s and was integrated into INIAP through the PIP.

A major objective of the Bean/Cowpea CRSP was to improve FSR in Ecuador. This implied building on national expertise, incorporating relevant experiences from other countries, and adapting social scientific methodologies in order to generate an economical and effective research design. The larger objective was partially achieved, as described below. This chapter focuses on methodology; more specifically, it describes the development of a research design that permits agronomic scientists to analyze smallholder agriculture in its regional and structural context.

CONCEPTUAL FRAMEWORK FOR BEAN/COWPEA CRSP RESEARCH

There is broad consensus among farming systems researchers that some sort of informal survey should be conducted by multidisciplinary teams prior to initiating agricultural R&D, but how institutions conduct preliminary or diagnostic field research varies. The Instituto de Ciencias y Tecnologías Agrícolas (ICTA) in Guatemala developed a technique called the *sondeo*. The format is open-ended, so the content of interviews varies according to what seems relevant to each region (Hildebrand 1981). A contrasting approach was developed for use in the East African Farming Systems Research Program of CIMMYT. This format is more formal, and it provides a detailed checklist to guide interviews (Collinson 1981, 1982). It is complemented by the general methodology developed at CIMMYT (Byerlee and Collinson 1980; Perrin et al. 1979). Other important approaches (Chambers 1981; Honadle 1982; Murphy and Sprey 1982; Rhoades 1982; Shaner et al. 1982) are intermediate with regard to degree of formalization. Alternatives are discussed and evaluated in Beebe (1985). The role of social scientists in these activities is considered in Horton (1984), Rhoades (1984), and DeWalt (1985). Fresco (1984) provides a useful comparison of anglophone and francophone approaches.

The appropriate unit of analysis is a critical issue. If it is established that regional and subregional variations are important determinants of farming systems, exploratory research should focus on systematic variation across space: the appropriate unit of analysis is a geographic area with definable agroclimatic characteristics. Within regions, further variation in farming systems can occur by social group. In this case, structured interviews with informants can elicit information about agricultural practices common to specific social groups residing in identifiable subregions.

Stated more generally, ecological and socioeconomic variables determine the organization of agricultural production in the sense that they delimit the alternatives open to producers. This is reflected in group-level variations in farming practices and in generic combinations of agricultural and nonagricultural activities. Social groups are located spatially in a systematic fashion, and regularities can be ascertained through regional analysis.

Exactly how ecological and socioeconomic variables determine the organization of crop and livestock production is still under investigation. Important principles have been enunciated by agricultural ecologists (Cox and Atkins 1979), but a consistently ecological approach to farming systems is unusual (Hart 1982). Nevertheless, the concept of a "recommendation domain" is predicated on the interrelation of ecological and socioeconomic characteristics (Harrison and Tripp 1984).

There are strong intellectual traditions that emphasize the systematic variation of human interaction with the physical environment, e.g., C. Smith (1976) in anthropology and D. Smith (1982) in geography. Harwood (1979) has insisted on the importance of physical characteristics, and Shaner (1984) suggests that systematic stratification, considering such components as the agroclimatic zone, provides a potentially cost-effective approach to FSR. Hart (1982) applies ecological analysis to farming systems, and Fresco (1984) describes francophone approaches that include the village and the subregion as levels of analysis. This literature collectively reflects one emerging tendency, namely the realization that agriculture has a regional organization that must be understood in order to place farm-level decisionmaking in its structural context.

The importance of regional variation and structural contexts has also been stressed in recent social scientific commentaries on FSR. Garrett (1984b) emphasizes how structural variables delimit the range of alternatives actually open to small-scale producers. Little (1985) argues that a focus on the individual farm needs to be supplemented by regional analysis. Maxwell (1986) demonstrates that appropriate farm-level modifications cannot be designed without attention to the economic and political aspects of a changing structural context. Biggs (1985) and Garrett (1987) emphasize organizational and institutional issues. These interpretations are basically complementary, especially in their emphasis on the interdependence of micro- and macrolevel structures. They are also broadly consistent with insights derived from human geography (Porter 1978).

Theoretical and empirical analyses alike suggest that agricultural production has a regional organization. The activities of large- and medium-scale landowners structure those of small-scale producers. Large-scale producers often employ smallholders, and the demand for labor on- and off-farm can be competitive. Estate owners are frequently sources of credit, so interventions requiring increased cash inputs must be evaluated in the context of the local credit network. Marketing is also regionally specific. Availability of productive inputs and access to buyers of agricultural goods are critical determinants of area farming systems. Because these factors are structured at a regional level, a specifically geographic and regional approach to the field is the most appropriate way to place small-scale producers in context. If national and/or international conditions change, these also need to be considered in analysis (Maxwell 1986).

Finally, small-scale agriculture is an eminently social activity. Children learn to farm by working with their parents. Adults discuss farming practices and share solutions to problems. Communities celebrate successful harvests, and complex systems of beliefs and rituals surround many agricultural practices. Farming is learned and shared. Indeed, it is the very sociability of agriculture that makes the diffusion of innovations possible.

A viable FSR design can build on these considerations. The social and cultural aspects of farming plus the systematic variation of farming practices by ecology provide the context for informant interviewing. Interviews can be structured to discuss how people who are like the informant practice agriculture and support their families. Responses will reflect systematic influences of ecological and socioeconomic factors, and this variation will distribute itself spatially. Preliminary research can thus capture how farming systems differ by region, reflecting ecological and socioeconomic variation. Selecting informants and interpreting their commentaries are considered in detail in Garrett et al. 1987 and Uquillas et al. 1986a.

In summary, the regional analysis of farming systems derives from two basic principles: variation in farming systems is systematic by subzone and social group; this variation is known to members integrated into agricultural communities. These principles have critical implications for research design. Specifically, informant interviewing is the data-collection technique of choice during the preintervention or diagnostic phases of FSR. Individuals are asked to report not about themselves but about people like themselves, not about their personal behavior but about practices common to a region. This technique generates qualitative, descriptive data that capture regional variation. These data have limitations, especially because they cannot be quantified and do not reflect individual differences. They can, however, provide reliable information about the farming systems in a region.

AN INTRODUCTION TO MANABÍ

Manabí is a challenge. It is a large and populous province located on the Pacific Ocean due north of Ecuador's largest city, Guayaquil. Because of its location, the province is a potential provisioner for coastal cities. Resources are limited, however, and the zone needs innovative and effective programs in agricultural research and development.

Young people leave Manabí if they can. As a counter to these migratory currents, many professionals reared or trained in the area develop regional allegiances. Consequently, provincial offices are staffed by many competent professionals committed to agricultural and rural development. Local institutions have a history of collaboration, and the Bean/Cowpea CRSP was able to mobilize interagency cooperation in ways that would probably have been more difficult in less peripheral regions.

In 1982, fully 64% of the economically active population worked in agriculture. Nevertheless, farming is problematic. Agroclimatic characteristics, topography, and limited investment in irrigation all limit production. The small size of most farms also makes exclusive reliance on agriculture difficult. Smallholders remain in farming by diversifying or intensifying. The principal alternatives are off-farm employment or intensification of on-farm production, principally through integration into the broiler industry.

When the Bean/Cowpea CRSP began work in Manabí, scientists knew little about farming systems in the region. The zone had been identified as appropriate for project activities because legumes were important in regional farming systems and in the local diet. Systematic research, however, was required to establish priorities for legume research.

PRELIMINARY EVALUATION OF LEGUME GERMPLASM

CRSP activities in Manabí began with a rapid reconnaissance of the province and the collection of germplasm during the spring of 1984. Flooding caused by El Niño in 1982–1983 had destroyed seed stocks, not only on farms, but also at the Portoviejo Experiment Station. The preservation, evaluation, and ultimate improvement of surviving legume cultivars was considered important because experimental research would require national as well as international germplasm.

A total of 155 samples of germplasm collected from 139 farmers was multiplied. Many seeds failed to germinate, and there was a high incidence of virus infestation. Plants with identical architectures were also known by different names (Chávez 1984). On-station research, therefore, identified issues that were subsequently addressed during diagnostic field research. Specifically, experimental research demonstrated that the production and storage of seed was a potentially important problem, as was loss to diseases, especially viruses. Finally, interviewers needed to pay close attention to the local names of cultivars because variation was likely to be pronounced.

The initial multiplication of germplasm also provided guidelines for subsequent agronomic research. Fifteen of the original 17 cultivars of lima bean (*Phaseolus lunatus*, climbing type) were selected for their tolerance to viruses and their pod-bearing capacity; nine of 36 cultivars of lima bean (bush type) and four with intermediary growth patterns were also selected for virus tolerance, early maturity, and productivity. Finally, 26 of the original 82 cultivars of cowpea (*Vigna unguiculata*) were selected for virus tolerance, early maturity, length of pod, and seed weight (this work is reported in detail in Linzán 1984). During the subsequent rainy season, selected lines were studied in trials with and without pesticides. Initial experiments were not conclusive, so research on this topic continued.

As a result of diagnostic field research, new trials were added during the 1985 dry season. Interviews and observations indicated that experimentation on planting distances was necessary, and this work began. Research on supports for climbing legumes was also initiated; preliminary results suggest that a good choice is horizontal wire from which a piece of plastic clothesline is suspended for each plant. Varietal research also continued, using local germplasm and lines introduced from the International Institute of Tropical Agriculture (IITA) and EMBRAPA.

The purpose of this work was to develop varieties and technologies appropriate for smallholders in Manabí. Diagnostic field research identified priority problems, and trials on smallholders' fields were initiated. Two promising lines, one of cowpea and the other of lima, earlier selected from farmers' fields, are currently being studied. Larger factorial experiments concerning planting distances and control of insects and diseases are also being conducted during both rainy and dry seasons. Collectively, this work illustrates the complementarity of socioeconomic and agronomic research, both on-station and in farmers' fields.

ANALYSIS OF SECONDARY DATA

The collection and analysis of secondary data, both agronomic and socioeconomic, began in late 1984. Ecological and soil maps were prepared and an extensive preliminary report was written. Many sources were consulted, including theses by students at the Universidad Técnica de Manabí (UTM), census data from the Instituto Nacional de Estadísticas y Censos (INEC), and studies by the regional development agency, the Centro de Rehabilitación de Manabí (CRM).

Census data indicated that Manabí, with a population of approximately one million, had strong migratory currents that produced low rates of population increase despite high birth rates. Although urban areas were growing, rural areas experienced absolute declines in population. Consistent with high birth rates is the fact that approximately half the population was economically dependent. In 1974, for example, 44% of the age-eligible population (12 years or older) was economically active, most (68%) in the agricultural sector.

Geographically, Manabí is dominated by two river systems, the Río Portoviejo/Río Chico and the Carrizal/Chone. Soils in the valleys were formed by alluvial deposits, and the region can generally be described as very dry tropical forest. Subregions have different climates, e.g., dry tropical forest, humid premontane forest, and spiny tropical montane. Lands with these characteristics have limited productivity, especially without irrigation. Large-scale irrigation does exist in the zone, but recent flooding damaged many canals and left the system virtually inoperative. Inadequate infrastructure and insufficient water were known to be important constraints on agricultural production in the region.

The distribution of landholdings in Manabí is very unequal, as reflected in a Gini coefficient of 0.76. Agricultural census data for 1974 indicated that farms of 200 ha or more represented only 1.2% of all farms but occupied 31.4% of the land, while these figures were 67% and 10% for units smaller than 10 ha. The continual parcelization of land is demonstrated by historical data: the number of farms less than 10 ha increased from 58% of all units in 1954 to 67% in 1974 (Uquillas et al. 1985c). Although more recent agricultural census data are not available, this trend has clearly continued because there has been no major land redistribution by agrarian reform in the zone.

Agricultural production in Manabí consists principally of export crops, such as coffee, cacao, and bananas. Only 5% of the area is dedicated to crops for internal consumption, including rice, casava, cooking bananas, cowpeas, and lima beans. Production of cowpeas and limas was concentrated (70%–80% in 1974) on farms of less than 10 ha. Livestock species varied by farm size: cattle were concentrated on large farms, while pigs and goats were typical of small units. Even small farms are integrated into a market economy, and fully 85% of all farms sell some or all of their production. Family labor predominates on small holdings, while occasional hired labor characterizes farms larger than 10 ha (Uquillas et al. 1985c).

Recently, the most dramatic change in the agricultural sector has been increased production of dry corn for feed in the burgeoning broiler industry. Hard corn is grown in the coastal highlands and used in lowland chicken houses. Valley smallholders able to change over to broilers have profited. Those with limited capital, however, have been excluded from participation in this growing agroindustry.

THE UTILITY OF PREPARATORY RESEARCH

Bean/Cowpea CRSP experiences suggest that preparatory research, specifically analyzing secondary data and drafting preliminary reports, can be cost-effective. The initial payoff in Manabí was in site selection. Agricultural census data for the two principal river valleys revealed important differences between them. Land was more subdivided in Río Portoviejo/Río Chico, so there were proportionally more smallholders. Sharecropping was more common, and cash rentals less so. More farms produced for household consumption, and legumes were much more prevalent.[3]

Data reflecting these regional differences were elaborated in the extensive preliminary report prepared by a small team led by the field sociologist. This document was then reviewed by a larger team of INIAP and Cornell scientists, who recommended that the section describing the physical and ecological conditions of different subregions be revised to minimize technical terminology, and that an executive summary focusing on the Portoviejo River valley be appended. These recommendations were implemented, and another team meeting was called to study the executive summary (Uquillas et al. 1985b). On the basis of background research, the team decided to focus field research in the Río Portoviejo/Río Chico valley. This decision was taken not because it would save time and money, but because it was *appropriate* to CRSP objectives. This example illustrates how preliminary research can enhance project effectiveness—even as it reduces the costs of fieldwork.

Background research also improves fieldwork by focusing inquiry on relevant issues and preparing interviewers to learn from the field. The Bean/Cowpea CRSP developed an interview guide that was originally applied in Imbabura (Garrett et al. 1982); it was modified and adapted to Manabí by the field sociologist, and a draft was discussed by the INIAP/Cornell team. Recommendations, especially those concerning details of legume cultivation during rainy and dry seasons, were incorporated into the schedule that multidisciplinary teams employed during field research in Manabí (Uquillas 1985).

Two CRSP documents were used to train interviewers. The executive summary was sufficiently short so that it was actually read and studied by team members. Also, authors of the longer paper were on hand to provide additional information upon request. The executive summary, however, furnished the ecological and socioeconomic information critical to effective field research; agronomic scientists found it informative and useful. The interview guide gave guidance for first-time interviewers and some uniformity of coverage across teams. Both documents provided concrete topics for discussions and a basis for cross-disciplinary dialogue. They enabled a multidisciplinary team, composed disproportionately of agronomic scientists, to begin field research with greater knowledge, confidence, and sophistication.

THE ORGANIZATION OF FIELDWORK

Informal interviews, such as the sondeo, are intended to identify common agrosocioeconomic characteristics of farmers so as to orient subsequent agronomic and socioeconomic research (Hildebrand 1981:426). With this objective in mind, a training session for the entire field team was organized. Training themes included the history of the INIAP/Cornell project, activities in Manabí, and techniques for field research. Particular emphasis was accorded the preliminary analyses of Manabí and the methodology for regional analysis that the CRSP was developing.

Training exercises were organized in which scientists divided into two teams and interviewed farmers near the Portoviejo Experiment Station. Subsequent discussions focused on the researchers' experiences in this pilot study and the utility of the interview guide. Thereafter, the logistics of fieldwork were considered, and issues concerning staffing, transportation, and finances were resolved. Earlier experiences in Imbabura had demonstrated that logistical problems needed to be anticipated and resolved before they arose. Planning facilitated fieldwork.

Field research was conducted by a rather large and diverse team. The 17 members represented four institutions: eight from INIAP, four from the regional development agency (CRM), three from the Manabí Technical University (UTM), and two from Cornell University. The team consisted of 13 agronomic scientists and four social scientists (one sociologist, one economist, and two agricultural economists). There were 15 males and two females, both agronomists.

Four teams were constituted, each with a social scientist and a representative of CRM. The social scientists were there to guarantee the collection of both agronomic and socioeconomic data, and the personnel of CRM were to enrich interviews with their years of extension experience. Each team was assigned one subregion of the Río Portoviejo/Río Chico basin. These subregions were delimited with agroclimatic data interpreted by knowledgeable scientists from CRM and INIAP. Once in the field, each team worked separately, but occasional general meetings permitted the exchange of ideas and evaluation of work in progress.

Diagnostic field research took place from 23 April to 3 May 1985. The four teams conducted more than 110 interviews, some of them group discussions. All teams had been instructed to seek out informants with a broad knowledge of the area and to focus discussions on phenomena typical of the region rather than peculiar to the respondent. These interviews, plus field observations, constituted the basis for preliminary team reports (Carrillo et al. 1985; Hinostroza et al. 1985; Maldonado et al. 1985; Uquillas et al. 1985d). Collectively, these reports identify similarities and differences across four areas of the river valley. Reports were written within a few days after fieldwork ended, a rapidity possible because structured interviewing using the CRSP interview guide elicits information that virtually writes itself.

These preliminary reports were used to design follow-up agronomic and socioeconomic research. Subsequently, the results of library and field research were synthesized and published (Uquillas et al. 1986b) in a document that focused on agricultural production, marketing, labor force, and consumption patterns among farmers in the Portoviejo River valley.

OVERVIEW OF PRINCIPAL FINDINGS

Together, the five reports mentioned above extensively document the organization of agricultural production in the Río Portoviejo/Río Chico valley. The richness of this information cannot be captured in a summary. However, a few of the principal socioeconomic findings from one subregion are highlighted here, followed by a discussion of the utility of fieldwork.

Throughout the study site, agricultural production is typified by intermediary levels of technology and unpaid family labor. Males and females, adults and children, all work, performing different tasks. Women manage farms when males migrate to engage in seasonal wage labor. These results echo other research (Balarezo et al. 1984; Safa 1987).

Despite these uniformities, the Portoviejo River valley divided itself into two zones. The lower valley is of greater interest to the Bean/Cowpea CRSP. Fieldwork there revealed three important changes in production during the last decade: Large-scale irrigation was constructed; high-value crops, including vegetables, coconut oil, soy beans, and marigolds, were introduced; and improved seeds were adopted for such traditional crops as maize, peanuts, cotton, and rice. Agriculture had changed rapidly.

The lower valley is typified by level fields, an incipient tendency toward monoculture, and crop rotation to maintain soil fertility. Smallholdings of less than two hectares predominate, and land is intensively exploited. Principal crops are short-cycle annuals—vegetables, maize, rice, peanuts, casava, and legumes, for example. The production and consumption of legumes are generalized. The zone is quite dry, so water availability is critical.

A large-scale irrigation system, the Poza Honda, was constructed to irrigate the entire valley, but flooding in 1983 destroyed the principal canals in a large sector, and they have not yet been repaired. People who live near water construct small dams to flood adjacent fields, but other farmers can grow crops only during the rainy season.

Historically, the Poza Honda permitted innovations in cropping systems, intensification of the agricultural calendar, and expansion of commercial production—all factors accelerating class formation and differentiation. Some farmers who began with better resources were able to intensify production. By increasing marketable surpluses and cash income, they positioned themselves to buy more land and expand their enterprises. Over time, both small- and medium-scale petty commodities producers have arisen, and these strata now employ wage labor.

Landless strata have also emerged. They engage in wage labor in the countryside and in nearby towns, working in fishing, fish processing, artisan production, and construction. These industries employ both males and females, but males uniformly command higher wages. This is consistent with CRSP findings in Imbabura (INIAP/Cornell Team 1982; Uquillas et al. 1985a). Jobs in the region are generally limited, so males frequently migrate to other coastal provinces for the harvests of coffee, cacao, and cotton. During their 2-to-4 month absence, their wives manage the farms. This adaptation, common throughout the world, has profound consequences for the organization of semiproletarian production (Chaney and Lewis 1980; Garrett 1986).

Marketing in the region centers on the city of Portoviejo. Only there can a wide variety of agrochemicals be purchased. The city's merchants serve a substantially larger market than do their counterparts in other towns. Producers deal principally with intermediaries rather than with customers, although transportation is adequate and distances short.

Despite the commercial orientation of smallholdings, production for home consumption remains important. Most of what people consume is produced locally. Legumes, a desirable foodstuff, are consumed throughout the year. They are eaten daily when available in the garden, and two to three times a week when they must be purchased. Most legumes are consumed green in soups and salads. Mature, dry legumes are also prepared as a savory called *manestra*. Animal protein is usually purchased. Beef and fish can be bought in markets and from itinerant vendors. Potatoes, a highland crop, and noodles, a processed food, are also purchased, along with toiletries, clothing, and the omnipresent Coca Cola, plus its national relative, Inca Cola.

Informants in the lower valley felt that families could live from their farms if they had two to three hectares of irrigated land, or at least six hectares of hillside lands. Hillside lands were seen as problematic, and families would require at least twice as much land as in the flats. Interestingly, informants' evaluations of what was necessary for subsistence were routinely and dramatically below professionals' calculations of minimal farm size.

THE UTILITY OF DESCRIPTIVE REGIONAL ANALYSIS

The Bean/Cowpea CRSP's adoption of a macro perspective on regional farming systems in Manabí resulted in the identification of marketing as a central socioeconomic issue requiring further research. Diagnostic research identified several problems with marketing channels. Farmers have limited liquidity and inadequate facilities for on-farm storage. Consequently, they must sell at harvest time when prices are lowest; price controls are not enforced. Farmers report limited access to official sources of credit, relying instead on informal systems. Professional moneylenders charge high interest rates. All these factors make it difficult for producers to prosper (Barril 1983).

These findings raised two fundamental questions: first, would producers and consumers, as well as merchants, benefit substantially from increased production? Second, could consumer demand absorb increased production if it were spaced more evenly throughout the year? Answers to these questions would determine whether scarce project resources should be devoted to legume research in the region.

A marketing study was designed that combined structured interviewing with participant observation. A total of 29 merchants, broadly representative of known marketing centers and channels, were interviewed. In addition market dynamics were observed during both wholesaling and retailing hours (detailed results are reported in Chávez et al. 1986).

As diagnostic research had suggested, the principal marketing chain is producer to large-scale wholesaler to intermediary to retailer to consumer. Producers bring legumes to the wholesale market in Portoviejo, where large-scale wholesalers purchase goods and resell them to medium-scale wholesalers. These intermediaries usually sell to retailers or to other medium-scale wholesalers from other large cities within the province or along the coast. Other marketing channels exist but handle little volume.

The difference between producer and consumer prices can be conceptualized as the surplus appropriated by merchants. An earlier study of marketing in the region (CRM 1978) found that profit margins varied by season, ranging from a high of 52% in March to a low of 28% in June. CRSP research, conducted in November, estimated an average profit margin of 50%. Seasonal variability in prices is marked, with lows immediately after harvest and highs at triple these levels during shortfalls. Merchants explain that demand for legumes is relatively stable throughout the year though supply is highly seasonal.

The CRSP marketing study suggested that increasing legume production and stabilizing availability would be a viable commercial strategy since the demand for legumes seems relatively inelastic. Under these circumstances, agronomic research could appropriately focus on modifications in planting dates and/or varieties to stabilize market availability. Since legumes are currently exported to other provinces, the potential market for Manabita production is substantial.

While marketing research was under way, INIAP's legume program proceeded on the assumption that CRSP research would continue in Manabí. The findings of diagnostic field research were interpreted, and priorities for INIAP's legume research were established.[4]

The relationship between diagnostic fieldwork and experimentation can be conceptualized in many ways. One approach is to emphasize problem definition through a process of elimination. Legumes are known to have a finite set of problems that agricultural R&D can address. The CRSP objective was to eliminate from the research agenda those problems that appeared unimportant to smallholders in the region and then to establish priorities among remaining topics. Field research is not designed to discover problems that scientists have never identified. Rather, its purpose is to select from among commonly recognized problems those whose solution would make a difference to specific groups of producers. FSR is applied, not basic, research.

Problem elimination is important to the design of experimental research. Legume storage in the Portoviejo River valley provides a useful illustration: legumes are stored exclusively for seed; consequently, there is no reason to study technologies for long-term, on-farm storage for human consumption. In another zone, however, this might be an appropriate theme.

Scientists found two principal on-farm techniques to store seed: legumes were either left on the vine and hung near the fireplace; or they were shelled, mixed with sand, and placed in a closed container. These are both fairly common postharvest technologies, but they are not completely effective. Informants reported insect infestations (*polilla, Callosobruchus* sp.). Scientists confirmed these reports and also observed that farmers were using certain chemicals in ways dangerous to human health. Finally, the germplasm trials that had been conducted on-station suggested that poor quality seed, infected with seed-borne diseases, was a common problem.

Collectively, these insights identified as a research priority the development of a technology to produce and store clean seed under smallholder conditions. This provided a framework for organizing supportive and related research and defined the context for work on improved varieties, planting distances, and infestations, including nematodes, insects, and diseases. The development of procedures for clean seed production and storage defined the parameters of associated research. Consequently, the research design had a rationale and logic frequently lacking in experimentation designed without intensive exploration of the site to be served.

The research agenda that emerged after fieldwork consisted of studies that are individually quite traditional. It is noteworthy, however, that several traditional topics are absent—for example, fertilization levels. Critics who fail to consider complementary aspects of research design (i.e., what is excluded as well as what is included) trivialize the contribution that a holistic analysis can make to R&D design.

IMPLICATIONS FOR MULTIDISCIPLINARY RESEARCH

Preliminary research, both on-station and in libraries, prepared CRSP researchers for much of what they observed during fieldwork. Indeed, there was little from a socioeconomic perspective that had not been anticipated on the basis of the general theoretical literature or the empirical analysis of Manabí. Certainly, a team composed solely of social scientists could have produced a more penetrating analysis of the organization of agricultural production in the province. In the context of this project, however, much of what is conceptually interesting in sociological terms could not be adequately explored. The Ecuador project differed from other CRSPs because social scientists enjoyed less disciplinary autonomy and more multidisciplinary collaboration (Garrett 1984c). There are both costs and benefits to this organization.

Our objective in Manabí was to adapt standard social scientific methodologies to provide a framework within which agronomists could conduct fieldwork successfully. Professionals with and without field experience improved their interviewing skills in both eliciting and interpreting commentaries. CRSP collaborators learned how hard smallholders work to maintain farms and support families under the disadvantageous conditions of Manabí. Interviewers focused on the details of agricultural production because they were of interest to both scientists and farmers. This focus allowed agronomic scientists to appreciate how production practices were influenced by factors other than knowledge of technological alternatives and professional recommendations.

In this way, agronomists developed some ownership of social scientific concepts. They saw firsthand how seasonal male migration affects the allocation of labor by task and how the availability of family labor conditions the organization of farming systems. It is possible to develop such understandings theoretically, but agronomists drew on what they saw and sought to interpret it. Because these insights were their own, CRSP agronomists expressed satisfaction with what they had learned. They had enjoyed fieldwork and thought it enhanced their understanding of agriculture in the region. Nevertheless, they found it difficult to specify exactly how fieldwork influenced experimentation decisions.

This observation can be interpreted in several ways: one could adopt the traditional position and argue that multidisciplinary fieldwork is marginal to the design and conduct of agronomic research; alternatively, one can ask how research priorities are actually established.

The provenance of existing strategies for agricultural development in Third World countries is not intuitively obvious. Conventional wisdom holds that research agendas in the natural sciences reflect consensus on puzzles important to the "scientific community." In many countries, however, critical contemporary literature is inaccessible because libraries cannot afford expensive journals. Contact with international peers is hard to establish and maintain because communication is difficult and travel expensive (Lacy et al. this volume.) Under these circumstances, national commodity programs find it difficult to reach the cutting edge of research.[5] National institutions also feel pressure to conform to an international division of labor. The IARCs facilitate research, but they also influence the direction of national programs. Finally, national programs have their own dynamics, which generally discourage innovation. All these factors mean that scientists cannot control their research agendas in an assertive, pro-active fashion. They can exercise control at the margin, but many parameters of their research are defined by outsiders.

Exactly how disciplinary, commodity, and national factors interact to determine research agendas is poorly understood. Consequently, it is not clear how much autonomy national commodity programs actually have. To the extent that the definition of a research strategy is mechanical rather than deliberate and judicious, programs are inherently unable to redefine agendas based on the regional analysis of farming systems.

Further complicating the problem of research strategy is a markedly divergent approach to the field in the social and biological sciences. Social scientists conduct research in the field, collecting data and exploring alternative interpretations. By contrast, biological scientists tend to equate research with controlled experimentation in laboratories and test plots; they therefore have difficulty incorporating insights from fieldwork into "real" (i.e., experimental) research. Fundamentally different conceptions of research, and consequently of fieldwork, inhibit communication in ways that need to be better understood if multidisciplinary collaboration is to be effective.

The farming systems approach allows scientists rationally and self-consciously to design a research program. This potential calls attention to some relatively unexamined influences that currently set the agenda for Third World commodity programs. Dependency is a complex phenomenon, and although national programs conduct research, they do not control basic aspects of their scientific agendas. A farming systems approach encourages nationals to take control of programming in ways that meet the needs of specific constituencies. Reflection on these issues may allow national scientists to make more deliberate and appropriate choices about research design in the future.

NOTES

Research was conducted under the Bean/Cowpea Collaborative Research Support Program (AID/DSAN/XIIG-0261). The authors have tried to reflect the stimulating contributions of those who worked intensively with the project in Manabí and who produced many of the papers cited in this chapter. Nevertheless, we accept responsibility for the interpretations presented here.

1. A model depicting phases of farming systems research and synthesizing diverse experiences was developed by collaborating scientists during a project workshop in Quito in August 1985. The following participants were included: INIAP/Ecuador—José Acuña, Diana Barba, Victor Hugo Cardozo, Rómulo Carrillo, Edmundo Cevallos, Napoleón Chávez, Francisco Muñoz, Arturo Villafuerte, Cristóbal Villasís, and Ely Zambrano; ICTA/Guatemala— Selvín Arriaga, José Manuel Díaz, and Porfirio Masaya; Cornell/USA—Patricia Garrett, Judith Hall, Wesley Kline, and Jorge Uquillas. The model was also employed in Espinosa and Garrett (1987) to illustrate how gender is a relevant consideration during all phases of FSR.

2. Research based on structured interviews must be carefully designed because the quality of information depends directly on the care with which informants are selected and interviewed. Knowledge of regional ecological and socioeconomic characteristics allows the team to identify appropriate informants. Preparatory research, specifically the analysis of existing agronomic and socioeconomic data, is essential to ensure coverage of all major ecological regions and social groups. Individual informants are selected so that they collectively represent the *range* of ecological and social situations manifested in the study site.

If researchers understand that experiences vary systematically by social position, they can identify respondents who are knowledgeable about specific themes. Preparation for field research is particularly helpful in anticipating the probable range of variation in the study site. In the field, social scientists (notably anthropologists and sociologists) are trained to analyze social, cultural, and economic differences within small regions, and their participation is critical on teams using structured interview techniques. A detailed interview guide that illustrates how structured interviewing can be adapted to farming systems research is available in English (Garrett et al. 1987) and Spanish (Uquillas et al. 1986a).

3. Agriclutural census data are available in Ecuador down to the county (*parroquia*) level, and our original intention was to analyze the parroquia data for Manabí, following the outline in Palacios and Garrett 1983. This was not possible. Team members did not have sufficient time to hand-copy the data on multiple variables for 90 parroquias. Moreover, adequate software for statistical analysis on the Apple II did not exist. Consequently, it was not feasible to

conduct a comprehensive statistical analysis for Manabí, paralleling that for Imbabura (Palacios and Garrett 1984). However, technology has changed dramatically in the short time since research began in Manabí. Lap-top computers now permit direct data entry in libraries and offices, and powerful statistical packages (such as SPSS and SAS) run on computers with hard disks. These innovations make it realistic to tally and analyze secondary data, at least under the favorable conditions that obtain in a country such as Ecuador. The application of microcomputers to agricultural development is discussed in Duff and Webster 1984 and Garrett et al. 1986. Obtaining USAID authorization to purchase microcomputers, however, remains an obstacle.

4. The CRSP had the freedom to decide whether to continue legume research in Portoviejo. By contrast, INIAP's Legume Program was administratively required to conduct research so long as the commodity program was assigned to the zone. It was necessary, therefore, that the Legume Program proceed as it did, using diagnostic research to define its work plan. The FSR approach to problem definition presumes the autonomy that the CRSP enjoyed; but it is also frequently employed by national programs that cannot elect to abandon regions or commodities. Thus, the commodity organization of national programs, based on the U.S. land grant university model, can conflict with a farming systems approach. FSR must, therefore, be creatively adapted to different institutional environments.

5. One notable exception is the bean program of ICTA/Guatemala directed by Porfirio Masaya, a host country PI on the Bean/Cowpea CRSP. The collaborative research support mode is intended to keep well-trained directors of national research programs in close communication both the such international centers as the Centro Internacional de Agricultura Tropical (CIAT) in Colombia and with peers such as Donald Wallace at Cornell University so that their programs can work on the cutting edge. The importance of CRSP support for good science conducted with and through national commodity programs needs to be highlighted.

REFERENCES

Balarezo, Susana, Osvaldo Barsky, Lucía Carrión, Patricia de la Torre, and Lucía Salamea. 1984. Mujer y transformaciones agrarias. Quito: CEPLAES-Corporación Editora Nacional-INFOC.

Barril, Alex. 1983. El crédito agropecuario en el Ecuador: antecedentes y comentarios sobre el acceso al sector campesino. CEPLAES Working Paper 83.1S. Quito: Proyecto INIAP/Cornell.

Beebe, James. 1985. Rapid Rural Appraisal: The Critical First Step in a Farming Systems Approach to Research. Networking Paper No. 5. Gainesville: FSSP.

Biggs, Stephen D. 1985. A Farming Systems Approach: Some Unanswered Questions. *Agricultural Administration* 18(1):1–12.

Byerlee, Derek, and Michael Collinson. 1980. Planning Technologies Appropriate to Farmers: Concepts and Procedures. Mexico City: CIMMYT.

Campbell, Carolyn. 1985. Rationale and Methodology for Including Nutritional and Dietary Assessment in Farming Systems Research/Extension. CRSP Working Paper 85.3E. Ithaca: INIAP/Cornell Project.

Carrillo, Rómulo, Napoleón Chávez, Alfredo Ugalde, and Marcín Carrillo.

1985. El area central del valle del Río Portoviejo: informe del trabajo de campo. Documento de Circulación Restringida 85. PRE.4. Portoviejo: Proyecto INIAP/Cornell.

CGIAR Technical Advisory Committee. 1978. Farming Systems Research at the International Agricultural Research Centers. Rome: FAO.

Chambers, Robert. 1981. Rapid Rural Appraisal: Rationale and Repertoire. *Public Administration and Development* 1(2):95–106.

Chaney, Elsa, and Martha Lewis. 1980. The Impact of Migration on Women's Food Production. Unpublished paper presented to BIFAD.

Chávez, Napoleón. 1984. Informe preliminar de los resultados del análisis de la boleta de recolección de semillas de leguminosas en Manabí. Documento de Circulación Restringida 84.PRE.1. Portoviejo: Proyecto INIAP/Cornell.

Chávez, Napoleón, Jorge Uquillas, and Miguel Guerra. 1986. La comercialización de leguminosas en el valle del Río Portoviejo. Documento de Trabajo ASE.9. Portoviejo: Proyecto INIAP/Cornell.

Collinson, Michael P. 1981. A Low Cost Approach to Understanding Small Farmers. *Agricultural Administration* 8(6):433–450.

———. 1982. Farming Systems Research in Eastern Africa: The Experiences of CIMMYT and Some National Research Services, 1976–81. International Development Paper No. 3. East Lansing: Agricultural Economics, Michigan State University.

Cox, George W., and Michael D. Atkins. 1979. *Agricultural Ecology: An Analysis of World Food Production Systems*. San Francisco: W. H. Freeman.

CRM. 1978. El mercadeo en el valle del Río Portoviejo. Portoviejo: CRM.

DeWalt, Billie R. 1985. Anthropology, Sociology, and Farming Systems Research. *Human Organization* 44(2):106–114.

Duff, Bart, and Paul Webster. 1984. The Application of Micro-Computer Technology to International Agricultural Research and Development. *Agricultural Administration* 17:135–148.

Espinosa, Patricio, and Patricia Garrett. 1987. The Relevance of Gender in Farming Systems Research: Experiences in Ecuador. *Agricultural Administration* 26(2):101–117.

Fresco, Louise. 1984. Comparing Anglophone and Francophone Approaches to Farming Systems Research. Networking Paper No. 1. Gainesville: FSSP.

Garrett, Patricia. 1984a. Farming Systems Research: An Introduction to the Literature. *The Rural Sociologist* 3(4):220–222.

———. 1984b. The Relevance of Structural Variables for Farming Systems Research. *Rural Sociology* 49(4):580–589.

———. 1984c. Social Science in the Bean/Cowpea CRSP. *The Rural Sociologist* 5(4):290–295.

———. 1986a. Social Stratification and Multiple Enterprises: Some Implications for Farming Systems Research. *Journal of Rural Studies* 2(3):209–220.

———. 1986b. Viable Objectives for Smallholder Programs: Variation by Social Strata. *Agricultural Administration* 22(2):39–55.

Garrett, Patricia, Paul Dillon, and Charles Staver. 1982. Metodología para el trabajo de campo. CRSP Working Paper 82.1S. Ithaca: INIAP/Cornell Project.

Garrett, Patricia, and Donna Goldstein. 1984. Some Methodological Issues in Pre-Intervention Farming Systems Research: Selecting Appropriate

Techniques for Data Collection. CRSP Working Paper 84.4E. Ithaca: INIAP/Cornell Project.

Garrett, Patricia, David Golden, and Joe D. Francis. 1986. The Measurement and Analysis of Inequality Using Microcomputers. *Social Science Microcomputer Review* 4(2):194–206.

Garrett, Patricia, Jorge Uquillas, and Carolyn Campbell. 1987. Interview Guide for the Regional Analysis of Farming Systems. CRSP Working Paper 86.2E. Cornell International Agriculture Monograph No. 113. Ithaca: Cornell University.

Harrison, L. W., and R. Tripp. 1984. Dominios de recomendación: un marco de referencia para la investigación en fincas. Documento de Trabajo 02/84. Mexico City: CIMMYT.

Hart, Robert D. 1982. An Ecological Systems Conceptual Framework for Agricultural Research and Development. In *Readings in Farming Systems Research and Development*. W. W. Shaner, P. F. Philipp, and W. R. Schmehl, eds., pp. 44–59. Boulder: Westview Press.

Harwood, Richard R. 1979. *Small Farm Development: Understanding and Improving Farming Systems in the Humid Tropics*. Boulder: Westview Press.

Hildebrand, Peter. 1981. Combining Disciplines in Rapid Appraisal: The Sondeo Approach. *Agricultural Administration* 8(6):423–432.

Hinostrosa, Francisco, Osvaldo Vargas, Lenín Linzán, and Winston Alcívar. 1985. La desembocadura del Río Portoviejo: informe del trabajo de campo. Documento de Circulación Restringida 85.PRE.3. Portoviejo: Proyecto INIAP/Cornell.

Honadle, George. 1982. Rapid Reconnaissance for Development Administration: Mapping and Moulding Organizational Landscapes. *World Development* 10(8):633–649.

Horton, Douglas E. 1984. Social Scientists in Agricultural Research: Lessons from the Mantaro Valley Project, Peru. IDRC Paper No. 219e. Ottawa: IDRC.

INIAP/Cornell Team. 1982. Características de los pequeños productores en zonas de Imbabura: informe preliminar. CRSP Working Paper 82.2S. Quito: Proyecto INIAP/Cornell.

Linzán, Lenín. 1984. *Informe anual técnico, Programa Leguminosas de Consumo Humano*. Portoviejo: INIAP.

Little, Peter D. 1985. Adding a Regional Perspective to Farming Systems Research: Concepts and Analysis. *Human Organization* 44(4):331–338.

Maldonado, Luís, Wesley Kline, Miguel Guerra, and Ángel Veles. 1985. El valle del Río Chico: informe del trabajo de campo. Documento de Circulación Restringida 85.PRE.3. Portoviejo: Proyecto INIAP/Cornell.

Maxwell, Simon. 1986. Farming Systems Research: Hitting a Moving Target. *World Development* 14(1):65–78.

Milford, Robert. 1983. Ecuador Agricultural Sector Study: Agricultural Production and Potential. Document No. LCBAY 4. Quito (unpublished manuscript).

Moscardi, Edgardo, Victor Hugo Cardoso, Patricio Espinosa, Rómulo Solís, and Ely Zambrano. 1983. Creating an On-Farm Research Program in Ecuador. Mexico City: CIMMYT.

Murphy, Josette, and Leendert H. Sprey. 1982. *Monitoring and Evaluation of Agricultural Change*. Wageningen, Netherlands: International Institute for Land Reclamation and Improvement.

Palacios, Juan J., and Patricia Garrett. 1983. Guía básica para el análisis de información censal agropecuaria. CRSP Working Paper 83.2S. Ithaca: INIAP/Cornell Project.

————. 1984. Estructura de la producción agropecuaria en la provincia de Imbabura: un análisis estadístico. CRSP Working Paper 84.2S. Ithaca: INIAP/Cornell Project.

Perrin, Richard K., Donald L. Windelmann, Edgardo R. Moscardi, and Jack R. Anderson. 1979. From Agronomic Data to Farmer Recommendations: An Economics Training Manual. Mexico: CIMMYT.

Porter, Philip W. 1978. Geography as Human Ecology: Decade of Progress in a Quarter Century. *American Behavioral Scientist* 22(1):15–39.

Rhoades, Robert E. 1982. The Art of the Informal Agricultural Survey. Training Document 1982–3. Lima: CIP.

————. 1984. Breaking New Ground: Agricultural Anthropology. Lima: CIP.

Safa, Helen I. 1987. Women in Latin America: the Impact of Socioeconomic Change. In *Latin America: Perspective on a Region*. Jack W. Hopkins, ed., pp. 133–143. New York: Holmes and Meier.

Shaner, W. W. 1984. Stratification: An Approach to Cost-effectiveness for Farming Systems Research and Development. *Agricultural Systems* 15:101–123.

Shaner, W. W., P. F. Philipp, and W. R. Schmehl. 1982. *Farming Systems Research and Development: Guidelines for Developing Countries.* Boulder: Westview Press.

Smith, Carol A. (ed.). 1976. *Regional Analysis.* Vols. 1 and 2. New York: Academic Press.

Smith, David M. 1982. *Where the Grass is Greener: Living in an Unequal World.* Baltimore: Johns Hopkins University Press.

Uquillas, Jorge. 1985. Guía de entrevistas. Documento de Circulación Restringida 85.PRE.2. Quito: Proyecto INIAP/Cornell.

Uquillas, Jorge, Diana Barba, Patricia Garrett, and Ely Zambrano. 1985a. Estratégias de reproducción en la economía campesina en Imbabura. Documento de Trabajo ASE.5. Quito: Proyecto INIAP/Cornell.

Uquillas, Jorge, Venus Arévalo, and Napoleón Chávez. 1985b. Resumen del diagnóstico agro-socioeconómico de Manabí. Documento de Circulación Restringida 85.PRE.1. Quito: Proyecto INIAP/Cornell.

Uquillas, Jorge, Venus Arévalo, Napoleón Chávez, and José Arroyave. 1985c. Diagnóstico agro-socioeconómico de la provincia de Manabí. Documento de Trabajo ASE.6. Quito: Proyecto INIAP/Cornell.

Uquillas, Jorge, Flor M. Cárdenas, Diana Barba, Ricardo Limongi, and Gonzalo Estrella. 1985d. Santa Ana: informe del trabajo de campo. Documento de Circulación Restringida 85.PRE.5. Portoviejo: Proyecto INIAP/Cornell.

Uquillas, Jorge, Patricia Garrett, and Carolyn Campbell. 1986a Guía de entrevistas para un análisis regional de los sistemas de producción agropecuaria. Documento de Trabajo ASE.8. Quito: Proyecto INIAP/Cornell.

Uquillas, Jorge, Wesley Kline, Rómulo Carrillo, Napoleón Chávez, and Lenín Linzán. 1986b. Características agrícolas y sociales del valle del Río Portoviejo. Segunda edición. Documento de Trabajo ASE.7. Quito: Proyecto INIAP/Cornell.

PART 4

Peanut CRSP

10

Social Science and Food Science Research in the Peanut CRSP

Gerald C. Wheelock, Hezekiah S. Jones, Bharat Singh, and Virginia Caples

The Peanut CRSP was initiated with a planning grant from USAID and BIFAD to the University of Georgia in August 1980. In February 1981, Alabama A&M University (AAMU) was selected from among several proposals from 1890 land grant institutions to assist in planning. A technical advisory committee (TAC) was also assembled to represent global peanut research interests. The TAC included USDA and land grant university plant, food, and social scientists, the peanut program coordinator from the International Crop Research Institute for the Semi-Arid Tropics (ICRISAT), and representatives from the African Groundnut Council, the Research Institute for Oils and Oilseeds (IRHO), Latin American and Caribbean research organizations (e.g., CARDI), and the World Bank. Later, U.S. producer interests were represented through the Peanut Council.

During the planning phase, in order to identify key researchable constraints to peanut production and utilization and to develop a global research plan, fact-finding trips were made to international peanut meetings at ICRISAT and to research sites in peanut-producing countries, where scientists from 20 nations were interviewed. Interviewees included several food scientists, but no social scientists studying peanut farming systems or utilization were identified within any national or university research organizations. However, at ICRISAT, the Economics Group provided some important insights into farming systems constraints on peanut production.

Most of these constraints centered on the greater labor demands planting and weeding peanuts relative to other crops. Planting corresponds with the onset of the rains. Because peanut seed stocks are more valuable than other crops, farmers are less likely to plant peanuts before sufficient rain has fallen. Weeding is equally critical to protect the farmer's investment in peanut seed. Consequently, more is at risk if drought occurs once peanuts are planted. More focused farming systems and market price–policy analysis appeared to be needed to understand peanut production and domestic market potential.

Peanuts are important both as a foreign-exchange earner and as a source of vegetable oil in the semi-arid tropics (SAT). Yet, in the countries surveyed, very little has been documented about peanuts as a foodstuff except for their wide use as a snack. Economists generally believed that peanut consumption would not normally vary among income groups since peanuts appeared to be eaten by nearly everyone, but only in small quantities. It was therefore decided that more information on market demand and home consumption patterns would be needed in order to better design product development research, (Cummins and Jackson 1982, Wheelock 1982).

Research proposals were solicited from U.S. institutions in the areas of: advanced line, variety testing and cultural practices; breeding and cultural practices; mycotoxin management; weeds, insects, diseases, and nematode control; food technology; physiology and soil microbiology; and socioeconomics. The TAC then matched identified country-level researchable constraints with the most relevant proposals. The result was the "Peanut CRSP Planning Report" (Jackson and Cummins 1981).

Socioeconomic proposals were few in number, especially from peanut-producing states. Furthermore, those submitted did not demonstrate potentially strong links with peanut scientists in the United States or social scientists in collaborating countries—a particularly important consideration for this tightly focused and budgeted single-commodity CRSP. Most proposals were broad-based food system or sociostructural studies of the niche occupied by peanut producers and users. At the time, it was believed that basic FSR on peanuts was already under way, and that specialized cash-crop and foreign-exchange issues, plus the high weather/price risk of peanut production, were the main concerns of collaborating country scientists. The TAC therefore recommended that none of the broader socioeconomic proposals be funded. However, several members of the committee concurred with the TAC's World Bank representative that, if socioeconomic studies were excluded in the global plan, a strong case could be made that there should not even be a Peanut CRSP!

A twofold compromise on socioeconomic issues was reached. First, it called for special economic analyses to be conducted by a social scientist currently studying markets and farming systems in Peanut CRSP countries. Evaluation of the potential impact of higher-yielding, lower-risk (drought- and aflatoxin-resistant) varieties on poorer farm families' diets and incomes was to be a major focus of this analysis. While shorter-season strains and more vigorous taproot growth of the young peanut plant have received some research attention in SAT national research centers, the primary thrust to increase food security has been toward other shorter-season legumes (e.g., chick pea and pigeon pea) and improved sorghums and millets. Breeding work on these less frequently traded commodities has also been more favored by international research projects. Perhaps the central but unstated issue of the entire Peanut CRSP is whether the dearth of research support for lower-risk peanut varieties for SATs is related to a true lack of genetic potential for peanuts in such climates, or whether it is due to protectionist policies of donor countries competing for the international peanut market.

Second, the compromise called for a multidisciplinary model, including social scientists and food scientists, to conduct utilization studies of food science constraints. In the first year of the Peanut CRSP, one such proposal was funded for Sudan. The Food Research Center of Sudan's Agricultural Research Corporation (FRC/ARC) and AAMU were named as host country and U.S. lead institutions, respectively. The principal objectives were to determine the role of peanuts in the diet and food budgets of Sudanese households and to explore the potential for improved or new peanut products and increased consumption. An initial survey phase would provide guidance in planning for the latter objective. Similar multidisciplinary projects were included in the second-year plan for Thailand and the Philippines, with the University of Georgia serving as U.S. lead institution.

Although it was the largest peanut-producing country in the CRSP, Sudan was not included in the program's agronomic plan. Sudanese scientists had expressed specific interest in drought tolerance and aflatoxin resistance as breeding objectives. However, as noted earlier, these constraints were not addressed in the proposals received from U.S. scientists. The TAC concluded that U.S. agronomists had little to offer their Sudanese counterparts at that time, but if such possibilities should develop in the future, agronomists from other collaborating African Peanut CRSPs at North Carolina State University, University of Georgia, and Texas A&M could then join food scientists already in Sudan. Coincidently or not, this strategy provided a convenient answer when, in 1982, U.S. peanut growers challenged USAID as to why a program was being funded that would help our major competitors in the world market. The answers were that the CRSP hoped to enhance peanut utilization around the world; the Sudan project was entirely utilization-oriented; all project countries involved were poor and their food balances showed deficits in carbohydrates and protein; and Senegal, an exporting country as was Sudan, was a convenient ally with whom to initiate collaborative research (with Texas A&M CRSP scientists) on health hazards from mycotoxins, the findings from which could be of great significance to U.S. peanut interests.

SOCIAL SCIENCE AND FOOD SCIENCE ON THE PEANUT CRSP IN SUDAN

The Food Science Peanut CRSP in Sudan is primarily a research service project focused on the role of peanuts in national food security. It was conceived as a multidisciplinary effort in terms of team composition, objectives, and implementation. It called for the establishment of laboratory and computer facilities in FRC/ARC, standardization and validation of basic measurement procedures, and corresponding services from each Sudanese and U.S. scientist on the team. Agricultural economists and sociologists from FRC/ARC and AAMU were responsible for establishing a computer facility that would enable comparable data analysis at both locations. They were also responsible for constructing survey instruments and coordinating input from the food scientists. Two instruments were needed initially: one to estimate demand for various peanut products, both in producing areas and in urban markets stratified by income levels; and one to evaluate the role of peanuts in food security at the farm level, vis-à-vis postharvest peanut storage, handling, utilization, marketing practices, and aflatoxin contamination levels.

The food scientists cooperated in the surveys, but they also worked to establish an aflatoxin determination lab and to rehabilitate other laboratory facilities. Tasks such as getting ethyl ether and other volatile chemicals into Khartoum (which proved very nearly impossible), installing and maintaining equipment, and standardizing and validating measurement procedures new to FRC, if not its scientists, were basic services provided by the project.[1]

U.S. social science input in Sudan has been 30%–40% of one scientist year for the first three years of the project. This time has been split between the rural sociologist (Wheelock) and the agricultural economist (Jones). In FRC/ARC, two agricultural economists have also worked on the project, but only one at a time at about 20%. Below, the findings and contributions of social scientists, as well as their recommendations for the multidisciplinary food science project of the Sudan Peanut CRSP, are described. These outcomes are then expanded by comparison with results from the more recently established Caribbean Peanut CRSP.

Peanuts and Foreign Exchange in Sudan

One of the first tasks for the social sciences was to examine the overarching and interrelated roles of peanuts as a cash and food crop in both international and domestic socioeconomic contexts. Over the last decade, the volume and value of Sudan's peanut exports have declined absolutely and relative to total exports. From 1974 to 1978, peanuts averaged about 16% of the nation's foreign-exchange earnings. Total peanut exports peaked at 280,000 tons in 1976 (Riley 1981). From 1979 to 1983, peanut exports dropped to less than 7% of average yearly earnings. That average was buoyed up by extraordinary exports of about 80,000 tons in 1980–1981 (Riley 1981), when drought cut U.S. peanut production by more than a third, and U.S. imports increased more than tenfold to 3.6 million pounds (USDA 1984:121). The percentage share of Sudan's total value of exports to the United States more than tripled, from 2.4% to 8% in 1980–1981, then returned to 2.6% the next year (Bank of Sudan 1983:45). U.S. farmers suddenly became very aware of Sudan's potential comparative advantage in peanut production. Sudanese farm prices were then somewhere below 50% of the world price, and one-sixth of the quota price of 27.5 cents per pound received by U.S. farmers (Bashir and Idris 1983). The Peanut CRSP was just being established, and U.S. grower interests had to be assured that peanut-exporting countries were not being helped to become even more competitive in the world market. However, subsequent events have replaced this concern with one of food security in Sudan and in Africa generally.

Increased domestic demand, combined with poor growing conditions for peanuts and related aflatoxin contamination problems, resulted in declining Sudanese exports in 1982 and 1983, and essentially no exports in 1984 and 1985. Domestic demand for peanut oil in cooking was boosted both by population growth and by diversion of all cotton seed oil to the domestic soap industry. Peanut cake production increased as a by-product of the oil industry, but its export market faltered when aflatoxin detections proved excessive for European livestock feed markets. Finally, drought in western Sudan reduced peanut production in favor of more drought-resistant food and export crops such as sesame, sorghum, millet, rosette, and gum arabic. Sesame and sorghum comprised 30% of exports in 1982 compared with 6.9% for peanuts (Table 10.1). In 1983, incentives for cotton farmers were substantially increased, resulting in a doubling of cotton's share of exports to 49%, while sesame and sorghum comprised 17% and peanuts only 2%.

Sudanese export declines have been followed by drops in peanut production from the 1977 peak of 1,027,000 metric tons (Table 10.2). Both area and yield have declined as labor shifted from rainfed agriculture to more drought-tolerant crops in western Sudan, to irrigated schemes in central Sudan, and to labor markets in Saudi Arabia and other Middle Eastern countries. Area planted has fallen from more than 2.6 million feddans (one feddan = 0.95 acres) in 1977 to less than a million in 1984. Most of the decline has been in semi-arid regions where rains were not sufficient for planting. The rains returned in 1985 and 1986, but peanut production in western Sudan was slow to recover. Priority has been given to sorghum. Few farmers in the western region had any peanut seed left, and labor supplies had been diverted by the drought. Peanut exports were curtailed even further by aflatoxin restrictions in the European Common Market. In sum, it appears that peanut production and prices will depend increasingly upon growth in domestic demand and decreasingly upon exports.

With several key variables in Sudan's peanut industry and agriculture changing dramatically from year to year, the challenge for socioeconomic analyses pertinent to FRC/ARC research plans and policy is great. A comparative advantage in peanut production for the world market probably still exists—if rainfall returns to normal in the rainfed peanut-producing areas

TABLE 10.1.   PEANUT, COTTON, SESAME, AND SORGHUM EXPORTS AS A PERCENTAGE OF
TOTAL MONEY VALUE OF EXPORTS IN SUDAN (1974-1983)

Year	Peanuts	Cotton	Sesame	Cake & Meal	Sorghum (dura)	Exports (Ls.million)
1974	14.9	35.5	13.5	-	-	-
1975	22.6	46.0	7.8	-	-	-
1976	20.2	50.7	9.0	-	-	-
1977	12.5	57.2	7.9	-	-	-
1978	10.2	51.8	9.5	3.3	1.3	202
1979	4.3	65.0	2.7	3.2	5.8	233
1980	2.2	42.5	9.2	5.0	15.8	271
1981	18.6	19.2	9.0	4.1	12.0	357
1982	6.9	25.1	7.9	3.0	22.2	483
1983	2.0	48.8	8.7	3.0	8.2	811

Source: Bank of Sudan 1981, 1983.

of western Sudan, if trade and foreign exchange policy continues to encourage exports, and if the area's labor supply stabilizes. Sudan could probably expand its trade with China, Japan, Saudi Arabia, Egypt, and other peanut and peanut-oil markets. If production and trade of peanuts were to resume, policymakers could further encourage production by calculating and announcing expected minimum prices before planting time in western Sudan (Sattar 1982; Wheelock and Jones 1983).

FRC/ARC can do nothing about the weather, international labor markets, or internal political problems affecting migration of labor. However, the institution's role in monitoring aflatoxin and researching its control is important to the development of Sudan's domestic market, with or without recovery in foreign markets. Also, assessment of current and potential supply and demand for peanut products relative to other domestic products is crucial to FRC/ARC's own planning process, as well as to its effectiveness in intragovernmental planning and policy (Wheelock 1985).

Peanuts and Food Energy Supplies in Sudan

When the source of Sudan's food energy supply was scrutinized, the relatively narrow objectives of the Sudan Peanut CRSP were further justified. Estimates for the country for 1979 to 1981 by FAO (1984) indicated a per

TABLE 10.2.   AREA PLANTED, YIELD PER FEDDAN,[a] AND TOTAL PRODUCTION OF
             PEANUTS IN SUDAN (1971-1982)

Year	Feddans (000)	Planted (change)	Yield (kg)	Feddan (change)	Total (000)	Production (change)
1971	1511	-	256	-	387	-
1972	1614	6.8%	348	35.9%	568	46.8%
1973	1748	8.3%	317	-8.9%	554	-2.5%
1974	1792	2.5%	517	63.1%	928	67.5%
1975	2321	29.5%	343	-33.7%	796	-14.2%
1976	1880	-19.0%	393	14.6%	738	-7.3%
1977	2661	41.5%	386	-1.8%	1027	39.2%
1978	2328	-12.5%	342	-11.4%	798	-22.3%
1979	2352	1.0%	362	5.8%	852	6.8%
1980	2129	-9.5%	332	-8.3%	707	-17.0%
1981	2346	10.2%	306	-7.8%	721	2.0%
1982	1853	-21.0%	270	-11.8%	497	-31.1%

Source: Bashier and Idris 1983, Bank of Sudan 1981, 1983.

[a]One feddan = 0.39 hectares = 0.95 acres.

capita availability of 2,291 calories (cal) per day excluding alcohol (23 cal);
by comparison, this figure is 3,455 for the United States. However, Sudan's
averages did not indicate the considerable caloric inequality that must be
present in one of Africa's largest and most climatically diverse countries.
Comparison with neighboring nations was therefore helpful. The irrigated
areas of the Nile and central Sudan have more in common with Egypt than
with the rainfed semi-arid tropics of western Sudan or the savanna and
tropical rain forests of the south. Hence, the latter regions should be
compared with other countries in the Sahel and to the south. Egypt was
estimated to have 3,174 cal per capita per day compared with only 1,691 and
2,079 in Uganda and Central African Republic, respectively. Central Sudan's
supplies may have been within 500 cal of Egypt's average, but supplies in
western and southern Sudan—which contain about one-third of the country's
population (18,378,000 in 1980)—would have been closer to the 2,000 cal
average of its neighbors to the south and west between 1979 and 1981.

Like most SAT countries of Africa, Sudan depends heavily upon the
peanut as a source of dietary oils and calories. FAO food balance sheets for

1979–1981 estimate that 43.2% of Sudan's fat supply and 12% of its per capita caloric supply (net of exports, feed, seed, and waste) came from peanuts and peanut products. Of Sudan's daily per capita supply of 2,291 cal, 220 were from peanut oil and 55 from peanuts. In 1983 and 1984, because of the peanut's intolerance for drought, fat and calorie supplies most certainly dropped dramatically, particularly in rainfed peanut-producing areas of western Sudan.

During good years in Sudan, substantial groundnut cake (a by-product of the oil presses) is available for export or domestic use as livestock feed. Between 1979 and 1981, for example, 180,000 mt per year were produced, but no products from peanut cake were included in the food balances. In this form, however, the groundnut is a prolific medium for *Aspergillis flavus* and mycotoxin by-products, including B1 aflatoxin. If groundnut cake is to be exported or used for animal or human consumption domestically, the production of this most potent of all carcinogens must be controlled.

Sample Survey of Peanut Producers and Consumers in Sudan and the Caribbean

Coinvestigators from the food and social sciences agreed upon survey objectives, instruments, and analytic procedures to coordinate core components of CRSP-wide questionnaire research across program sites in Sudan and the Caribbean. Prior to the initial survey in Sudan, rigorous field survey techniques and quantitative methods of demand analysis were new to the AAMU and FRC/ARC food scientists. At the same time, nutritional subject matters were new to the social scientists. Overcoming the lack of experience in each other's disciplines was taken seriously by all concerned, and there was considerable give and take in defining objectives and procedures. The social scientists took leadership responsibility for survey objectives, sampling design (for both households and peanuts), questionnaire construction, and interview strategies. With the whole team's participation, these issues were thoroughly worked out to fit within budgetary and personnel constraints.

Two major multidisciplinary field survey objectives were identified to fill knowledge gaps on demand for various peanut products and to understand the food security role of peanuts at the household level. First, for estimating income elasticities of demand and other purposes, purchases of peanuts in various forms (raw, roasted, paste, or peanut butter) were documented in urban samples. To ensure that all income levels were sufficiently represented, the sample was stratified by low-, middle-, and high-income subdivisions. A second survey of producers was aimed at understanding the importance of peanuts as a cash crop and documenting variation in peanut cultural practices (pre- and postharvest) that might be associated with aflatoxin contamination of farm-stored peanuts. Peanut samples for laboratory analysis were also collected from the farmers interviewed.

In Sudan, the urban study was conducted in Khartoum, the capital. Two farm samples were selected to represent major peanut-growing areas: one was drawn from four irrigation-scheme communities in central Sudan; the other included five rainfed agricultural villages in western Sudan (Singh 1984, 1985a, 1986a). On the more recently established Caribbean Peanut CRSP, similar procedures were used to interview urban samples in Trinidad, Jamaica, and St. Vincent, plus farm samples in the latter two countries (Okezie 1984; Singh 1985b and 1986b). The next sections briefly outline some of the major socioeconomic and other findings of these surveys.

Sources of New Demand for Peanuts and Peanut Products

To estimate growth in aggregate demand for peanuts and to document differences in markets for various peanut products, the Sudan and Caribbean utilization surveys collected data on quantities and values of peanut and peanut product purchases. These surveys sought to provide input for planning more useful product development research on peanuts and/or for redirecting research toward more promising commodities. At the same time, survey research skills would be enhanced within the respective food research centers.

To estimate potential growth in aggregate demand for peanuts in the domestic markets of CRSP countries, a standard model was elaborated based on growth in population and—to the extent that consumption increases with income—upon growth in income. Assuming domestic requirements would grow in proportion to the population and that income elasticities of demand for peanuts and peanut products, including oil, would average 0.5% (Mellor 1966:66), demand in Sudan and the Caribbean would be expected to increase about 3% and 2% per year, respectively. Population growth estimates in the two areas range around 2.9% and 1.8%. In Sudan, income is stagnant, but supplies are produced domestically. In Trinidad, the income effect may be negative since peanuts are imported and incomes have fallen. Therefore, price has probably increased and quantity purchased declined. Still, to the extent that domestically produced food is more available than imports (food and nonfood), more peanut and peanut oil may be consumed.

It would be expected that high-income households would purchase peanut products different from those bought by low-income households. Products requiring more value-added processing would generally be preferred by higher-income households, while those with little or no such processing or sorting would be more frequently purchased by lower-income households. Domestically roasted or parched peanuts are more likely to be purchased from street vendors and consumed as snacks, while peanut paste, butter, and oil are more likely to be consumed at home. Accordingly, the former products may be more frequently consumed by low-income households, and the latter by high-income ones. Boiled peanuts are more frequently consumed in rural peanut-producing areas. Since peanut butter and oil are more likely to be used to complement a variety of foods (in soups and salads, on bread, or in cakes and candies), higher-income households with more diverse diets may be more likely to consume these products. Similarly, fancy imported and canned nuts would not figure in low-income household diets.

Thus far, social scientists' analysis of the available survey data has contributed to the existing research policy and planning dialogue within collaborating food research centers. Farmers' interest in growing peanuts relative to interest in alternate crops was directly communicated to food scientists, as were consumer preferences. Less directly examined were more macrolevel questions as to how declining export surpluses affect domestic utilization in Sudan or how domestic production and supplies would respond to import controls in Caribbean countries.

Country-by-country comparisons of the survey data on demand elasticities for peanut products have helped target some of these issues. Extrapolations from 1-month estimates derived from the survey of urban households in Khartoum yield estimated purchases of nearly 15 lbs of shelled or processed peanuts (excluding oil) per person per year in households with double the average sample food purchase budget, but only 6.2 lbs for persons in households with half the average food budget (Table 10.3). In the Caribbean, these estimates range from a low of 5.1 lbs for all budget levels in Jamaica, where imports have recently been prohibited, to 11.9 lbs in urban St. Vincent, where growing conditions permit two crops per year. Those with 50% of average incomes purchased 9.1 lbs per capita, while those with double the average purchased 17.5 lbs. In Trinidad, where all peanuts are imported, the urban household survey yielded an estimated range of 7.8–15.5 lbs per capita (Table 10.3).

Household samples were drawn from three strata of residential subdivisions (high, middle, and low income) to ensure sufficient variation to estimate income elasticities of demand for the various products. Therefore, these per capita estimates are not comparable to the UN/FAO food balance sheet (FBS) estimates discussed earlier. However, it is obvious that in all countries sampled, the stratified urban samples report more peanut purchases than their share of FBS estimated supplies. This would support the hypothesis of a positive income elasticity of demand for peanuts.

To test that hypothesis, income elasticities were estimated directly from the survey data. For each sample, the natural logs of reported household purchases of peanut butter and total peanuts (including peanut butter) were regressed on natural logs of income or amount of total food expenditures (depending upon the quality of the data) and of household size. That is quantities of peanut purchases were taken as a function of income or food

TABLE 10.3. ELASTICITIES OF DEMAND FOR SELECTED PEANUT PRODUCTS[b]

	Khartoum		Jamaica		St. Vincent		Trinidad	
	Peanut butter	All peanuts	Roasted peanuts	All peanuts	Peanut butter	All peanuts	Peanut butter	All peanuts
Food purchases per week	1.03^a	$.63^a$	$-.14$	$-.09$	-	-	-	-
Gross family income	-	-	-	-	$.47^a$	$.41^a$	$.29$	$.55^a$
Household size	$.41$	$.22$	$.84^a$	$.75^a$	$.39^a$	$.30$	$.66^a$	$.44^a$

Source: Surveys conducted by FRC/ARC, CARDI, AAMU Food Technology Peanut CRSP (Okezie 1984, Singh 1984).

[a]Elasticity significant at the .05 level.

[b]See Table 10.4 for details.

expenditures and household size. When logical adjustments were made for country differences, the results were reasonably consistent across samples. In Sudan, the lowest-income country with the least diverse diet, particularly among vegetable oils and legumes, the food purchase elasticity (net of family size) for peanut paste was an elastic 1.03; for all peanuts, it was .63 (Table 10.3). Household size was not a significant factor. These income elasticities are consistent with the 0.8 reported by Mellor (1966:66) for Africa, but they are higher than the corresponding figure for pulses and nuts. Considering that all estimates reported here include the more highly processed peanut butter that is eaten as a complement to the salads, soups, bread, and confections more frequently consumed by middle- or higher-income households, these figures may not be unreasonable.

In Caribbean countries, household size was positive and significant in all equations, but income coefficients (net of household size) showed mixed results. In St. Vincent, where peanut surpluses are produced for export, the income elasticity of demand for peanut butter was .47 and .41 for all peanuts. Both figures are noteworthy in spite of significant net effects for household size (Table 10.3). In Trinidad, where most peanut products are imported from the United States, these figures were .29 and .55. Again, net of income effect, the household size effect was positive, particularly for peanut butter. For example, for each percentage increase in family size, peanut butter purchases increased .66% in the Trinidad sample. The higher income

TABLE 10.4.   ELASTICITIES OF DEMAND AND DETAILS OF THE ORDINARY LEAST
SQUARES ESTIMATES FOR PEANUT PRODUCTS

Natural Logs[a]	Khartoum Jan 1984		Jamaica May 1984		St. Vincent May 1984		Trinidad May 1984	
	Peanut butter	All peanuts	Roasted peanuts	All peanuts	Peanut butter	All peanuts	Peanut butter	All peanuts
Food purchase per week								
B	1.03*	.63*	-.14[b]	-.09				
SE	0.29	0.16	.10	.11				
Gross family income								
B					.47*	.41*	.29	.55*
SE					0.13	0.12	.16	.16
Household size								
B	.41	.22	.84[b]*	.75*	.39*	.30	.66*	.44*
SE	.45	0.25	.21	.23	0.16	0.17	.19	.18
Constant	-3.15	.79	1.46	2.07	.67	1.19	.25	.91
Number	99	99	137	137	210	210	179	179
F-value	7.4	9.0	8.1	5.3	11.4	10.0	9.6	11.2
DF	(2,96)	(2,96)	(2,134)	(2,134)	(2,207)	(2,207)	(2,176)	(2,176)
R-square	.13	.15	.11	.07	.10	.09	.10	.11

Source: Surveys conducted by FRC/ARC, CARDI, and the AAMU Food Technology
Peanut CRSP (Okezie 1984, Singh 1984).

[a]When no peanut purchases were reported by a household, a small positive
value (.001) was added to allow computation of natural logarithms.

[b]Little or no peanut butter was available in the area surveyed; therefore
the coefficients are for roasted peanuts.

*Significant at the .05 level.

elasticity coefficient for all peanut products can be explained by quality and
price differences.

Processed peanuts found in urban Trinidad grocery stores were fancy
salted peanuts, vacuum-packed in the United States. These imports were
seldom available in Jamaica or St. Vincent. Also, roasted peanuts sold as
snacks to children or men by street vendors would not have been as
uniformly reported as store-bought household purchases. Accordingly, roasted

peanut prices reported by Trinidad households were higher than in the other samples, but peanut butter on the average was reported to have cost less.

In Jamaica, the income or food purchase elasticities of demand were not significant. However, purchases of both roasted peanuts (.84) and all peanut products (.75) increased roughtly in proportion to household size (Table 10.3). In Jamaica, where imports have recently been stopped in order to encourage local production, commercial peanut butter processing is in its infancy. The lack of a positive income elasticity of demand for peanut products in Jamaica may simply reflect the absence of peanut products on the shelves of high-income suburban grocery stores. Local products may be more accessible to lower-income people, but their quality may not be acceptable to higher-income shoppers, who opt for other snacks or local meat and dairy products instead. Locally processed peanuts may thus be the more affordable protein snack for low-income, large-family households. The survey data suggest that local vendors buy direct from farmer–middlemen and then roast, package, and sell their own products. In this instance, the import controls appear to be fostering grassroots entrepreneurship. Furthermore, they appear to be doing so without distorting consumer prices. While the average peanut butter price paid by the Jamaican urban sample was the highest of the three Caribbean samples, the average price for roasted peanuts was lower. Jamaican households reported purchasing less than half as much peanut butter; but, in spite of their lower average income and food budget, they purchased nearly the same amount of roasted nuts (Table 10.3). Of course, the survey data do not provide information on prices of locally produced peanuts before import restrictions. Since the survey was conducted soon after imposition of the new import controls, it is also possible that higher-income households have now found local suppliers and vendors, and prices may have been driven up accordingly.

To understand the effects of currency devaluation and import restrictions on the emergence of a domestic peanut industry, additional surveys are being planned with scientists of the Food Technology Institute in Kingston, Jamaica. At the time of the first survey, small producers and processors were participating in the newly stimulated domestic market, and low-income consumers were buying their products on a par with other consumers. How will small producers, processors, and consumers fare as the future unfolds? Is the production and processing technology sufficiently divisible that small producers and processors can meet domestic demand efficiently? And will low-income consumers still be able to buy the products? Comparison with St. Vincent, an exporter of surpluses, and Trinidad, strictly an importer of peanuts, provides an excellent opportunity to study indigenous entrepreneurship in food production and technology. Trinidad's recent currency devaluations are increasing economic pressures to internalize more value-added industry. Peanut processing may be a candidate.

To help guide their work, host country food scientists on the CRSP expressed a definite desire to institutionalize social science food-demand and food-policy analysis. A CRSP plan for long-term collaboration in these areas was well received by the cooperating scientists. Also, host country commitment was evidenced in Sudan by the reassignment of a PhD in economics within ARC to the FRC, plus support of PhD training for the original FRC/ARC economist. In addition, the Food Technology Institute in Jamaica is consulting with CRSP social scientists on the country's nascent peanut butter processing industry. Through continued collaboration among all Peanut CRSPs (including those of Thailand, the Philippines, and the University of Georgia), a larger aim is to develop an internationally standard food demand–analysis capability.

Along with income and food purchases, the impacts of family age and sex composition upon food product demand are now being evaluated (Huang and Raunikar 1985). Statistics can be calculated using computer capabilities at the various food research centers. Dialogue among Peanut CRSP collaborators is needed to ensure standardized use of statistical tools. To the extent that these results help food scientists differentiate growth markets for peanut products (and food products in general), consumers, producers, and processors will all benefit.

Moreover, these benefits could be extended to U.S. producers as well. In 1980, several factors combined to undermine U.S. peanut exports, including drought in the southern United States, peak petroleum prices that increased production costs, and the erosion of export markets caused by a strong dollar. However, U.S. peanut export markets have since expanded. Research to increase demand for peanuts in developing countries would therefore enhance the positive trend in post-1980 U.S. peanut exports. More important, it would help supply middle- and higher-income markets in developing countries with more acceptable domestically produced peanut consumer goods. Improved domestic peanut products range from peanut butter and peanut drinks for human consumption to peanut cake safe for use in domestic livestock feed. In turn, producers and small- to medium-scale processors in developing nations could enhance their own food security with the increased cash income.

Incidences of Aflatoxin in Sudan and the Caribbean: Sociogenic or Biogenic Causes?

Small-farm production of peanuts involves a wide variety of cultural practices that may affect aflatoxin (B1) contamination. Several of these practices were monitored in the farm-level surveys, including planting and harvest date of last crop, kind of crop rotation and intercropping practiced, soil type and washing or cleaning of harvested nuts, gleaning of loose nuts from the field after harvest, and storage practices. Peanut samples from the same farms were to be collected and analyzed for aflatoxin contamination.

Samples from Sudanese farms were very small (100 cc or less); in many cases, no peanuts were available because the entire crop had been sold. Aflatoxin analysis requires larger samples, so individual samples were pooled for larger areas. All pooled samples were analyzed at FRC/ARC, but none showed B1 aflatoxin contamination of 20 parts per billion (ppb) or more (Khalid et al. 1986). Insofar as international standardization tests have not been run on the newly installed equipment, these data must be considered preliminary.

In Jamaica and St. Vincent, only eight of 141 samples were found to be contaminated at levels of 20 ppb or greater. These tests were of international standard and are considered reliable. When these values were classified by cultural practices, seven of the eight contaminated samples (87.5%) were found to have been harvested during aflatoxin-prone months. Furthermore, it was discovered that the contaminated samples were grown on farms with several similar cultural practices, including growing peanuts in rotation after sweet potatoes, intercropping peanuts with corn, and post-harvest gleaning (Singh 1985b:279). When combined with harvest during aflatoxin-prone months, these practices were related to higher probabilities of contamination.

From these limited survey data, both biogenic and sociogenic hypotheses as to the causes of contamination can be formulated. Biologically, the indicated cultural practices in combination with aflatoxin-prone harvest months could have resulted in greater incidence of aflatoxin contamination in the peanut samples collected. Incidence of contamination increases when wet harvest weather, conducive to growth of *Aspergillus*, follows drought-induced defects in shell formation. However, an Israeli study of similar design reported no correlation between crop sequence and incidence of *Aspergillus flavus* (Ishag 1986; Joffe and Lisker 1969). But, this study included no root crops in the rotations. Regarding soil type and the practice of washing peanuts, total kernel mycoflora were constantly higher on medium and heavy soils than on other soils.

Alternately and sociologically, these contaminated samples may have been culls retained by small but thrifty, labor-intensive farm operators for emergency use as food, feed, or fertilizer. Sampling procedures may have simply resulted in more contaminated peanuts (culls) from these farms. Survey evidence supports this hypothesis: findings suggest that the 141 farmers providing peanut samples generally practiced more labor-intensive methods and were more likely to have gleaned peanuts from fields during the critical harvest month than were the 174 that did not provide samples. Similarly, they were more likely to have washed the peanuts harvested during the critical month. Chi-square tests of these findings are significant at the .05 level. In any event, it would seem important to determine whether the probability of aflatoxin contamination is greatly increased when peanuts are grown in rotation with fleshy root crops, such as sweet potatoes. This would be particularly desirable before beginning any extension program to promote peanuts in home gardens.

CONCLUSIONS

Collaborative food science and social science research findings of the kind reported here should be of value to social, food, and agronomic scientists in making future research decisions about peanut production, storage, processing, and marketing, plus the relative importance of peanut-related research in future agricultural research budgets. Agronomic experiments suggested by the farm surveys of cultural practices conducive to aflatoxin growth lay beyond the scope of the Food Science project, but through the Peanut CRSP's management entity, the TAC, and host country collaborators, this and other cross-disciplinary issues are discussed and negotiated. Likewise, commodity research coordinators in each country meet and negotiate technical issues and research budgets domestically and with international donors. In this way, multidisciplinary research to optimize the role of peanuts in host country economies and diets should complement the role of other commodities in the overall effort to maximize the benefits to each country's population, especially the poor, from each nation's public research dollar, and commodity and human resource mix.

More specifically, within the CRSP's multidisciplinary collaborative research mode, students are trained, trained scientists are equipped, and participating scientists become better-informed teachers; research collaborations are forged between scientists and disciplines; methods and measurement procedures are developed and refined in accordance with international standards; alternative biogenic and sociogenic hypotheses are considered; improved technologies are designed and tested for use on small farms, in low-income homes, and in small cottage industries; research findings are debated and published for wider application or dialogue; and higher R&D payoffs or more refined research issues result.

NOTES

This chapter was supported in part by the Peanut Collaborative Research Support Program, USAID Grant No. DAN-4048-G-SS-2065-00. Recommendations do not represent an official policy position of USAID.
1. While provision of these services could be taken for granted by many CRSP projects, this was not the case in Sudan. Basic cultivar selection projects in which all necessary information is contained within a few seeds

would be much easier to implement; but with Sudan's already considerable production potential and the lack of U.S. sources of drought-resistant genetic material, more complex utilization issues were identified as the constraints to be dealt with at this time.

REFERENCES

Bank of Sudan. 1981. 22nd Annual Report. Khartoum: International Printing House.
————. 1983. 24th Annual Report. Khartoum: International Printing House.
Bashir, Abdel Razing El, and Babikir Idris. 1983. Impact of Marketing and Pricing Policies on Production of Groundnuts. Paper prepared for the Agricultural Price Policy Workshop in the Democratic Republic of Sudan, Khartoum.
Cummins, D. G., and C. R. Jackson. 1982. World Peanut Production, Utilization and Research. Special Publication No. 16. Experiment, GA: University of Georgia, Georgia Experiment Station.
FAO. 1984. Food Balance Sheets: 1979–81 Average. Rome: Statistics Division.
Huang, Chung L., and Robert Raunikar. 1985. Spatial Market Estimate on Consumption of Broiler Meat. *Agribusiness* 1(2):153–163.
Ishag, H. M.. 1986. Personal communication. ARC, Khartoum.
Jackson, Curtis R., and D. G. Cummins. 1981. Peanut CRSP Planning Report. Experiment, GA: University of Georgia, Georgia Experiment Station.
Joffe, A. Z., and N. Lisker. 1970. Effects of Crop Sequence and Soil Types on the Mycoflora of Groundnut Kernels. *Plant and Soil* 33:531–533.
Khalid, Anna S., A. K. El Karib, and B. I. Magboul. 1986. Post-harvest Evaluation of Farmers' Stock Peanuts from Two Regions of Sudan for Crop Year 1983–84. In 1985 Annual Report of the Peanut CRSP. David G. Cummins and Tommy Nakayama, eds., pp. 163–168. Experiment, GA: University of Georgia, Georgia Experiment Station.
Mellor, John W. 1966. *The Economics of Agricultural Development*. Ithaca: Cornell University Press.
Okezie, Onuma B. 1984. Peanut Utilization in Food Systems in Developing Countries. (FS/AAMU/CARDI). In 1983 Annual Report of the Peanut Collaborative Research Support Program (CRSP). David Cummins, ed., pp. 159–162. Experiment, GA: University of Georgia, Georgia Experiment Station.
Riley, Peter A. 1981. Africa's Peanut Exports Steadily Declining: Few Prospects to Benefit from Current Favorable World Prices. Washington, DC: International Economics Division, Economic Research Service, USDA (draft).
Sattar, Abdus. 1982. Study of Cost of Production and Comparative Advantage of Crops under Different Farming Systems in Sudan 1980/81. Khartoum: Democratic Republic of the Sudan Ministry of Finance and Economic Planning.
Singh, Bharat. 1984. An Interdisciplinary Approach to Optimum Food Utility of the Peanut in SAT Africa (FT/AAMU/S). In 1983 Annual Report of the Peanut Collaborative Research Support Program (CRSP). David G.

Cummins, ed., pp. 71–82. Experiment, GA: University of Georgia, Georgia Experiment Station.

———. 1985a. An Interdisciplinary Approach to Optimum Food Utility of the Peanut in SAT Africa (FT/AAMU/S). In 1984 Annual Report of the Peanut Collaborative Research Support Program (CRSP). David G. Cummins, ed., pp. 132–148. Experiment, GA: University of Georgia, Georgia Experiment Station.

———. 1985b. Peanut Utilization in Food Systems in Developing Countries (FS/AAMU/CARDI). In 1984 Annual Report of the Peanut Collaborative Research Support Program (CRSP). David G. Cummins, ed., pp. 266–284. Experiment, GA: University of Georgia, Georgia Experiment Station.

———. 1986a. An Interdisciplinary Approach to Optimum Food Utility of the Peanut in SAT Africa (FT/AAMU/S). In 1985 Annual Report of the Peanut Collaborative Research Support Program (CRSP). David G. Cummins and Tommy Nakayama, eds., pp. 150–171. Experiment, GA: University of Georgia, Georgia Experiment Station.

———. 1986b. Peanut Utilization in Food Systems in Developing Countries (FA/AAMU/CARDI). In 1985 Annual Report of the Peanut Collaborative Research Support Program (CRSP). David G. Cummins and Tommy Nakayama, eds., pp. 336–347. Experiment, GA: University of Georgia, Georgia Experiment Station.

Solomon, Hossana. 1985. Peanut Purchase and Income Elasticities for Urban Households of Caribbean Countries: Trinidad, Jamaica and St. Vincent. MSc thesis, Agricultural Economics, Alabama A&M University.

USDA. 1984. Agricultural Statistics 1984. Washington, DC: U.S. Government Printing Office.

Wheelock, G. C. 1982. Socioeconomics of Peanut Production and Utilization. In World Peanut Production, Utilization and Research. David Cummins and Curtis R. Jackson, eds., pp. 106–126. Special Publication No. 16. Experiment GA: University of Georgia, Georgia Experiment Station.

———. 1985. Organizing for Serendipity in the Peanut CRSP. *The Rural Sociologist* 5(4):296–299.

Wheelock, G. C., and H. S. Jones. 1983. Groundnut (peanut) Production, Utilization and Policy in Sudan. (Unpublished manuscript). Normal, AL: Peanut CRSP.

PART 5

Small Ruminant CRSP

11

Targeting Production Systems in the Small Ruminant CRSP: A Typology Using Cluster Analysis

Keith A. Jamtgaard

Agricultural R&D programs that propose to alter production practices in some fashion are faced with the prior task of identifying the potential beneficiaries of their efforts. This typically involves choices within three criterial areas: broad policy questions; socioorganizational structures; and production systems. An example of the first might be whether research on a given topic (e.g., small ruminants) is needed in the first place, and, if so, in which countries. Within the countries selected, political-economic, as well as scientific, criteria may be considered in targeting populations and regions. Even after these policy choices have been made, much of the work of targeting still remains, however.

The second step centers on diversity in the social organization of agricultural production systems within the R&D area. This requires choosing among different types of producers of a commodity, or, at the very least, being aware that different social relations of production may limit the usefulness of given technologies. In Peru, for example, systems with very different social relations of production include independent commodity producers, cooperatives, plantations, and peasant communities.

The third step is to target beneficiaries by production systems. Commodity-oriented R&D might be presumed to hold an advantage over broader spectrum approaches such as FSR (farming systems research) since they can simply target "the producers of commodity X," but, in fact, commodity programs may encounter *more* difficulties. FSR typically targets a single socioorganizational type of producer, i.e, "peasants." Moreover, FSR recognizes that peasants usually manage risk by raising a variety of plant and animal species. Thus, from the outset, FSR is sensitive to the complexity of peasant production systems. (From this standpoint, perhaps one of FSR's shortcomings is that the simplicity gained by targeting production systems is traded for increased technical complexity since the whole system must be addressed—not just one commodity within it.) Even so, FSR projects still must choose among production systems (Bernsten et al. 1984).

195

Commodity-oriented programs face an analogous problem. A single commodity can fit into many different production systems. The question is which of the many systems incorporating the commodity to target. This chapter describes and evaluates a set of empirical procedures devised by SR-CRSP sociologists that helped answer this question for the SR-CRSP/Peru. This case is instructive for other agricultural R&D initiatives faced with difficulties in defining target populations.

A TARGET POPULATION FOR THE SR-CRSP/PERU

Diversity in the Social Organization of Production

Peru manifests enormous socioorganizational and environmental diversity in production, even within a single category such as "peasants." Small-scale independent farmers work irrigated river basins in the coastal desert. Only a few hours away, peasant communities (*comunidades campesinas*, or CCs) cultivate mountain slopes at over 3,600 m in the high Andes. Farther to the east, medium-sized farmers in the Amazon basin pursue a thoroughly distinct tropical agriculture. Large cooperative enterprises created by the agrarian reform of 1968–1980 also operate throughout the major agroecological zones of the country.

Each of these forms of production is embedded in a fundamentally different social structure, with distinct relations of production, legal structures, linkages with the state, and scales of operation. For instance, the cooperative sector is an assortment of entities constructed primarily from the large haciendas expropriated by the central government during the agrarian reform. They are still closely affiliated with the state. Private producers, whom the government perceives as being among the most productive farmers, have also benefited from government policies aimed at increasing agricultural outputs.

Peru's peasant communities, however, are the most numerous of the rural sector. From the beginning of the SR-CRSP/Peru in 1980, it was clear that CCs were significant producers of livestock, holding an estimated 52% of the nation's sheep; another 15% of the national flock are owned by cooperative institutions, and the remaining 33% by independent producers (DCCN 1980).[1] As much as 80% of Peru's alpaca herds are in the hands of peasant producers (Vidal and Grados 1974, cited in Flores Ochoa 1977:41). Moreover, about 44% of all alpaca are raised within officially recognized CCs[2] (DCCN 1980). Peasant communities also play a commanding role in producing Peru's major plant food staples, notably potatoes, barley, and maize (DCCN 1980).

Diversity in Production Systems

Despite their numerical and economic importance, peasant communities have been historically disfavored by development projects, agrarian policymakers, and credit institutions. Given the SR-CRSP mandate to assist the "poorest of the poor," however, such communities constituted the program's logical target group. Yet, even after narrowing its socioorganizational choices to CCs, the SR-CRSP still faced difficulties in specifying its target population. Two problems often arise when generalizing about cropping and animal husbandry in Peruvian CCs; both result from the tremendous environmental variation that exists from one end of the country to the other—or even within a single community, from its highland pastures over 4,000 m to the valley floor 1,000 m below.

This variation obfuscates comparisons of data from one community or region with basic production parameters from the larger population of all CCs. Moreover, when designing development programs with applicability to some subset of CCs, it is exceedingly difficult to distinguish even the most general production differences among communities. The tendency has therefore been to view Andean peasant communities as impossibly diverse and to confine observations to individual communities or small regions, or, conversely, to make monolithic generalizations about all CCs.

Nevertheless, to target its R&D population, the SR-CRSP/Peru still needed to answer two questions. The first was: How important are small ruminants in the economy of different types of peasant communities? From the very beginning of program activities in Peru, two general types of CC production systems were evident: pastoral and agropastoral.

Peruvian peasants everywhere value small ruminants for their ability to utilize high-altitude grasslands and other areas not under cultivation. In many highland CCs in the central Andes, people's livelihood primarily depends on their herds of alpaca, llama, and sheep; these communities may be characterized as "pastoral." However, small ruminants are also important for agropastoral CCs. While many such communities likewise utilize highland pastures, they often follow a rotational fallowing system (Custred and Orlove 1974; Orlove and Godoy 1986) in which fallow fields are grazed and manured by herds, and crop residues are a critical dry-season feed resource for herds (Jamtgaard 1984). In fact, small ruminants and the manure they provide are criterial to the continued functioning of this production system (Winterhalder et al. 1974).

Animal husbandry is subject to quite different constraints under these two production systems. For example, since agropastoral households actively engage in both cultivation and herding, their labor needs are very different from those of households pursuing only one or the other (Orlove 1977; Vincze 1980). This presents both opportunities and costs. As noted above, plant and animal crops enjoy some mutual benefits in agropastoralism. At the same time, however, the two compete for land and labor, thus necessitating complex mechanisms for integrating the two sectors of production (McCorkle 1986, 1987). Awareness of such constraints is critical in designing successful interventions to increase outputs from the CC livestock sector.

The second question the SR-CRSP needed to answer was: Which of these two types of peasant communities controls more small ruminants? In other words, given limited program resources, which group should be targeted? In the absence of any solid information, it was initially assumed that pastoral communities held more small ruminants and should therefore be the primary target group. But SR-CRSP social scientists pointed out that the program could have greater impact if the universe of small ruminant producers could be empirically delineated and the major producer types defined.

Gathering firsthand data on a population as large and diverse as that of all Peruvian peasant communities was manifestly impractical. However, program sociologists located an exceptionally rich data set in Peru's Dirección de Comunidades Campesinas y Nativas (DCCN), which generously made this information available to the SR-CRSP. These data derived from a 1977 survey that recorded important production and other indicators in 2,716 CCs, or 99% of all officially recognized peasant communities at the time (DCCN 1980).[3] For Peru, this is a unique data set, both because its scope is so broad and because its unit of analysis is the peasant community. With this information, SR-CRSP sociologists were able to elaborate a useful typology of CC production systems.

A PRODUCTION SYSTEMS TYPOLOGY

Approaches to typology construction are traditionally classed as heuristic or empirical. In the former, categories are delineated by reference to a theoretical framework, and the researcher essentially specifies the criteria for bounding the categories. In the latter, categories are developed to conform to salient differences within the data themselves, often employing algorithms such as cluster analysis. However, this heuristic/empirical dichotomy is less useful than are approaches that directly consider the need to measure objects and assign them to groups (Bailey 1973). If research includes a stage in which observations will be assigned to categories, and the objects to be classified lack features that conclusively locate them in one or another type, then typology construction should come after measurement. The goal should be to achieve the best fit between the categories needed and the empirical observations.

For SR-CRSP sociologists, analysis of Peruvian CCs began with an image of different theoretical categories: pastoral; agropastoral; and agricultural. However, these served mainly as guideposts for evaluating the results of the empirical analysis. Cluster analysis was selected for this task because of the lack of criteria for clearly delimiting boundaries among these theoretical categories. Two kinds of production indicators from the DCCN study formed the basis for typology construction: CC herd populations by species, and hectares of principal plant crops under cultivation in each CC.[4]

In the vertical ecology of the Andes, production of many of the most common plant and animal species is altitudinally bounded (Custred 1977; Dollfus 1981; Gade 1975). Knowing which species a community raises usually provides some basic information about its ecological resources. For instance, camelids (especially alpaca) are today most often found above 4,100 m. Sheep and potatoes are increasingly important at the lower limits of this zone (about 3,900 m). Barley, wheat, and broadbeans are the chief crops between 3,900 and 3,300 m, and maize dominates the zone between 3,300 and 2,400 m. Cultigens like sugarcane, fruit trees, and coffee are generally grown at lower altitudes.[5] Therefore, certain production figures can sometimes furnish a crude indicator of the ecozones exploited by a community. If a CC primarily produces livestock, its access to arable land is likely to be minimal. Conversely, many maize-growing CCs lack access to the high-altitude rangelands necessary for significant livestock production.

In reality, communities display enormous diversity in their particular combination of ecozone access and utilization. Anthropologists have documented the historic Andean ideal of maintaining vertical control over multiple ecozones (Masuda et al. 1985; Murra 1972). Many contemporary peasant communities still do so (Brush 1977; Masuda 1981; and many others). Hence, the typology presented here is not claimed to represent any absolute or "true" characterization of CC production systems. SR-CRSP sociologists had a specific goal: to reduce the great variation in CC systems to relatively few categories capturing principal differences among them. As Everitt (1980:6, italics his) notes:

> [I]n many fields the research worker is faced with a great bulk of observations which are quite intractable unless classified into manageable groups, which in some sense can be treated as units. Clustering techniques can be used to perform this *data reduction....* In this way it may be possible to give a more concise and understandable account of the observations under consideration. In other words simplification with minimal loss of information is sought.

Procedures

Analysis was performed in four stages: (1) selection of the variables to be analyzed; (2) data preparation, including logarithmic transformation, standardization of variables, and treatment of outliers; (3) factor analysis in order, to collapse the number of variables into frequently occurring combinations; and (4) cluster analysis of the scores derived from the factor analysis.

Selection of variables. Analysis began with the full range of production indicators listed in Table 11.1. The DCCN study incorporated additional data on forests, overall community area, native pastures, and human demographics, but these were omitted in the SR-CRSP analysis because they lacked the same sense of "production." If the goal of this undertaking had been to develop a typology of natural resources, or to classify communities according to overall production potentials, then including these and other measures might have been desirable. But the SR-CRSP's aim was to define and rank production systems in terms of small ruminant husbandry.

Data preparation. Nearly all of the production indicators listed in Table 11.1 had highly skewed distributions. For example, while 97% of CCs raised some sheep, just three communities accounted for over 5% of the total 7,807,851 head. The median number of sheep per community was 1,000, with a mean of 2,875—also indicating a highly skewed distribution. Initial attempts at clustering suggested that a relatively small proportion of communities were unduly influencing the results. The exact proportion of CCs with high values varied by plant and animal species, averaging about 10% for each species. Since the communities exhibiting extreme values differed from one species to another, too many CCs were involved simply to remove them all from analysis.

This problem was solved with a logarithmic transformation of the variables. In cluster analysis, the "arbitrariness involved in scaling and combining different variables" means that "there is rarely any justification for using the particular values rather than values obtained from some monotonic transformation; for example, their logarithms or square roots" (Everitt 1980:68). Transforming production indicators to their logarithms dramatically reduced the effect of extreme values, while retaining a semblance of their original variation.

Another problem was that the variables displayed widely differing scales. In order to permit joint analysis of such disparate indicators as "hectares of barley" and "head of sheep," these were standardized to a mean of 0 and an SD (standard deviation) of 1. This was also helpful in scoring the variables for cluster analysis, since the Euclidean D dissimilarity measure that was employed in this analysis is sensitive to differences of scale (Everitt 1980).

No attempt was made to standardize the data with respect to size criteria, such as community land area or human population; that is, production indicators were not adjusted to form such ratios as "sheep per hectare of

TABLE 11.1.   PRODUCTION INDICATORS COLLECTED IN THE DCCN SURVEY

Livestock (Head)	Crops (Hectares)
Cattle[a]	Potatoes[a]
Sheep	Maize
Goats	Barley
Llama and alpaca (combined)	Wheat
Swine[a]	Alfalfa
Burros, horses, and mules (combined)	Broad beans
	Coffee
	Rice[b]
	Tobacco[b]
	Sugarcane
	Oranges

[a]These indicators had loadings of .40 or above on more than one factor during factor analysis, and were therefore dropped.

[b]These indicators had communality estimates of .15 or lower during factor analysis, and were therefore also dropped.

community land" or "hectares of maize per inhabitant." This might have given a more accurate image of the actual deployment of resources, particularly in smaller CCs, but it would have eliminated the effect of the volume of production itself, which was also important.

Taken together, the foregoing steps permitted comparisons among variables while still signaling whether a community was a large- or small-scale producer. The next step was to exclude outlier cases and CCs with insufficient data. Only eight CCs registered zero on each of the variables of interest and hence were excluded prior to the logarithmic transformation. To identify outliers, a disjoint cluster analysis was performed with 50 clusters specified; clusters consisting of only one observation were then removed. Four CCs were eliminated in this manner. Finally, the variables for the remaining 2,704 CCs were once again standardized.

Factor analysis. A factor analysis was performed prior to clustering[6] in order to determine which variables or groups of variables would best capture differences between production systems and to organize this information in a compact form. In this stage of analysis, many different solutions were iteratively examined, and a number of indicators were eliminated rather quickly (Table 11.1). For example, those for swine, cattle, and potatoes were dropped because they were found in many combinations of production systems, and hence did not characterize any one system. For the opposite reason (i.e., nonco-occurrence with any other indicators), rice and tobacco were also dropped.[7] This operation greatly reduced the number of variables, thus facilitating cluster analysis both in terms of computing resources and in the interpretation of results.

A "varimax" rotation was also performed; this provided a much clearer identification of variables to factors. Since the eigenvalue noticeably dropped from the fourth to the fifth factor, a four-factor solution was chosen. Each of the four factors had an eigenvalue greater than 1 following rotation.

Next, factor-based scores were computed. These were used instead of common factor scores because of the likelihood of measurement error in the data. Also, using all of the information from variables with smaller factor loadings might be misleading (Kim and Mueller 1978). As it turned out, each of the four factors had three variables loading on it (Table 11.2). The observations were assigned factor-based scores by multiplying the standardized values by 1 for each variable with a high loading, and by 0 for the others. The results were then summed for each factor. Each of these factor scores had a mean of 0 and an SD of about 2.3 (Table 11.2).

The factor-based scores also incorporate a sense of production scale. Higher figures indicate greater commitment to the production activities that make up the factor, while lower figures point to their absence. However, at this stage of analysis, a community that ranks high on one factor can rank even higher on another. A CC's score on each of these factors simply indicates the relative importance of that kind of production vis-à-vis the population of CCs studied. Zero indicates that a CC scored close to the population mean; a positive or negative number means it scored above or below the mean, respectively.

Given the strong relationship in the Andes between vertical ecozone and production activity, labels were tentatively assigned to the four factors in Table 11.2 based on the production zone best represented by the variables emerging from the factor analysis. Sierran agriculture (I) was assigned its title because three of the principal, nonpotato crops (barley, wheat, and broadbeans) are produced above 3,300 m, often without irrigation. A high score on this factor signals large hectarages planted to these crops, but it may mean either major production of only one crop or minor production of some combination of the three.

Although most of Peru's 2,716 CCs lie in the Andes, some are found on the coast and on the eastern slopes of the mountains.[8] Nonsierran agriculture (II) represents three crops typically raised at lower altitudes—coffee, sugarcane, and oranges. A high score on this factor simply indicates a CC's

TABLE 11.2. CONFIGURATION OF THE FOUR FACTORS USED IN SUBSEQUENT ANALYSES

Factor Label	Components[a]
I. Sierran Agriculture	Hectares of barley, wheat, and broad beans (SD = 2.4)
II. Non-Sierran Agriculture	Hectares of coffee, sugarcane, and orange trees (SD = 2.3)
III. Intermontane Valley	Hectares of maize, alfalfa, and head of goats (SD = 2.2)
IV. Livestock	Head of sheep, camelids, horses, and burros (SD = 2.2)

[a]Factor scores were computed by summing the multiplication of the standardized scores of each of the variables identified with the factor by 1, and for the variables not identified with the factor, by zero. They each have a mean of zero. Standard deviations (SD) varied as indicated.

substantial commitment to these crops relative to the total population of predominantly Andean CCs.

Probably the most difficult factor to label was **III**. A key distinction among CCs was the presence of maize fields. Alfalfa and goats were often associated with maize.[9] All three of these crops are frequently raised in the Andean mountain valleys; hence the name intermontane valley.

The livestock factor (**IV**) likewise implied access to a particular altitudinal zone. Since most sierran communities primarily rely on extensive grazing, and since mountain rangelands are the principal feed source for their herds, a high score on this factor suggested access to native grasslands, usually located above the limits of cultivation.

Cluster analysis. In this stage, the four factors were used to generalize about CCs' involvement in different production sectors by developing a typology of the combinations of factor-based scores across all of the sample CCs. From a technical perspective, a challenging feature of this undertaking was the large number of observations to be classified. Cluster analysis is not a single technique, but rather a family of algorithms that group observations according to criteria of similarity or difference. However, analytic alternatives rapidly shrink when numerous observations are to be classified. This practically necessitated the use of a nonhierarchical clustering algorithm. The procedure selected was based on the k-means algorithm (MacQueen 1967),[10] employing Anderberg's (1973) centroid sorting method as implemented in FASTCLUS of SAS version 82.3. Euclidean distance was the measure of dissimilarity.

A major uncertainty in this or any cluster analysis is how many groups to accept since this is equivalent to determining how many categories the typology will have. This decision must therefore be carefully considered. After testing numerous possibilities, including solutions ranging between four and 20 groups, a 14-group solution was accepted[11] (Table 11.3); but as in many statistical techniques, objective criteria offer little "proof" of one typology's superiority over any other. The final decision is largely subjective. In this analysis, solutions with fewer groups seemed to mask important differences among production systems, while those with more groups seemed to dwell on minor variations in scales of production rather than on new combinations of systems or substantial scale differences within already defined systems.

The 14 clusters can themselves be used as "building blocks" for higher-level generalizations. Indeed, some sort of generalization is necessary to answer the SR-CRSP's initial question about the importance of agropastoral communities for small ruminant production in Peru; hence, Table 11.3's aggregation of the clusters into four broader categories: Lowland, Agropastoral, Pastoral, and Agricultural.

Perhaps the most distinctive feature of this typology (and of the alternative solutions examined) is the numerous clusters for lowland CC production systems relative to the small number (123) of CCs involved. Of the 14 clusters identified by the algorithm, six had noticeably high scores on factor II. This is neither an important finding nor a problem for understanding the other categories. It is merely a consequence of including an entire factor just to distinguish a few CCs.

Eight clusters emerged for the numerically more important highland CCs. From Table 11.3, clusters 7, 8, and 9 were typed as Agropastoral. Compared to the other clusters, they had important activities in both plant and animal agriculture. CCs in cluster 7 had major commitments to factors III and IV, and a lesser one to I. This contrasts moderately with cluster 8's strong emphasis on I, diminished involvement in IV, and nonparticipation in III. Cluster 9 clearly represents the largest highland CCs, with major investments in all sierran production sectors—factors I, III, and IV.

Two clusters were classed as Pastoral. The first (10) is a fairly clear-cut case of CCs with substantial livestock activities and little more. CCs in cluster 11 simply appeared to be more involved with livestock than anything else. Note that size of production is a consideration here; cluster 11 appears to be primarily composed of small highland CCs.

The three remaining clusters (12, 13, 14) were categorized as Agricultural because of their low scores on factor IV. Cluster 12 represented CCs with large investments in III, but little else. Cluster 13 also scored high on III, but even higher on I. CCs in cluster 14 paralleled those in cluster 11 in their low scores on all factors. Discounting cluster 14's score on

TABLE 11.3. MEAN SCORES ON FOUR MEASURES FOR 14-CLUSTER SOLUTION, GROUPED BY GENERAL CATEGORIES[a]

Category Label	Cluster	N	%[b]	Factor I Sierran Agri- culture	Factor II Non- Sierran Agri- culture	Factor III Inter- Montane Valley	Factor IV Livestock
Lowland	1	9	.3	-1.95344	24.96425	1.20431	-0.18355
	2	19	.7	-0.84408	8.91746	1.88506	0.74285
	3	38	1.4	-2.14259	3.53655	0.42143	-1.42240
	4	24	.9	-2.09161	14.07012	1.17883	-1.03576
	5	14	.5	-2.15002	8.65796	-0.06523	-4.73965
	6	19 123	.7 4.5	2.85802	5.47319	2.63845	0.43129
Agropastoral	7	273	10.1	0.58379	-0.41116	2.54995	1.98740
	8	296	10.9	2.77679	-0.43071	-1.64558	0.47271
	9	148 717	5.5 26.5	5.29509	-0.37591	3.51572	2.03488
Pastoral	10	350	12.9	-1.82401	-0.43258	-1.70847	2.87303
	11	539 889	19.9 32.8	-1.12328	-0.43220	-1.82030	-0.21976
Agricultural	12	338	12.5	-1.52349	-0.41930	1.77389	-0.77548
	13	288	10.7	2.13457	-0.43058	1.15632	-1.21898
	14	349 975	12.9 36.1	-1.37510	-0.41812	-0.63908	-3.24633

[a]The 14 categories derived from the cluster analysis have been reordered under the labels provided to reflect the interpretation given here.

[b]Percents do not always sum to 100 due to rounding.

II, which is already at its minimum, its next highest score was on III. Thus, cluster 14 might best be described as very small CCs with some production emphasis in maize, alfalfa, and goats.

Discussion

Table 11.3 indicates that of the 2,704 CCs analyzed, the largest number were Agricultural (975, or 36%). The second largest type consisted of Pastoral communities (a third of the total). Agropastoral CCs accounted for 717, or

27% of the population. Finally, 123 communities were categorized as Lowland.

SR-CRSP social scientists' original question concerned the distribution of plant and animal resources across different types of production systems. Table 11.3 is suggestive in this regard, but not conclusive. Since we already know that many of the CCs typed as Pastoral or Agricultural are small (clusters 11 and 14, respectively), simply knowing numbers of CCs may not be particularly helpful. More conclusive information may be obtained by examining the values of the original crop and livestock population figures for the four categories.

Table 11.4 shows that Pastoral communities are of primary importance in camelid production. They hold nearly three-fourths of the llama and alpaca found in the 2,704 CCs. The remaining fourth is held by Agropastoral CCs. However, Pastoral and Agropastoral communities are equally important in terms of sheep population, with 45% and 44%, respectively, of the flocks in the sample. Cattle are more evenly distributed across different production systems. But even here, Agropastoral CCs hold a dominant position, with 47% of all cattle.

Agropastoral communities are important actors in plant crops, too. Across the three key crops (potatoes, barley, and maize), Agropastoral CCs are outstripped by Agricultural CCs only in maize. Agropastoralists control about half of potato and over two-thirds of barley production. Moreover, Agropastoralists make up over a third of all inhabitants in the sample CCs (Table 11.5),[12] thus representing the most important production system in terms of human subsistence production as well.

For other R&D programs wishing to duplicate these procedures, a question arises as to what constitutes suitable data and whether such data are likely to be available. For the case described here, it would be difficult to imagine a better information source. The DCCN study addressed the same unit of analysis as did the SR-CRSP; it gathered the kind of production data needed; and it was relatively current. But if these data had not been available, how useful might alternative sources have been?

Even though data may not be available according to the desired unit of analysis (whether peasant communities, individual farmers, cooperatives, eor other units), they can still be useful. When a data set mixes different socioorganizational types of producers, additional information on the degree to which each type controls production in the aggregate unit would be required. One possibility would be to include units with a minimum predetermined level of participation in the production variable of interest. Alternatively, the procedures described here could be applied, but with careful examination of each cluster for the degree to which the socioorganizational type of interest is present.[13]

TABLE 11.4.   AGRICULTURAL PRODUCTION INDICATORS BY PRODUCTION SYSTEM TYPE

A. Animal Crops

	Sheep		Cattle		Camelids	
Production System	Head	%[a]	Head	%	Head	%
Lowland	178,436	2.3	170,733	6.5	1,450	0.1
Agropastoral	3,502,251	45.1	1,230,090	46.6	368,864	26.8
Pastoral	3,416,596	44.0	729,207	27.6	989,428	72.0
Agricultural	659,968	8.5	507,686	19.2	15,228	1.1
Total	7,757,251	99.9	2,637,716	99.9	1,374,970	100.0

B. Plant Crops

	Potatoes		Maize		Barley	
Production System	Ha	%	Ha	%	Ha	%
Lowland	8,175	2.6	34,320	15.7	1,555	1.3
Agropastoral	157,792	50.4	88,794	40.6	83,882	68.0
Pastoral	94,189	30.1	6,059	2.8	16,601	13.5
Agricultural	52,874	16.9	89,436	40.9	21,381	17.3
Total	313,030	100.0	218,609	100.0	123,419	100.1

[a]Percents do not always sum to 100 due to rounding.

TABLE 11.5.   HUMAN POPULATION[a] BY PRODUCTION SYSTEM TYPE

	Population	
Production System	N	%
Lowland	263,137	10.2
Agropastoral	895,583	34.6
Pastoral	654,690	25.3
Agricultural	773,826	29.9
Total	2,587,236	100.0

[a]Population data were obtained from the 1972 census as published in DGOR 1977, and then integrated with the production typology discussed in the text.

Other problems concern the content of the data gathered. Even in the absence of desired production indicators, valuable insights can be gleaned. For instance, data on camelids disaggregated by alpaca and llama would have been useful for the SR-CRSP since these species are often raised in somewhat different ecozones. Such information might have clarified the factor-based scores and otherwise enhanced the analysis. Even so, the simple inclusion of aggregate data on camelids significantly contributed to typology development.

CONCLUSION

The identification and enumeration of major producer types helps target limited research resources to those beneficiaries who best match the goals of a project. On the SR-CRSP/Peru, it was initially assumed that pastoral communities owned most of the livestock held by Peruvian peasants. Through careful statistical analysis of empirical data, however, SR-CRSP sociologists demonstrated that this supposition was in error. Peruvian agropastoralists are nearly equally important producers of livestock. Hence, they needed to be included in the program as well.

Based on these and other findings, the program focused its efforts to validate livestock technologies for peasant communities on the dual character of small ruminant production in the Andes: pastoral and agropastoral. Sites for field research were therefore selected to represent these two very different groups of producers. Recommendations for interventions to improve small ruminant production in Peruvian peasant communities now draw upon field research and experimentation in these sites.

Such findings might be taken to mean that scarce R&D resources must be thinly spread across very different kinds of producers, but, in fact, this kind of analysis can conserve limited resources since it allows projects to more tightly target their efforts on a reduced set of like producers. Other R&D programs can apply the procedures described here to do the same.

The usefulness of such analyses lies not only in the typology generated, but also in the identification of producer units falling into each of the categories. This makes sampling from a large population easier, more accurate, and more cost-effective.[14] Added benefits are increased understanding of the characteristics of the target population; greater awareness of the limits to generalizing from research results; and a set of parameters that can serve as benchmarks for monitoring and evaluating changes in production. These represent just a few kinds of contributions that social scientists can and do make to the sensitive design and successful implementation of international agricultural research and development.

NOTES

This study was conducted as part of the USAID Title XII SR-CRSP under grant numbers AID/DSAN/XII-G-0049 and AID/DAN/1328-G-SS-4093-00 in collaboration with the Instituto Nacional de Investigación y Promoción Agropecuaria (INIPA). Additional support was provided by the University of Missouri–Columbia. The author gratefully acknowledges the contribution of DCCN members José Portugal, Victoriano Cáceres, Ivan Pardo Figueroa, and Juana Jeri. Thanks are also due Mario Tapia and Jorge Flores for encouragement in locating the data source.

1. Production data disaggregated by socioorganizational criteria are rare. These rough estimates were obtained by combining figures on livestock transferred to the associative sector toward the end of the agrarian reform (Caballero and Álvarez 1980) with figures on livestock owned by officially recognized peasant communities (DCCN 1980). The remainder was attributed to independent producers.

2. Likewise, these estimates are confounded by the fact that many alpaca producers reside in peasant communities unrecognized officially.

3. The DCCN study sought to evaluate the effects of the agrarian reform, when the central government expropriated most of the large, privately held haciendas in Peru, formed cooperative enterprises on these lands, and in some cases distributed land to neighboring peasant communities.

4. One question in this approach is: what relevance do production indicators have across communities? To give an example, all areas planted to barley are not equal. Soil quality, management practices, water availability, and still other variables can account for great production differences. Likewise for livestock; many factors combine to determine the yield from different herds of the same size and species. Still, certain basic tasks in raising a given plant or animal species impose some similar constraints upon its producers regardless of ecozone. As in FSR, the truly critical part of analysis is understanding the particular array of plants and animals exploited, along with their relative importance within the production system as a whole.

5. These altitudinal boundaries represent the upper limits for Andean cultigens, with livestock occupying the nonarable lands above. There appear to be no effective lower ecological limits for many plant or animal crops, perhaps including alpaca (Flores Ochoa 1982). Most small ruminants can be produced on land suitable for maize, although Andean peasant common sense and, indeed, agroecological rationality dictate against this. Opportunity costs, of which peasants are keenly aware, may serve as more effective limits.

6. Either principal components or common factor analysis is often used prior to cluster analysis (Dowling 1987). Factor analysis was chosen in this case because of its greater flexibility in handling measurement error.

7. Interestingly, these results suggest an approach to distinguishing monocultural production systems, though this alternative was not pursued since monocultural community production systems are few in Peru and are largely located at lower altitudes.

8. The numerous indigenous settlements of the Amazon Basin (*comunidades nativas*) differ from CCs in both socioorganizational structure and legal status. However, some CCS are located at the edge of the jungle region, as well as along the coast.

9. This does *not* mean that numerous CCs in Peru supplement caprine

diets with maize and alfalfa, but simply that the three activities co-occur with sufficient frequency to be considered together. The label attached to the factor is less important for this analysis than is the usefulness of the factor for distinguishing production systems.

10. The k-means algorithm is sensitive to the ordering of the data (Milligan 1980), particularly for data sets with less than a hundred observations (SAS Institute 1982). However, it provides satisfactory results when compared to other iterative and hierarchical cluster techniques.

11. After 18 iterations, no observations shifted to new clusters, thus terminating the procedure.

12. In previous publications (DGOR 1977), data from Peru's 1972 population census were organized by peasant community. This analysis shows how the 1972 population was distributed across the production system categories discussed here.

13. A danger with this kind of aggregate data is the "ecological fallacy" (Robinson 1950), although proper specification of the analysis can greatly reduce this problem, too (Langbein and Lichtman 1978).

14. A template has been developed for use with spreadsheet programs that essentially performs this function by incorporating the key features of the procedures described here. After entering production data from a real or hypothetical observation (e.g., a CC), one can quickly learn which typological category most closely matches the observation. By slightly varying the different indices, one can also detect how near the boundary of a category an observation is located.

REFERENCES

Anderberg, M. 1973. *Cluster Analysis for Applications*. New York: Academic Press.

Bailey, K. D. 1973. Monothetic and Polythetic Typologies and their Relation to Conceptualization, Measurement and Scaling. *American Sociological Review* 38:18–33.

Bernsten, R. H., H. A. Fitzhugh, and H. C. Knipscheer. 1984. Livestock in Farming Systems Research. In Proceedings of Kansas State University's 1983 FSR Symposium. Cornelia Butler Flora, ed., pp. 64–109. Manhattan, KS: Kansas State University.

Brush, Stephen B. 1977. *Mountain, Field, and Family*. Philadelphia: University of Pennsylvania Press.

Caballero, José María, and Elena Álvarez. 1980. Aspectos cuantitativos de la reforma agraria (1969–1979). Lima: Instituto de Estudios Peruanos.

Custred, Glynn. 1977. Las punas de los Andes centrales. In Pastores de puna: Uywamichiq punarunakuna. Jorge Flores Ochoa, ed., pp. 55–85. Lima: Instituto de Estudios Peruanos.

Custred, Glynn, and Benjamin Orlove. 1974. Sectorial Fallowing and Crop Rotation Systems in the Peruvian Highlands. Paper presented to the 41st International Congress of Americanists, Mexico.

DCCN. 1980. Comunidades campesinas del Perú: Información básica. Lima: Ministerio de Agricultura y Alimentación.

DGOR. 1977. Comunidades campesinas del Perú: Información censal población y vivienda 1972 (19 vols.). Lima: SINAMOS.

Dollfus, Olivier. 1981. *El reto del espacio Andino.* Lima: Instituto de Estudios Peruanos.

Dowling, Grahame R. 1987. Dialogue on Systems as Clusters: Identifying Systems. *Behavioral Science* 32:149–152.

Everitt, Brian. 1980. *Cluster Analysis.* New York: Halsted.

Flores Ochoa, Jorge. 1977. Pastores de puna: Uywamichiq punarunakuna. Lima: Instituto de Estudios Peruanos.

———. 1982. Causas que originaron la actual distribución espacial de las alpacas y llamas. In Senri Ethnological Studies 10. Luís Millones and Hiroyasu Tomoeda, eds., pp. 63–92. Osaka: National Museum of Ethnology.

Gade, Daniel. 1975. *Plants, Man and the Land in the Vilcanota Valley of Peru.* The Hague: Dr. W. Junk, B.V.

Jamtgaard, Keith. 1984. Limits on Common Pasture Use in an Agro-Pastoral Community: The Case of Toqra, Peru. SR-CRSP Technical Report No. 42. Columbia: Department of Rural Sociology, University of Missouri.

———. 1986. Agro-Pastoral Production Systems in Peruvian Peasant Communities. In Selected Proceedings of Kansas State University's 1986 FSR Symposium: Farming System Research & Extension—Food and Feed. Cornelia Butler Flora and Martha Tomecek, eds., pp. 751–765. Manhattan: Kansas State University.

Kim, J., and C. W. Mueller. 1978. Factor Analysis: Statistical Methods and Practical Issues. Sage University Paper Series on Quantitative Applications in the Social Sciences, Series No. 07-014. Beverly Hills and London: Sage.

Langbein, Laura I., and Allan J. Lichtman. 1978. Ecological Inference. Sage University Paper Series on Quantitative Applications in the Social Sciences, Series No. 07-010. Beverly Hills and London: Sage.

MacQueen, J. 1967. Some Methods for Classification and Analysis of Multivariate Observations. Proceedings of the Fifth Berkeley Symposium on Mathematical Statistics and Probability 1:281–297.

Masuda, Shozo (ed.). 1981. *Estudios etnográficos del Perú meridional.* Tokyo: University of Tokyo Press.

Masuda, Shozo, Izumi Shimada, and Craig Morris (eds.). 1985. *Andean Ecology and Civilization: An Interdisciplinary Perspective on Andean Ecological Complementarity.* Tokyo: University of Tokyo Press.

McCorkle, Constance M. 1986. Integrative Strategies of Labor Organization for Crop-Livestock Production in an Indigenous Andean Community. In Selected Proceedings of Kansas State University's 1986 FSR Symposium: Farming System Research & Extension—Food and Feed. Cornelia Butler Flora and Martha Tomecek, eds., pp. 513–531. Manhattan: Kansas State University.

———. 1987. Punas, Pastures, and Fields: Grazing Strategies and the Agropastoral Dialectic in an Indigenous Andean Community. In *Arid Land Use Strategies and Risk Management in the Andes: A Regional Anthropological Perspective.* David L. Browman, ed., pp. 57–79. Boulder: Westview.

Milligan, G. W. 1980. An Examination of the Effect of Six Types of Error Perturbation of Fifteen Clustering Algorithms. *Psychometrika* 45:325–342.

Murra, John V. 1972. El "control vertical" de un máximo de pisosóecol gicos en la economía de las sociedades Andinas. In *Visita de la Provincia de*

León de Huánuco (1562). Iñigo Ortiz de Zúñiga, visitador. Vol. 2, pp. 429–476. Huánuco: Universidad Hermilio Valdizan.

Orlove, Benjamin S. 1977. *Alpacas, Sheep and Men: The Wool Export Economy and Regional Society in Southern Peru*. New York: Academic Press.

Orlove, Benjamin S., and Ricardo Godoy. 1986. Sectoral Fallowing Systems in the Central Andes. *Journal of Ethnobiology* 6(1):169–204.

Robinson, W. S. 1950. Ecological Correlations and the Behavior of Individuals. *American Sociological Review* 15:351–357.

SAS Institute. 1982. SAS User's Guide: Statistics. Cary, NC: SAS Institute.

Vidal, Orlando, and Eduardo Grados. 1974. La alpaca, el vellón y la esquila. Boletín de Divulgación, octubre. Lima: Asociación de Criadores de Alpacas del Perú.

Vincze, Lajos. 1980. Peasant Animal Husbandry: A Dialectic Model of Techno-Environmental Integration in Agro-Pastoral Societies. *Ethnology* 19:387–401.

Winterhalder, Bruce, Robert Larsen, and R. Brooke Thomas. 1974. Dung as an Essential Resource in a Highland Peruvian Community. *Human Ecology* 2(2):89–104.

12

Veterinary Anthropology in the Small Ruminant CRSP/Peru

Constance M. McCorkle

The primary research mandate of the Small Ruminant CRSP (SR-CRSP) is to design and test appropriate and affordable technology to enhance the productivity of resource-poor stockowners' herds of sheep, goats, llama, and alpaca in developing countries (DCs). Correctly contextualized in a social science of agricultural development (DeWalt this volume) and carefully targeted to reach its intended beneficiaries (DeWalt and DeWalt, Jamtgaard this volume), research to increase food and income from livestock products holds forth one of the greatest promises for increased human well-being throughout the developing world. Two-thirds of the globe's domesticated ruminants are found (WILRTC 1978:25) in DCs, where even "the poorest of the poor" in rural areas often keep at least a few small ruminants.

To fulfill this promise, however, improvements in animal health are critical, for without them rarely can any other improvements in livestock productivity be realized. Especially in DCs, where animal diseases abound and where herds are more susceptible because of climatic and nutritional stress, stockraising "most of all . . . requires a mastery of disease risks through good husbandry and adequate veterinary protection" (Moris 1981:79).

The SR-CRSP has been a leader in pioneering an exciting new field of study to address this need: ethnoveterinary R&D, or "veterinary anthropology" (McCorkle 1986). As a named and recognized branch of research, veterinary anthropology is barely a decade old.[1] In broad topical and disciplinary terms, the field spans ethnomedicine, ethnosemantics, and international agricultural development, drawing upon the skills of sociocultural (especially ecological and economic) anthropologists, linguists, and veterinary scientists (epidemiologists, immunologists, microbiologists, parasitologists, pathologists, pharmacologists, physiologists), plus specialists in still other fields such as animal husbandry, range science, water management, and agricultural economics.

Veterinary anthropology can be briefly defined as the systematic investigation and practical application of folk veterinary knowledge, theory, and practice within a holistic but comparative and production system–specific framework. In this context, it forms one component in mixed farming systems research. Its goal is to increase livestock production and productivity through improved management of animal health, as informed by an interdisciplinary understanding of folk veterinary medicine and related husbandry techniques. Key elements of this approach include the following:

1. An explicit recognition that the complexity of exogenous (i.e., external to etiological agents and their hosts) and endogenous variables impinging upon animal health lies beyond the ken of any one social or technical science

2. An emphasis upon in-depth, firsthand field research among stockowners under real-world husbandry conditions in order to achieve a meaningful, holistic comprehension of the complex structures in which animals and their owners are embedded

3. The use of anthropological fieldwork methods, combined with the laboratory expertise and technical skills of veterinarians and animal scientists

4. Perhaps above all else, equal attention to emic and etic, i.e., the folk and scientific, in the description and analysis of animal health problems and solutions

5. Finally, a firm commitment to making research results useful for hands-on livestock development and extension, coupled with a constant awareness that the ultimate goal is increased *human* rather than *animal* well-being

Topics typically addressed from these perspectives include veterinary ethnosemantics and ethnotaxonomy; ethnoveterinary pharmacology, manipulative techniques (e.g., bonesetting, obstetric, cosmetic, and vaccination skills), and magicoreligious operations; and appropriate methods and personnel for local veterinary extension. The overarching subject of veterinary anthropology is folk management of animal health in the context of the pastoral or farming system as a whole, and its relation to larger ecological, socioeconomic, cultural, political, historical, and other realities.

It is not possible to address all these issues here. (For full detail, see McCorkle 1986). Instead, the aim is to illustrate some of the approaches, applications, and broader implications of this new area of international agricultural R&D, drawing upon SR-CRSP activities in highland Peru between 1980 and 1987.

EMIC AND ETIC,
ANTHROPOLOGICAL AND BIOLOGICAL

One of the most basic tasks of veterinary anthropology is the investigation of folk knowledge systems and the associated semantic and taxonomic systems that guide and encode animal management practices. An appreciation of the shape, scope, and accuracy of a people's etiological, anatomical, physiological, diagnostic, therapeutic, and epidemiological information about livestock ills is essential. Without this, developers cannot even begin to evaluate what, how, or if native veterinary practices should be altered, nor can they communicate their evaluations and relevant development strategies in a way that is comprehensible, culturally inoffensive, and congruent with indigenous cognitive and social systems pertaining to animal husbandry.

The first part of the veterinary anthropologist's task is to translate folk ways of conceptualizing, describing, and combating animal ills into Western scientific terms.[2] Predictably, this is not easy. Medical science, whether human or animal, classes diseases and stipulates treatments and prophylaxes according to the etiological information afforded by sophisticated laboratory analysis. In contrast, at least pending practical necropsy, ethnoveterinary distinctions and therapies typically rely on the recognition of morbid signs, more rarely on epidemiological observation, sometimes on sorcery, or on any combination of these.

Below, a combined ethnographic and veterinary-medical analysis of one major category of livestock disease recognized by the Quechuas of highland Peru is presented. Folk and scientific understandings are systematically compared along the following parameters: clinical signs and diagnosis; etiology; treatment; and prevention and control (for parallel analyses of nine other disease designations, see McCorkle 1982, 1983a, 1988). These data derive from the author's SR-CRSP fieldwork in 1980 in the peasant community of Usi, Department of Cuzco.

Next, an example is given of the successful application of veterinary anthropology to combat another type of livestock disease. This example stems from ongoing work in ethnopharmacotherapy in the peasant community of Aramachay, Department of Junin, by SR-CRSP social scientists and collaborating veterinary scientists from IVITA (Instituto Veterinario de Investigaciones Tropicales y de Altura, of the Universidad Nacional Mayor de San Marcos). The SR-CRSP has been conducting intensive interdisciplinary crop/livestock research and technology testing in Aramachay since March 1983, under the direction of the University of Missouri Sociology Project. Finally, both specific and general implications of these two cases for livestock development programs in Peru and other DCs are discussed, along with the overarching importance of integrating social, biological, and folk science in any development initiative.

Q'icha in Usi

Quechua stockowners in Peru invariably report *q'icha* as one of the most destructive diseases plaguing their herds of sheep, llama, alpaca, and cattle. The translation of q'icha is simply diarrhea.

Clinical signs and diagnosis. Q'icha is both named and diagnosed by its most obvious clinical sign. Usiños uniformly apply this diagnosis across all species to any case of diarrhea. At the same time, they remark a number of additional signs, many of which are merely the general indications of parasitism: weakness; fatigue; listlessness; loss of appetite; and, in one informant's words, overall "stupefaction." Villagers also cite other indications that can accompany the diarrhea: e.g., fever; blood in the urine and feces; foaming at the mouth; blind staggers; and, in sheep, yellowing and dropping of the wool. In fact, some of these symptoms are unrelated to the diarrheas. Many others that *are* related go unmentioned, such as bloating or swelling of various parts of the anatomy; differing consistencies and colorings of the feces; anemia, as evidenced by paleness of eye, nose, and mouth membranes; and more (cf. Ensminger 1970; Fulcrand Terrisse 1978).

Etiology. Scientifically, the jumble of symptoms that Usiños gloss as q'icha corresponds to at least seven distinct ailments spanning endoparasitic, bacterial, viral, and toxemic etiologies. Folk ideas as to the causes of q'icha are much more colorful, however.

One of the most dramatic explanations is that malevolent foreigners have polluted community water supplies and grazing grounds with diarrhea-inducing substances broadcast from airplanes! More commonly, however, villagers adduce a variety of supernatural causes for this and other livestock ills, such causes as the anger of a mountain spirit (*apu*) or of the *Pachamama* (earth mother) at a stockowner's failure to pay these dieties proper respect and ceremony; a punishment from God for wrongdoing; a neighbor's vindictive sorcery; and, in certain cases, a herd's desire to follow its deceased master into death. Another frequently cited cause of diarrhea is a fascinating panoply of twisting, gusting, sacred, and evil winds (*wayra*). Curiously, from informants' recitation of clinical signs, these wind-induced ailments sometimes appear to gloss plant poisoning from a native loco weed (*Astragalus* spp.; Quechua *husq'a*, Spanish *garbancillo*).

Supernatural diagnoses may be made singly or in combination or sequence with other, more naturalistic etiologies. An example of the latter is some stockowners' apt attribution of q'icha to internal parasites. However, this etiology is often cited only upon observation of massive worm infestation at slaughter. For example, initial ethnodiagnoses of general or supernaturally induced q'icha may be revised to *qallutaka* (lit., slug) when practical necropsy reveals a fluky liver crawling with the *p'alta kuru* or flat worms of hepatic distomatosis.

Folk theories as to how these and other worms enter livestock vary. One posits that animals ingest them during early morning grazing when pastures are still moist with dew. The tiny worms or worm eggs are said to be encased in the dew droplets. Another theory holds that the dewy grass itself infects the herds. Also, a few villagers link q'icha to the muddy, muck-filled corrals of the wet season; all stockowners agree that the disease is most troublesome at this time of year. Others add that sometimes q'icha results from livestock's eating too much fresh, young grass. Although Usiños are unable systematically to correlate these more naturalistic ethnoetiologies and their associated management practices with specific types of q'icha, comparison with findings in Western veterinary science indicates that they are essentially empirically correct for some diarrheal ills.

Of course, damp conditions generally favor the spread and growth of a number of diarrhea-inducing agents and/or their hosts, as, for example, the stomach and gut worms of verminous gastroenteritis, or various bacteria. For example, when sufficient moisture is present, the larvae of the common stomach worm crawl up grass blades, coming to rest with evaporation and moving onward and upward with additional moisture. Once they pass the 1-inch mark, below which some 98% of most infective larvae are found, they are more likely to be consumed by livestock. (Along with erosion control and forage sustainability, this is one of the principal reasons for avoiding overgrazing.) Similarly, the hardy grass mites that host the larvae of other intestinal worms migrate upward during the cool dimness of early dawn; but as the sun emerges and the day grows warmer, they retreat into the protective soil (after Ensminger 1970).

Also, humid pastures and heavy rains favor the snails that host the embryos and cercariae of the liver fluke, which promotes the constant diarrhea of hepatic distomatosis. Wet, filthy corrals certainly provide the ideal environment for a variety of bacteria that produce diarrheas in both ovines (e.g., *Escherichia coli* and *Clostridia perfringens*; see Ensminger 1970:457) and camelids (e.g., *Clostridia wilchi*; see Flores Ochoa 1979), as well as for the microscopic protozoa of coccidiosis, which cause the bloody diarrhea commonly known in English as "red dysentery." However, like many infectious agents, the coccidia oocysts are readily destroyed by direct sunlight and complete drying (Schillhorn van Veen 1986).

Finally, diarrhea may sometimes accompany enterotoxemia or "overeating disease" (Alexander 1982). This is a toxic condition that can arise from abruptly placing animals on rich, high-carbohydrate diets—as when, at the end of the long, lean dry season, starving stock gorge themselves on the fresh, young pasturage of the early rainy season.

Treatment. Treatments for q'icha differ as much as do ethnoetiologies. When sacred or evil winds are diagnosed, cures vary according to the type of wind involved and largely rely on magical techniques. In the case of sorcery, stockowners may hire the dehexing services of a shaman, although these specialists are becoming rare and their services increasingly dear. For other supernatural causes, stockowners may perform appropriate propitiatory rites. However, the most popular cures are more naturalistic and consist of drenching (the force-feeding of liquids) with any of a host of herbal infusions and decoctions mixed with other ingredients such as lemon juice, human urine, salt, and oil. An adjunct therapy is to rub such preparations onto the sick animal's body, especially in the area of the liver. An alternative cure is to feed it handfuls of salt.

The practical value of some of these treatments is obviously debatable. Supernatural cures do not afford animals even the psychosomatic benefits they can produce in humans, although such cares do comfort the worried stockowner. And heavy salt feedings may only worsen certain conditions. However, Usiños express considerable satisfaction with their herbal remedies, avowing that these often work. If nothing else, force-feeding liquids may combat diarrheal dehydration. It is also likely that at least some of the herbs employed have anthelmintic, or deworming (Choquehuanca 1986) and constipative properties.[3] Furthermore, as Elisabetsky (1986) notes for human ethnomedicine, recent scientific findings on skin permeability are at least suggestive for additional research on topical applications of folk veterinary medicaments.

Usiños know that commercial drugs to combat q'icha and other livestock ills are readily available in nearby towns, but they hardly ever purchase such preparations, for good reasons. Modern veterinary medicines are usually too expensive for the peasant pocketbook. A related complaint centers on travel expenses and the time involved in obtaining and administering commercial drugs. Moreover, particularly for sheep, the drugs are not cost-effective; better simply to slaughter the animals. Finally, informants report that on the few occasions they attempted store-bought cures (usually for the much more valuable and beloved camelids), their money was thoroughly wasted. They say the medicines worked only for a week or two, or not at all; that they cured some animals but not others; or even that they hastened the creatures' death!

In part, such failures are due to Usiños' imperfect understanding as to which drugs to purchase. Additionally, villagers are often uncertain about the proper posology of alien medicaments. Applied too sparingly or irregularly, no drug is effective. Conversely, excessive doses of powerful modern drugs can further sicken or even kill the scrawny, malnourished animals that comprise many Indians' herds. Ethnic domination mechanisms also figure in commercial treatments' failure. *Misti* (mestizo) store owners habitually foist off their oldest, shoddiest, or most slow-moving merchandise on Indian clients. In consequence, the few pharmaceuticals villagers do purchase are sometimes long past their effective shelf-life, or are even contraindicated.

Prevention and control. Prophylaxes logically follow from etiologies. In the supernatural realm, for example, prevention consists of keeping animals away from windy areas, avoiding wrongdoing and quarrels with covillagers, and performing ceremonies properly—particularly the annual reproductive and protective rites (*t'inka*) for herds. These rites are festive affairs that feature dramatic events such as the forced inebriation of llama; "marriages" of herd-animal couples; burnt offerings to the earth mother; libations cast to the various "winds"; propitiation of powerful mountain, aquatic, and lightning spirits; and more (cf. *Allpanchis Phuturinga* 1971; Aranguren Paz 1975; Flores Ochoa 1977; Mayorga et al. 1976; McCorkle 1983a, 1983b; Nachtigall 1975; Tschopik 1951; Valderrama and Escalante 1976).

In the natural realm, given "dew-ridden grass" etiologies of q'icha, Usiños do not graze stock in the early morning before the dew has risen. Dirty-corral explanations lead some people to rotate corrals during the rainy season, but only one villager reported any systematic effort to clean and disinfect corrals.

While there is some merit in keeping animals away from windy areas (e.g., to minimize cold stress and, perhaps, exposure to certain aerially transmitted ailments[4]), this has little direct impact on the risk of acquiring a diarrheal disease. Neither do pastoral rituals, although they may serve various "library" and instructional functions, encoding and transmitting valuable pastoral information in their symbology, incantations, and ceremonial paraphernalia and enactments (Flores Ochoa 1977). On the other hand, avoidance of damp, filthy surroundings is an apt preventive measure for a number of parasitic and other ills that induce diarrhea in Usi's livestock. Aside from the few measures just listed, though, Usiños do little to prevent or control q'icha and the many other diseases afflicting their herds.

Indeed, village stockowners follow almost none of the tenets of preventive medicine set forth by veterinary science, such as the prompt isolation or slaughter of animals with transmissible diseases; general sanitation in all management operations, (e.g., docking, shearing, castrating, ear-branding, and birthing); periodic cleaning and disinfecting of animal quarters, and the provision of clean, dry bedding; regular mineral feeding; dipping, dosing, spraying, dusting, and vaccinating against both parasitic and nonparasitic ills; eradication of toxic flora; subdividing herds by different age/sex/species susceptibility to contagion; or avoiding overgrazing and regularly rotating pastures. Expectedly, Usiños' inaction in many of these regards is linked to constraints on capital, labor, and land. In others, however, lacuna in folk veterinary knowledge are implicated, particularly in etiological and epidemiological information.

In sum, comparative analyses such as that of q'icha in Usi provide important insights into ethnoveterinary systems. Specifically, they help pinpoint within indigenous knowledge and management systems where animal health could potentially be improved. Veterinary anthropology also suggests *how* improvements can be brought about, as the following case-study materials illustrate.

Utashayli in Aramachay

In the central sierra of Peru, the community of Aramachay identified ovine manges, produced by a variety of biting and burrowing ectoparasites, as one of their primary herd health concerns. Like Usiños, Aramachay stockowners are well aware of the existence of commercial veterinary pharmaceuticals to combat this problem. Indeed, until the late 1970s, villagers regularly employed commercial sheep dips and other modern methods of ectoparasitic control. But, with Peru's rampant inflation and crumbling economy, by the 1980s these remedies had become too expensive for all but a few families (after Fernández 1986).

Community members met with SR-CRSP personnel to discuss this problem. During the meeting, a village shepherd recalled a traditional home remedy for ectoparasites of horses, burros, and cattle. An all-but-forgotten therapy, it consisted of rubbing the leaf of a local wild tobacco, named *utashayli*, into the afflicted animal's hide. Villagers wondered whether this topical treatment could be modified to serve as a dip for sheep. With the assistance of SR-CRSP social scientists and veterinarians, they organized several initial trials to test this idea. As per the long-standing use of nicotine-based parasiticides in both folk and modern veterinary medicine worldwide, the trials were successful. Indeed, stockowners felt the utashayli dip was even more effective than the commercial preparations they had previously used (Fernández 1986).

SR-CRSP veterinarians therefore embarked upon laboratory research to establish the minimum effective frequency and concentration of the dip (Bazalar and Arévalo 1985), ultimately finding that a solution of 500 g of ground utashayli in 6.25 l of water applied once a year renders a treatment that is 97% effective on one of the major ectoparasites (*Melophagus ovinus*, or sheep ticks) as of the twenty-second day after dipping (Bazalar and Arévalo 1986). Additionally, the project is testing the tobacco compound in combination and comparison with *tarwi* water. Tarwi (*Lupinus mutabilis*) is a bitter, alkaloid-laden but high-protein legume that is edible only after prolonged steeping. The resulting infusion has long been used in the southern sierra as an effective folk remedy for ectoparasites of alpaca

(Bustinza 1985). Project veterinarians in both southern and central Peru are analyzing still other plant materials in the ethnopharmacopoeia (artichoke leaves, squash seeds, various herbs) that are employed to combat ovine endoparasitism (Arévalo and Bazalar 1986; Bazalar and Arévalo 1986; Choquehuanca 1986). SR-CRSP economists are evaluating the cost-benefit ratios of all these treatments relative to one another and to commercial remedies, taking into consideration all relevant factors: price of materials and travel or other expenses involved in obtaining them; labor, water, and fuel resources required to prepare the treatments; and spin-off benefits for human well-being, such as increased cultivation and consumption of such high-quality foods as tarwi . At the same time, SR-CRSP sociologists in Aramachay are investigating how to organize the cultivation and/or controlled harvesting of these plant resources to ensure an adequate and equitable supply. They are also helping the community to establish social, economic, and juridical mechanisms for preparing the medicament, financing and maintaining dipping structures, and universally enforcing the treatment. In this endeavor, extant lines of authority, community decisionmaking processes, and common-interest associations are respected and put to use as basic sociostructural building blocks in collaborating with community members to disseminate new vetcrinary information and develop improved husbandry practices that fit comfortably into existing ideological, socioeconomic, and production systems.

VETERINARY ANTHROPOLOGY AND DEVELOPMENT

In accord with findings in veterinary anthropology from other parts of the globe (e.g., Schwabe and Kuojok 1981; Sollod and Knight 1983; Sollod et al. 1984; Wolfgang 1983; Wolfgang and Sollod 1986), the case of q'icha in Usi suggests that stockowners such as those discussed here could improve herd health and productivity solely by incorporating additional veterinary information into the indigenous knowledge system. For example, Usiños' premortem ethnodiagnoses of q'icha are often confused. Villagers generally fail to recognize prodromes and syndromes that would permit them to distinguish one diarrheal ailment from another, and to treat and prevent it accordingly. The same is true for other diseases as well. For example, stockowners sometimes cite tapeworms as the cause of the wracking cough that is variously symptomatic of verminous bronchitis (infestation by lungworms) or the viral infections of pulmonary adenomatosis and pneumonia.

There is an important caveat here, however. For some livestock ills, Quechuan diagnostic and therapeutic skills rival those of Western veterinary medicine. Predictably, these are diseases that have patent manifestations, such as manges or contagious keratoconjunctivitis (pink eye). In the latter, for instance, Usiños reportedly achieve 100% cure rates, even though folk diagnosis and therapy are partially cast in supernatural terms.

Nevertheless, for q'icha and many other diseases, these Andean stockowners could certainly benefit from increased diagnostic information, if only to distinguish endoparasitism from plant poisoning. Indeed, better understanding of the developmental symptomology of any ailment allows for earlier and more positive diagnosis. Simple and inexpensive education into the prodromes and syndromes of the economically most destructive diseases plaguing their herds permits stockowners everywhere to take more prompt and appropriate management action, whether it be quarantine, treatment, or slaughter.

In the same vein, Usiño etiologies are significantly incomplete. Villagers themselves confess they often have no idea of the causes of their animals' ailments. Lacking modern laboratory tools and techniques and access to the in-depth veterinary information these provide, Usiños, like many DC stockowners, are understandably ignorant of the microscopic life cycles of certain endoparasites, the existence of hosts and vectoring agents, and even simple excremental cycles. For example, villagers in both Usi and Aramachay were unaware of the role of the intermediate snail host with which their pastures are visibly infested and which leads to the constant diarrhea of hepatic distomatosis.

Like stockowners everywhere (McCorkle 1986), the Andean groups described here do control considerable empirical veterinary knowledge. At the same time, as nearly all researchers of ethnoveterinary epistemology have observed, many folk diagnoses, explanations, and curative or preventive steps are "incorrect in major or minor parts" (Schwabe and Kuojok 1981:237). While they are not the whole problem, such gaps in ethnoveterinary knowledge in part explain Usiños' inaction in prevention and control. Without insulting existing etiologies, both supernatural and natural, development personnel can readily explain that there are still other sources of disease that must also be guarded against[5] (except, perhaps, when expatriate developers are confronted with "malevolent foreigner" explanations).

Admittedly, limited-resource stockowners typically lack the capital, labor, or technology to devote to intensive systems of animal husbandry (McCorkle 1983b; Vincze 1980). They may therefore be unable systematically to destroy the agents, hosts, and vectors of disease. However, with increased etiological and epidemiological information, they can still take advantage of at least some basic, low- or no-cost controls: not herding where agents, hosts, and vectors of disease abound or where, at certain times of the day or year, they are most active, for example, or instituting or reinforcing household- or community-level pasture rotation systems; not constantly quartering animals in their own excrement; exercising simple hygienic habits in management operations; recognizing and thus avoiding contaminated water; creating herd subdivisions; and so forth.

For both prevention/control and treatment, the case of utashayli in Aramachay illustrates the very real benefits of teaming social and biological, folk and scientific know-how to tackle specific development goals. There, SR-CRSP efforts in ethnopharmacotherapy emphasize compounds and applications that are based upon cheap or even free materials available locally, and that are readily comprehended and easily prepared within the community. Equal attention is given to community social systems for managing veterinary health programs. This integrated approach obviates the negative reciprocity and human indignities of dealings with oppressive, superordinate ethnic groups. It also frees stockowners from dependency upon expensive external inputs over whose quality, price, and supply they have no control.

Indeed, spasmodic breakdowns in supply of modern technological inputs to rural populations are commonplace in developing countries. Breakdowns may be due to civil strife, simple infrastructural inadequacies, political and financial machinations within government agencies, or an unstable economy. As Lawrence et al. (1980) have dramatically documented for another part of the globe, asystematic extension of Western veterinary technology can ultimately result in more acute animal health problems than if it had not been adopted in the first place. The well-being of human groups who depend upon livestock for a crucial part of their subsistence is accordingly imperiled.

SOCIAL, BIOLOGICAL, AND FOLK SCIENCE

In the findings and hypotheses of veterinary anthropology to date, some consensus on development and extension strategies is emerging: to wit, that educational, managerial, marketing, and other such interventions are often more appropriate, economical, and effective than is modern drug therapy as applied in mass vaccination and treatment schemes or other costly top-down, "tech-fix" programs such as wholesale eradication of disease-bearing pests. Not surprisingly, findings also indicate that interventions grounded in indigenous practice and/or evaluated and coordinated by local stockowners or native veterinary practitioners are likely to be more successful.

A larger lesson is that ethnological investigations coupled with biomedical research can return indigenous knowledge "improved through scientific analysis, to the people that most contributed to it and most desperately need it" (Elizabetsky 1986:125). In the process, knowledge that might otherwise be lost is rescued, and low-cost medicines can be developed that are free of the sales, delivery, distribution, consumption, and misinformation problems attached to modern commercial pharmaceuticals in DCs.

At an even broader level, these lessons are equally applicable to other arenas of international agricultural development. Veterinary anthropology is only one, fresh example of an overarching approach to development that melds anthropological, biological/technical, and folk or "people's" science (Chambers 1986; Richards 1985) in order to understand and successfully build upon indigenous knowledge systems in designing and implementing sensitive, cost-effective, bottom-up interventions. Moreover, in this process the bearers of such knowledge ideally take an active role as coresearchers and developers.

This approach provides two critical kinds of development intelligence: first, as for q'icha in Usi, it can identify where the indigenous knowledge base could most benefit from increased information; second, as with utashayli in Aramachay, it taps this same system, its human bearers, and their social institutions to generate solutions that are culturally acceptable, technically comprehensible, ecologically sound, and sociostructurally, economically, and even politically feasible—i.e., "appropriate" in every sense.

No one science can accomplish this on its own. It is therefore imperative that social and biological/technical scientists join forces in the R&D process. It is equally imperative that this process begin with existing folk science and, throughout, involve the people whose livelihood will be affected. In sum, whether in veterinary health, livestock or crop production generally, or any other arena, "bringing people in" is critical to true development.

NOTES

This study was conducted as part of the USAID Title XII SR-CRSP under grant number AID-DSAN-XII-G-0049 and AID-DAN-1328-G-SS-4093-00, with additional support from the University of Missouri–Columbia. The chapter is reprinted, with revisions, from *Human Organization* 48, forthcoming, copyright Society for Applied Anthropology 1989. In Peru, the SR-CRSP's primary institutional collaboration is with the Instituto Nacional de Investicación y Promoción Agropecuaria (INIPA). Preparation of this chapter would not have been possible without the commentary and collaboration of SR CRSP veterinary scientist: A. F. Alexander, Colorado State University; Hernando Bazalar, IVITA-Huancayo; Zenon Choquehuanca, SR CRSP Community Studies Project, Quishuara; and Mowafak Salman, Colorado State University. Likewise for the informational, editorial, and fieldwork inputs, respectively, of UMC SR-CRSP social scientists Mariá Fernández, Jere Gilles and Michele Lipner, and Lidia Jiménez. Thanks are also due DVMs Donald Blenden of UMC and Tjaart Schillhorn van Veen of Michigan State University for sharing their views on the "diarrhea complex."

1. This exogamous marriage of seemingly strange bedfellows is a direct outgrowth of the conscious melding of social and biological sciences on integrated, interdisciplinary livestock development projects such as the SR-CRSP (Blond n.d.) or the Niger Range and Livestock Project, or NRLP (Swift 1984), which focus upon immediate production problems of DC smallholders.

The SR-CRSP and the NRLP began work in veterinary anthropology contemporaneously (ca. 1980) but in ignorance of each other's efforts. Interestingly, on the SR-CRSP, social scientists spearheaded the move into this area, while veterinary scientists led the way on the NRLP. Clearly, the topic is of equal disciplinary interest to social and biomedical scientists; they have independently sought each other out to tackle this unorthodox branch of research.

2. This comparative or "translation" exercise should not be taken to imply any ethnocentrism. The issue is *not* how closely folk knowledge and practice parallel Western veterinary medicine, or whether indigenous beliefs and practices are "right" or "wrong" in any absolute sense. Rather, it is the extent to which they promote productive animal management given the resources (ecological, technological, socioorganizational, informational, etc.) actually or potentially and realistically available to stockowners. For further discussion of this point, see McCorkle 1983a and 1986, the chapter conclusion, and more broadly, Brokensha et al. 1980.

3. Interestingly, these same concoctions are used for human diarrhea. Unfortunately, at the time of fieldwork in 1980, SR-CRSP did not yet have the facilities and personnel to analyze the plants in question.

4. There is some controversy in the veterinary literature over the role of aerosol transmission (the classic route for respiratory ailments) in diarrheal diseases. While certain diarrhea-inducing viruses and bacteria can be spread in this fashion, most researchers feel that contagion is more closely related to direct contact, as in crowded and poorly ventilated quarters, than to airborne routes (Don Benden personal communication). In fact, the strong winds on open ranges that Quechua stockowners are referring to when they speak of wayra would likely offer some protection from contagion by diluting rather than enhancing aerosol transmission of diarrheal agents.

5. Fernández (1986) includes an instructive account of action anthropology to disseminate veterinary information in a peasant community of highland Peru. Significantly, the case she independently encountered also involved ignorance of the life cycle of the liver fluke and its snail host.

REFERENCES

Alexander, A. F. 1982. Personal communication from Alexander (then professor and head of the Department of Pathology, College of Veterinary Medicine and Biomedical Sciences at Colorado State University) to McCorkle in Denver, CO.

Allpanchis Phuturinga. 1971. Ritos agrícolas y ganaderos del sur-andino. Cusco: Revista del Instituto de Pastoral Andina Vol. 3.

Aranguren Paz, Angélica. 1975. Las creencias y ritos mágicos religiosos de los pastores Puneños. *Allpanchis* 8:103–132.

Arévalo T., Francisco, and Hernando Bazalar R. 1986. Ensayo de la eficacia contra *Fasciola hepática* de la shepita y alcachofa en ovinos alto andinos naturalmente infectados. Paper presented to the 5th Congreso sobre Agricultura Andina, Puno, Peru.

Bazalar R., Hernando, and Francisco Arévalo T. 1985. Ensayo de la eficacia del *Utashayli* contra *Melophagus ovinus* en ovinos alto andinos naturalmente infestados. Paper presented to LAPA, Huancayo, Peru.

————. 1986. Uso de hierbas en el control de parásitos externos e internos a nivel de comunidades campesinas de la sierra central del Perú. Informe Técnico. Huancayo: Convenio UNMSM. IVITA/SR-CRSP.

Blond, R. D. (ed.). n.d. Partners in Research: A Five Year Report of the Small Ruminant Collaborative Research Support Program. Davis, CA: SR-CRSP ME, University of California–Davis.

Brokensha, David, D. M. Warren, and Oswald Werner (eds.). 1980. *Indigenous Knowledge Systems and Development*. Lanham, MD: University Press of America.

Bustinza Ch., Victor, et al. 1985. Piel de alpaca. Puno: Instituto de Investigaciones para el Desarrollo del Altiplano.

Chambers, Robert. 1986. *Rural Development: Putting the Last First*. London, Lagos, New York: Longman.

Choquehuanca, Zenon. 1986. Personal communication from Choquehuanca (SR-CRSP veterinarian) to McCorkle during joint fieldwork in Quishuara, Peru.

Elisabetsky, Elaine. 1986. New Directions in Ethnopharmacology. *Journal of Ethnobiology* 6(1):121–128.

Ensminger, M. E. 1970. *Sheep and Wool Science* (4th ed.). Danville, IL: Interstate Printers & Publishers.

Fernández, María E. 1986. Participatory-Action-Research and the Farming Systems Approach with Highland Peasants. SR-CRSP Technical Report No. 72. Columbia: Department of Rural Sociology, University of Missouri.

Flores Ochoa, Jorge A. 1977. Enqa, enqaychu, illa y khuya rumi. In *Pastores de puna: Uywamichiq punarunakuna*. Jorge A. Flores Ochoa, ed., pp. 211–237. Lima: Instituto de Estudios Peruanos.

————. 1979. *Pastoralists of the Andes: The Alpaca Herders of Paratía*. Philadelphia: Institute for the Study of Human Issues.

Fulcrand Terrisse, Bernardo. 1978. Enfermedades de ovinos y su tratamiento. Cusco and Ayaviri: Centro de Estudios Rurales Andinos 'Bartolomé de las Casas' and Instituto de Educación Rural 'Waqrani.'

Lawrence, J. A., C. M. Foggin, and R. A. I. Norval. 1980. The Effects of War on the Control of Diseases of Livestock in Rhodesia (Zimbabwe). *Veterinary Record* 107:82–85.

Mayorga, Sylvia, Félix Palacios, and Ramiro Samaniego. 1976. El rito aymara del "despacho." *Allpanchis* 9:225–241.

McCorkle, Constance M. 1982. Management of Animal Health and Disease in an Indigenous Andean Community. SR-CRSP Technical Report No. 5. Columbia: Department of Rural Sociology, University of Missouri.

————. 1983a. Meat and Potatoes: Animal Management and the Agro-pastoral Dialectic in an Indigenous Andean Community, with Implications for Development. Ph.D. dissertation, anthropology, Stanford University.

————. 1983b. The Technoenvironmental Dialectics of Herding in Andean Agropastoralism. SR-CRSP Technical Report No. 30. Columbia: Department of Rural Sociology, University of Missouri.

————. 1986. An Introduction to Ethnoveterinary Research and Development. *Journal of Ethnobiology* 6(1):129–149.

————. 1988. Manejo de la sanidad de rumiantes menores en una comunidad indígena andina. Lima: Comisión de Coordinación de Tecnología Andina.

Moris, Jon. 1981. Managing Induced Rural Development. Bloomington: International Development Institute of Indiana University.

Nachtigall, Horst. 1975. Ofrendas de llamas en la vida ceremonial de los pastores. *Allpanchis* 3:133–140.

Richards, Paul. 1985. *Indigenous Agricultural Revolution: Ecology and Food Production in West Africa.* Boulder: Westview Press.

Schillhorn van Veen, T. W. 1986. Some Considerations in the Approach to Measure and Prevent Animal Health Problems in Traditionally Raised Livestock. Paper presented to the workshop on Les Methodes de la Recherche sur les Systémes d'Elevage en Afrique Intertropicale, Dakar.

Schwabe, Calvin W., and Isaac Mahuet Kuojok. 1981. Practices and Beliefs of the Traditional Dinka Healer in Relation to Provision of Modern Medical and Veterinary Services for the Southern Sudan. *Human Organization* 40(3):231–238.

Sollod, Albert E., and James A. Knight. 1983. Veterinary Anthropology: A Herd Health Study in Central Niger. In *Proceedings of the Third International Symposium on Veterinary Epidemiology and Economics*, pp. 482–486. Edwardsville, KS: Veterinary Medicine Publishing.

Sollod, Albert E., Katherine Wolfgang, and James A. Knight. 1984. Veterinary Anthropology: Interdisciplinary Methods in Pastoral Systems Research. In *Livestock Development in Subsaharan Africa: Constraints, Prospects, Policy.* James R. Simpson and Phylo Evangelou, eds., pp. 285–302. Boulder: Westview Press.

Swift, Jeremy (ed.). 1984. Pastoral Development in Central Niger: Report of the Niger Range and Livestock Project. Niamey, Niger: USAID.

Tschopik, Harry Jr. 1951. The Aymara of Chucuito, Peru. Part 1: Magic. The American Museum of Natural History Anthropological Papers No. 44, Part 2.

Valderrama, R., and Carmen Escalante. 1976. Pacha t'inka o la t'inka a la madre tierra en el Apurimac. *Allpanchis* 9:177–191.

Vincze, Lajos. 1980. Peasant Animal Husbandry: A Dialectical Model of Techno-environmental Integration in Agro-pastoral Societies. *Ethnology* 20(4):387–403.

WILRTC (Winrock International Livestock Research and Training Center). 1978. The Role of Ruminants in Support of Man. Morrilton, AR: WILRTC.

Wolfgang, Katherine. 1983. An Ethnoveterinary Study of Cattle Health Care by the Fulbe Herders of South Central Upper Volta. Unpublished thesis, Hampshire College/Tufts University.

Wolfgang, Katherine, and Albert Sollod. 1986. Traditional Veterinary Medical Practice by Twareg Herders in Central Niger. Tahoua, Niger and North Grafton, MA: Integrated Livestock Production Project, and Tufts University School of Veterinary Medicine.

6

Commentary by Technical Scientists

13

A Plant Breeder's View of Social Sciences in the CRSPs

Matt J. Silbernagel

As a plant breeder on the Bean/Cowpea CRSP, I have worked closely with agricultural economists on the program and have interacted with anthropologists and sociologists on this CRSP as well as others. As a result of these experiences, I am more firmly convinced than ever that not only should the social sciences be involved in international agricultural development programs, but also that chances for the successful completion of most biologically based technical interventions under DC conditions are greatly reduced without the essential information provided by these disciplines.

The CRSP mandate calls for special research attention to smallholder farm families and to the role of women in development. Smallholders produce most of the food in DCs. And, certainly for beans and cowpeas, women do most of the production, harvesting, storage, marketing, and preparation for consumption. These are therefore very valid mandates and ones that should not be neglected, especially in times of budget reductions.

CRSP OBJECTIVES AND SOCIAL SCIENCE ROLES

To fulfill CRSP mandates, high levels of social science inputs are required, and research goals must be carefully defined in terms of both their biological and social soundness. The USAID log frame is a useful tool in helping program participants (as well as reviewers, administrators, and others) to see their individual roles holistically. The log frame sets timelines, input and output requirements, and the social, economic, and political conditions necessary to reach concrete objectives. Any modifications to the original framework must be carefully reviewed by the CRSP MEs, technical committees, boards of directors, and USAID before approval.

Ultimately, external evaluation panels rate CRSP projects and programs according to their accomplishment of the objectives set forth in the log frame. Evaluators also must consider how well and to what degree biological intervention packages relate to the needs of smallholders and women. However, this is very hard to do without on-farm testing of potential production packages. And imperative to such testing is social science analysis of the acceptance or rejection of production packages, their spread to other smallholders, and their positive or negative impacts on family income and nutrition and on regional marketing and food systems.

From the perspective of USAID and its need to justify its programs to Congress, this kind of social science documentation of pre- and postintervention conditions is usually the best way to quantify the biological, agronomic, economic, and social effects (and effectiveness) of development efforts. Such documentation is often the critical factor in decisions to continue or cancel donor funding. Agricultural development endeavors must compete for scarce funds against programs in health, education, road systems, and other fields—all equally important in DCs. Administrators therefore examine the relative cost/benefit ratios of various programs to calculate which ones will obtain the most "bang for the buck." Biological research alone does not generate that kind of assessment information.

Within DCs, host country scientists must compete even more fiercely for scarce governmental support of their agricultural programs. They, too, need success stories and good cost/benefit assessments of their contributions, both actual and potential, in order to convince their own governments that money spent on plant breeding will pay off economically, socially, and politically. Here again, biological research needs proper social science input.

In assessing the value and importance of social science research in production agriculture, a key question is: how do we measure the contributions of such research? This is not an easy question to answer, since presumably social science achievements cannot be directly calculated in bushels per acre. Biological scientists can measure their success by the productivity of new disease-, insect-, or drought-resistant cultivars. But social research may have greatly contributed to such biological achievements by discovering which plant, seed, or cooking characteristics are most desired by producers, consumers, and marketers in a disease-, insect-, or drought-resistant context.

Likewise, evaluation of new cultivar acceptability, area production figures, marketing volumes, changes in prices and/or per capita consumption, and so forth, are beyond the capability of the biological scientists. Usually, anthropologists, sociologists, and economists compile this kind of information.

Careful impact documentation should lead to continued funding of existing projects and/or the expansion of successful R&D models to other crops. Perhaps one way to determine how much social scientists have contributed to CRSPs will be to see how long and well the CRSP model is used by development entities such as USAID and how long it takes other agencies to adopt the use of more interdisciplinary research teams. In other words, CRSP achievements will be measured against those of agricultural development projects staffed solely by biological scientists. Once that comparison is made, the only question remaining will be: "why did it take us so long to see the advantages of this approach?"

TENSIONS AND CHALLENGES IN CRSP RESEARCH

Part of the answer to the above question lies in the special tensions and challenges of conducting research under the CRSP model. The chapters in this volume present some fine examples of how cross-disciplinary teams can evaluate, formulate, and execute successful research programs. However, they also note that the process is not easy; it requires considerable effort and compromise for all involved.

One problem in such cross-disciplinary endeavors is that all of us have for so long been compartmentalized by our respective academic and administrative experiences. Thus, we find we are often woefully ignorant of other fields and their professional terminology, research methods, publication styles and audiences, etc. This is equally true for biological and social sciences. The more we interact on many different levels, thought, the more we understand each other and the more we appreciate the value of, and develop genuine respect for, the different disciplines that are needed to ensure the success of a specific goal-oriented project. In this regard, the CRSPs have made some significant strides, as this book attests.

To reach this point, however, some strong biases have to be overcome. First and foremost is the territorial instinct. For the biological scientist, this translates as, "I know what I need to do, so why should scarce resources be diverted to social science studies?" Social scientists, on the other hand, may feel that this same biological scientist is in great need of precisely the kinds of insight and research guidance that only they can provide. This situation represents a kind of intellectual snobbery on both sides. Only after we all realize how much we need one another in order to reach the greater common goal do we begin to appreciate the wisdom of the people in USAID who designed the CRSP approach to solving world food and hunger problems.

This brings up another important point: the tensions between conducting applied research versus "hard science." CRSPs are by definition and necessity goal-oriented *service* projects. Therefore, participants should expect to serve. While this role may call for some real ingenuity and innovative approaches, ultimately it boils down to technology transfer. U.S. scientists involved in CRSPs should be well established in their respective fields, because under present university systems this kind of work will not lead to promotions in the academic world. Likewise, both biological and social scientists should realize before they get involved that neither group is merely providing a service to the other. Instead, all inputs should address a common program goal. There is no room for the independent operator.

A further challenge is that of addressing long-term research objectives on short-term and sometimes unstable budgets. Sadly, this appears to be a fact of life when it comes to USAID-funded activities, and it applies equally to all disciplines. Recent budget cuts under the Gramm-Rudman act curtailed some CRSP activities. Many CRSP social scientists have felt that they and their projects were disproportionately cut relative to biological scientists. However, a number of CRSP biological activities have also been cut or revised. In the opinion of some biologists, these activities may have been more relevant to project goals at this point than was continued social research—especially if the latter would provide only an ever-broadening view of a dynamic flux of people, environments, economics, politics, crops, donor agencies, expatriate specialists, problem diagnosis, recommended solutions, and so on and on. The fact remains that most agricultural production projects depend primarily on biological inputs to generate new advances in agricultural technology.

At least in the realm of plant breeding, what is needed now is much more focused biological information that breeders can use to develop improved cultivars. Furthermore, once a long-term breeding program is launched, at least 10 years of concentrated effort from biological scientists is required to achieve any concrete results in the form of improved cultivars. In short, goals cannot be redefined indefinitely, because each time a new objective is added, it takes longer to reach the ultimate goal.

This is not to say that CRSP priorities cannot or should not change. Rather, it is simply to recognize the hand that feeds us. USAID objectives for the CRSPs are to increase the production and utilization of specific basic food crops in DCs. It is not our job to decide whether wheat needs more research attention than do beans. Nor is it our place to question whether CRSP research should be directed at small (poor) farmers, or whether host country food needs might best be met by a few large mechanized farms. Likewise, our research and training activities include a mandate to consider the role of women in development. In other words, the primary task at this point is to complete the objectives at hand, not to develop new ones.

THE FUTURE

Continuation of USAID funding for CRSPs will depend to a considerable degree on these programs' contributions not only to DCs but also to our domestic U.S. economy—contributions that derive from increased scientific knowledge and new agricultural advances gained through CRSP research. Documentation of quality research in refereed international journals is the foremost criterion on which we will be judged. Trip reports and workshop reports are also important. All such documents should make explicit how CRSP activities help domestic programs. Moreover, these documents should be systematically distributed to U.S. administrators. In every way possible, we should also inform the general public (grower groups, service clubs, etc.) of benefits to domestic programs.

Each CRSP and CRSP project should use videotapes, printed information, and other materials and media to stress that these programs are aimed at *famine prevention* in DCs and that they promote the development of scientific knowledge and U.S. agriculture. For example, we should emphasize that the CRSPs create "centers of expertise" that put participants in the forefront of their scientific fields by pulling together, from around the world, leading scientists in government and university research, including key IARC scientists.

Despite its tensions and challenges, the CRSP concept of interdisciplinary goal-oriented research within the framework of a global plan is an excellent new model. It affords all participants unique opportunities to accomplish objectives not attainable within the normal limitations of conventional narrow-spectrum, unidisciplinary research. This model is so sound that I believe it can and will become the norm within domestic research programs. To make it work most effectively, however, more directed, cross-departmental graduate student training will be required, along with academic reward systems that give greater recognition and promotional consideration to scientists engaging in such interdisciplinary team research.

14

The Interdependence of Social Science and Food Science

Tommy Nakayama

The social consequences of technology development have created an active arena of litigation, with subsequent limitations on the scope of applied technology. Recourse to such terms as "size neutral" constitutes an attempt by agricultural research entities to divorce technology development from its social consequences for both small "family" farmers and large corporate enterprises; likewise for projects that focus on research (the CRSPs' mandate) rather than research plus extension—the latter is left to national programs. Again, this represents an attempt to sidestep the potential social impacts of technology development.

In the ultimate analysis, however, such rhetorical postures cannot shield either biological or social scientists from the actual consequences of technology development. Some of the chapters in this volume leave the impression that biological scientists have been antagonistic toward, or at best benignly neglectful of, social scientists. Wherever the truth may lie in such perceptions, the fact is that social impacts cannot be ignored. Perhaps an illustration from one natural scientist's perspective of where social scientists can make important contributions in agricultural development may be helpful.

A PLANT/PEOPLE MODEL
OF FOOD DELIVERY SYSTEMS

An early contribution to international agricultural research came from economics, by way of what was basically an application of the second law of thermodynamics (Table 14.1). This law states that the energy available to a system equals the total energy in the system minus the unavailable energy. This simple statement has had numerous interpretations, but its essence has guided many technology development efforts. An example is the steam engine: as with many scientific innovations, the impetus to find the theoretical limits to the efficiency of this invention was primarily economic.

TABLE 14.1.   AN ANALOGY OF THE SECOND LAW OF THERMODYNAMICS APPLIED TO FOOD
              SYSTEMS

---

o $\Delta G = \Delta H - T \Delta S$

o   free energy = total energy - unavailable energy

o   available food = total food produced - unavailable food

o   consumed food = total food harvested - food lost, wasted, or used
     elsewhere

Applying this analogy of the second law of thermodynamics in food science generates the equivalent equation that "available food equals the total food produced within a system minus that lost, wasted, or used elsewhere" (Table 14.1). With this equation, a simple plant/people model of food delivery systems with sharply distinct phases can be derived, as illustrated in Figure 14.1.

As the figure shows, when seed is sown, there is no available food because no food is produced; hence, system entropy is very high. That is, the molecules of the system are widely scattered in a random fashion. During the growth period, of course, the molecules are reordered into specific ratios and alignments, and the total food produced reaches a maximum. At the same time, the randomness in the system is also reduced. Thus, at harvest time, the available food becomes positive and has value. Because of its value, it is at about this time that farmers must be on guard against crop theft—one type of loss and hence a source of system entropy.

After the harvest, the total potential for food formation is nil, and the only way to increase available food is to prevent waste. Thus, all actions from the harvest onward are concerned with preservation, utilization, and distribution mechanisms aimed at decreasing randomness. The molecules again become dispersed, and randomness is very high. The purpose of food processing is to preserve the low entropy of the food. This means preventing spoilage and waste, and maximizing availability and acceptance. The latter factors are highly dependent upon characteristics of both the food and the consumer. Information about these characteristics can be used to increase the probability of consumption (Table 14.2). With consumption, the total energy in the food system decreases.

The equation in Table 14.2 is not derived from first principles, but rather is a summation that accords with food scientists' experience. Food value is derived from such things as, first, the quantity of the food, multiplied by a factor that assesses quality and recognizes that all foods are not equivalent. The resulting value is in turn multiplied by a host of probability factors that determine the food's utilization. Of course, all of these must be reckoned per unit cost, as shown in the denominator of the equation in Table 14.2. The

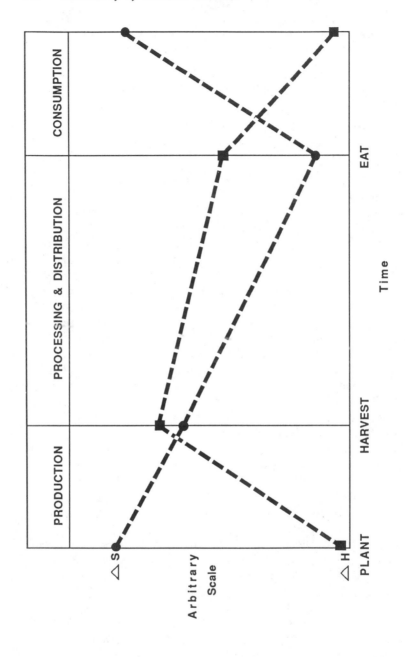

FIGURE 14.1. THE THREE PHASES OF THE FOOD DELIVERY SYSTEM

TABLE 14.2. RELATIONS AMONG ATTRIBUTES IN THE FOOD DELIVERY SYSTEM

o	value of food = [amount] X [quality] X [probability of consumption]
o	maximize for efficiency:

$$\frac{\text{value of food}}{\text{cost}} = \frac{\text{[amount] X [quality]}}{\text{cost}} \text{ X [probability of consumption]}$$

probability factors for utilization include, inter alia, the probability of sale at a certain price; the probability that the foodstuff is acceptable for social or cultural reasons; and the probability that it has the right qualities of, for example, taste and color. Because these probability factors are multiplied in the equation, if they prove to be very low any technological efforts centering on that foodstuff are all for naught. This is what is meant by such sayings as, "No food is nutritious unless it is eaten by somebody."

Food scientists primarily select out the factors involved in acceptance and endeavor to test only this probability, by way of consumer panels and other assessment techniques. They focus on this issue not because of ignorance of other factors, but because of a lack of training in how meaningfully to assess these other parameters. Food technologists must therefore seek help in these areas. Too often, they merely ignore these parameters or attempt to make such judgments themselves. This is equivalent to having social scientists act as, say, chemists. Workable solutions require the collaborative efforts of *both* natural and social scientists.

SOCIAL SCIENCE CONTRIBUTIONS

Several of the chapters in this book illustrate some of the ways that social scientists contribute to the food and nutrition sciences. DeWalt and DeWalt highlight one of the most critical messages of the social sciences for food sciences: namely, the goals of nutrition research need to be closely targeted to those in need. Moreover, these authors show how needs may differ by region and social class. In the course of their discussion, they also illustrate many of the key operational activities that social sciences can perform for and with the natural sciences, such as targeting, understanding crop and food systems and predicting impacts of new technology on food consumption, recommending improvements, and monitoring and evaluating program outcomes.

The chapter by Cattle also lays out some of the ways that social scientists can facilitate research and disciplinary integration, from the design phase forward. In field operations, for example, social science inputs are important in selecting research sites and sample populations, establishing interview techniques and policy, building a team, managing personnel, communicating among many different groups, and more. In particular, serving as guides in unfamiliar territory, social scientists can interact with local populations to enhance project operations and can translate between projects and people to the benefit of both.

Paolisso and Baksh's chapter offers an excellent example of how social science inputs can both refine focused hypothesis testing and generate new questions for food and nutrition research. Equally important is their contribution to methodological strategies in collecting and analyzing data on food systems. Expressing the effects of malnutrition in terms of social modes and behaviors, emotions, responsiveness, and other factors directly contributes to an understanding of the human consequences of technological interventions, both proposed and attempted.

However, because the results of such investigations are presented in anthropological or sociological terms, social scientists need to interpret their findings clearly for technologists. The successful communication of results and agreement on their meaning are important to efficient teamwork. Clearly, mutual respect and understanding are required. While this book demonstrates the value of bringing together diverse disciplines to explore common goals, and while much progress has been made in this regard, mutual education remains a continuing need.

As several authors point out, the inclusion of social scientists in the planning phase of projects is certainly one way to increase interdisciplinary communication and respect, and to overcome the service role that later attachment to a project tends to foster for social sciences. Working together in planning, social scientists can guide natural scientists in the applied arena with suggestions as to cost, shape, color, seasonality, social acceptability, and other factors in proposed directions in food and nutrition R&D.

Where projects have the same time frame, however, cooperation becomes a parallel effort, and thus must be continued at appropriate steps in the design and development of technology. At various points in this process, social scientists should be asked whether a given technology is socially acceptable, environmentally sound, and economically feasible. It is perhaps unrealistic to expect them to give an immediate yes or no answer to such questions; but answers as to whether the project should proceed or change direction seem reasonable. Working thus in tandem, continual input from social scientists as to the acceptability of proposed technology might be one good way effectively to deploy their skills. And since the ultimate success of any technology depends upon its social benefits, it is fitting that it be monitored and assessed by experts in this arena; the social scientists.

In sum, it is clear that social scientists have an integral role to play in the successful development of agricultural technology for the benefit of "real people." Although this volume deals with developing countries, there is a lesson to be learned here from the history of U.S. agriculture, which has evolved through the expansion of cropland, increased utilization of mechanical power, and exploitation of the production sciences. But further developments, whether in the United States or abroad, will of necessity entail increased application of the social sciences.

NOTES

Preparation of these comments was supported in part by the Peanut CRSP, USAID Grant No. DAN-4048G-SS-2065-00. Opinions expressed or recommendations made are those of the author and do not represent any official position or policy of USAID.

15

Social Sciences in Agricultural Research: An Animal Science Perspective

R. E. McDowell

Social scientists are advised that moving from no or low to "in" or "of" involvement in agricultural research can and will require time, despite any legislative actions by Congress. For meeting human food needs, alleviating malnutrition, and stimulating economic development, the sacred cow in agricultural research for over three decades has been the technical aspects of crop production, with plant breeders playing a dominant role.

History reveals that there is good reason for an emphasis on cropping. In what could be termed "Phase 1" of U.S. involvement in international agricultural R&D, seeds, fertilizers, and livestock were successfully exported to Western Europe in the late 1940s, and they served to combat hunger in Asia. However, unrecognized problems of livestock and crop disease, as well as poor responses to prevailing soil conditions, led to a short life for this model of assistance to low-resource countries. Phase 2 therefore emphasized the control of crop and livestock diseases. During these first two phases of assistance, feedback on social issues came mainly from expatriate representatives of various organizations, including religious orders serving as missionaries. These organizations focused on such "crisis solutions" as medical assistance and donations of food, seeds, and animals. Their members' technical training in either agricultural or social science was low or nonexistent. Generally, the religious workers felt themselves capable of handling any cultural constraints, since often their aim was to "westernize" local peoples.

In the early 1970s, Phase 2 was replaced by an emphasis on rapid rises in food production. The World Food Conference of 1974 sought 2% and 4% annual growth in grain production in countries and developing countries, respectively. The general thesis was that technology could be made available, whether by exporting technicians skilled in agronomic practices, by developing more appropriate plants for grain production, or by directly transferring technology (e.g., importing bull semen to upgrade cattle by crossbreeding). At the same time, U.S. agricultural universities, almost exclusively, became the trainers of foreign nationals in aspects of agronomy.

Phase 3 saw greatly increased support from governments and donor agencies for programs like the green revolution. But the green revolution triggered concern among social scientists over inequities in the distribution of benefits from agricultural R&D. Animal scientists in particular were criticized because many social scientists believed that livestock programs promoted competition between humans and animals for food. In principle, the social sciences had some valid points. But evidence shows their judgments about smallholders' failure to adopt recommended cropping practices was hasty and lacked an essential variable: it did not appreciate the fact that most smallholders engage in mixed crop/livestock operations, with these two subsystems fulfilling equally important roles (McDowell 1986).

Because the interdependence of the two subsystems went unrecognized, such social criticisms lacked full validity. Both then and now, smallholders' low adoption of improved plant varieties was largely a result of their dependence on crop residues for animal feed. As plant breeders selected for dwarfing and higher grain yields, the feed value of residues declined through increases in the low digestible plant fraction (hemicellulose) and the indigestible fraction (lignin). Coupled with some rise of phenols in stems and leaves in order to enhance plant resistance to disease, increases in these fractions made the crops unacceptable to smallholders practicing mixed farming. Critical on-farm services rendered by animals, namely traction and manure, were likewise ignored.

Crop scientists insisted that their priorities in plant selection did not conflict with smallholder needs. It was not until late 1987 that crop and animal scientists gathered to discuss the problem. This was a timely meeting, as evidence showed that certain plant cultivars with high grain yields maintained acceptable feeding value in their residues; therefore, decline in feed value was not always a necessary outcome of improving food crop yields.

Coupled with shortcomings of the green revolution, a long drought in the early 1970s in Sahelian Africa stimulated a reassessment of agricultural R&D policies. In addition to other lacks, it was recognized that not enough was known about traditional agricultural systems, social institutions, smallholders' objectives, the economic environment, and the constraints under which these systems were operating. This triggered Phase 4 of technical assistance: farming systems research (FSR).

In this phase, a methodology to account for the complex interactions between socioeconomic and technical factors emerged. Better understanding of socioeconomics has proved useful both in the United States and overseas. In the United States, some examples of important issues raised by FSR include the social impact on dairying of bovine growth hormone to stimulate milk production, and the effects of recommendations from animal science research in intensive systems as these relate to animal welfare. Overseas, increased knowledge of traditional systems has enhanced the potential usefulness both of international technology and of more locally appropriate technology.

As in the three previous phases of U.S. technical assistance, however, donor agencies are showing some disenchantment with FSR. Growth in agricultural production is now challenged on a cost-benefit basis. Most development professionals give high scores to FSR because of its more holistic approach. Unfortunately, what might be considered unrelated events are undermining support for FSR. Among these are political pressures arising from grain surpluses in the United States and elsewhere. An example is the decision to forbid use of U.S. funds to support research overseas on crops produced in surplus in the United States.

This brief historical review of technical assistance leads to two conclusions. First, biologists and social scientists got off to a stormy start, but many problems have since been resolved. Second, collectively, all the sciences need to exert more effort to achieve a coordinated focus and to reinstate support for agricultural research in developing countries.

SOCIAL SCIENCE INPUTS
TO ANIMAL SCIENCE R&D

Social scientists have made some extremely important contributions to livestock research. These can be illustrated from experiences at the International Livestock Center for Africa (ILCA), established in 1974, with headquarters in Ethiopia and field teams in numerous countries. During its first five years, ILCA focused almost exclusively on studying traditional production systems in the semi-arid, subhumid, humid, and highland zones of Africa. In 1974–1975, few personnel with multidisciplinary experience were available. Nevertheless, for the field studies, teams of four to six members were formed, composed of at minimum one social scientist (anthropologist, sociologist, or economist), one agronomist, and one animal scientist.

Contrary to DeWalt's comments (this volume) on the IARCs, ILCA organized a policy group led by senior staff, which included economists and other social scientists. This group worked to ensure that the social sciences directly participated in research planning. Component research was increased in 1980, with social scientists continuing as team members. The multidisciplinary field teams' evaluations of traditional systems made it clear that, almost invariably, introducing technologies put forth in initial hypotheses would have failed. Some examples will serve to illustrate how this partnership between social and animal sciences contributed to ILCA's program.

ILCA joined with Ethiopian government agencies to develop a milk program for small farms in the highlands. The government planned to distribute crossbred cattle, but ILCA team surveys showed that the 2.8 ha farms were already heavily stocked with an average of one donkey, one cow, a pair of bullocks, one young head of cattle, and seven sheep and goats. Plans were to lower stock numbers so as to improve feed resources. Technicians chose the donkey and small ruminants for removal, but farm women refused to forgo either. Drawing upon social scientific insights, the bullock team was replaced with two cows for work and milk. This strategy permitted the milk program to move forward.

With crossbred cows, milk volume per farm was high. But women did not relish processing 10–20 liters of milk per day. Also, they liked to keep the crossbred cows constantly tethered because this facilitated manure collection (dung cakes are used for cooking and heating). Another problem was that as national economic conditions deteriorated, government milk collections were reduced from 365 days per year to 130 in order to correspond with the number of fasting days when animal products are not to be consumed. With social scientists' help, improved methods of butter making, home preparation of cheeses, management of tethered animals, and assistance in marketing thus were introduced. These steps made it possible to maintain the whole program.

Also in Ethiopia, ILCA introduced the use of ox-drawn scoops for constructing ponds to store water for both human and animal use. Farmers agreed to use their own oxen in pond construction. However, as social scientists on the field teams discovered, the farmers feared loss of prestige if they accepted public, in-village training in handling the scoop. On-station training in scoop operation resolved the problem.

In ILCA's semi-arid program in Mali, social scientists demonstrated the interdependence between pastoralists and cultivators in exchanging manure and milk for grain. This insight helped resolve conflicts over land use infringements. Social scientists also helped to show that high pea-yielding varieties of cowpeas were unacceptable to smallholders because of decreased forage yields. This led to a program emphasis on dual-purpose cowpeas instead of high grain-yield varieties.

In Nigeria and other countries, alley-cropping of leguminous trees and food crops is spreading rapidly, mainly thanks to social scientists. They showed that, while the technology is sound, its method of on-farm use must be quite flexible. In ILCA's subhumid program around Kaduna, Nigeria, intercropping of forage legumes to provide dry-season feed and reduce weed problems required large inputs of social scientific information in order to become effective.

In sum, ILCA is proof of the importance of disciplinary integration. The major reason ILCA teamwork is effective is mutual agreement on objectives, interactions to identify problems arising in ongoing research, and annual program reviews.

PROBLEMS IN INTEGRATION

McCorkle (this volume) and other Small Ruminant CRSP studies provide excellent examples of how social science research is important in targeting agricultural R&D thrusts. But from an animal scientist's perspective on the strong needs for sustained integration of crops and livestock in small farm systems, problems still remain in melding the different disciplines.

For example, the SR-CRSP's 5-year summary (Blond n.d.) cites examples of social science contributions to understanding small ruminant production. However, these are not reflected in the three major research thrusts of the SR-CRSP's strategic plan for 1990–2000: (1) hair sheep production systems; (2) agropastoral production systems; and (3) animal health. None of the three enunciates social issues as an objective. The only suggestion for social science inputs is found in the implementation plan for hair sheep production, which includes characterizing the social, economic, and biological activities of traditional farming systems. This sounds suspiciously like nothing more than the usual surveys. Similarly, economists' possible inputs are vague. Such potentially marginal roles do not represent real progress in interdisciplinary integration.

In the chapters in this book dealing with the Sorghum/Millet, Bean/Cowpea, and Peanut CRSPs, FSR is frequently mentioned, but, in fact, only studies of cropping systems are presented. There is no mention of crop residues and problems of smallholder adoption of new plant-crop varieties when their animal feeding value is less than or equal to that of traditional varieties. A useful social science contribution would be to determine possible trade-offs between increased grain yields and farmers' acceptance of decreased animal feedstuffs. Already in Africa, smallholders are slow to or do not adopt new bird-resistant varieties of sorghum because of the lower animal feeding value of both the grain and the stovers from these varieties.

In the chapters on plant crop and nutrition CRSPs, plant breeders are criticized for not paying sufficient attention to qualities such as taste, cooking quality, and storage. Such statements assume that all desirable plant traits are positively correlated. Plant breeders sometimes give the impression they can select for almost any trait, but they may not always make clear what the trade-offs may be. For example, maize that stores well on-farm (such as some traditional varieties) fetches a low market price because it does not process well in commercial systems. Illustrating from animal science, cattle can be bred to produce milk with over 4% protein, but doing do decreases total yields of milk, calcium, vitamins, and lactose by about 50%. Markets will not support the high protein milk, nor will farmers tolerate sharp declines in total yields. The point here is that social scientists should carefully review trade-offs before they criticize their biological/technical colleagues.

Another social issue is recognizing that when new technology is introduced into production systems, not all people will benefit equally. Some will gain and others will lose. Social scientists need to help biologists decide whether overall benefits exceed losses. To give a hypothetical example, what if 10 poultry enterprises could produce all the eggs usable in a market at lower-than-usual prices, but at the cost of diminishing household income for 100 traditional producers? Would such a poultry program be warranted in social terms? From the animal science standpoint, the 10 more efficient producers are acceptable.

Implied in several chapters and explicit in one is the thesis that livestock and poultry compete with humans for food. With poultry production expanding in almost all developing countries, this thesis is gaining more adherents, despite the fact that data are seldom put forth to support it. Animal scientists are skeptical because this competition theory ignores a farmer's own, valid economic decisionmaking.

An example comes from Mexico, where sales of maize by smallholders is declining. Smallholders who adopt recommended practices for growing new varieties of maize find they are at a price disadvantage in the commercial market (Hart and McDowell 1985). Those with some water available instead cultivate small plots of alfalfa, which is harvested almost daily and sold to urban poultry and pig raisers. Smallholders grow native varieties of maize for household food needs mainly because native maize stovers sell for up to four times more than stover from improved varieties (McDowell 1988). The lesson is that when grain prices are low smallholders will seek alternate crops and markets.

Therefore, an alternative thesis is that grains going to feed poultry and swine may stimulate total grain production. Data from India and countries in Africa show a positive correlation between increases in grain and livestock production mainly because of increased feed from more crop residues. An additional reason for a positive correlation between rises in grain yield and more livestock is market demand. As human population grows in size and wealth, there is greater demand for more and better food.

ILCA investigators have consistently shown that sales of livestock and their products furnish the capital for improving crop production. Cash income is low because most agricultural produce is consumed within the household, and funds for fertilizer, seed, or pesticides are scarce. In the absence of adequate credit mechanisms, grain output increases only when there is cash to purchase inputs. Cash from selling livestock products serves as a catalyst for the farm system. Another type of crop–livestock association is the sale of cattle for draft power. Work oxen are often a pivot in farming.

These associations highlight the need to recognize mixed farms as having two major subsystems, crops and animals. Both contribute to family welfare. However, there remain major concerns in building complementary linkages. Western perceptions of the use of animals and their products for human foods is often ethnocentric. Harris (1985) shows that many non-Western cultures use far more types of animals and parts of animals (viscera, blood, marrow); thus, livestock in these societies contribute relatively more to supplementary needs in protein, minerals, and vitamins. Seemingly, the social sciences should be primary advocates of the strong crop–livestock associations characteristic of mixed farm operations.

Finally, nowhere in this volume is mention made of the need for joint training at the university level between the social and biological sciences as a means of strengthening interactions. How many CRSP-sponsored trainees in the social sciences have been encouraged to take courses in agriculture and animal science, and vice versa? Most campuses now agree that this is a pressing need. Still other major problems remain, such as convincing national agriculture research services to allocate some of their limited resources to support social science components. The bottom line is that social science inputs are essential to agricultural R&D, but they must be made in a "progressive" rather than a "digressive" fashion, as has occurred so frequently in the past.

REFERENCES

Blond, R. D. (ed.). n.d. Partners in Research: A Five Year Report of the Small Ruminant Collaborative Research Support Program. Davis, CA: SR-CRSP ME, University of California–Davis.

Harris, M. 1985. *Good to Eat: Riddles of Food and Culture.* New York: Simon and Schuster.

Hart, R., and R. E. McDowell. 1985. Crop/Livestock Interactions as Determinants of Crop and Livestock Production. Cornell International Agriculture Mimeo No. 107. Ithaca: Cornell University.

McDowell, R. E. 1988. Importance of Crop Residues for Feeding Livestock in Smallholder Farming Systems. Proceedings of a Workshop on Plant Breeding and Nutritive Value of Crop Residues, p. 12–21. Addis Ababa: ILCA.

———. 1986. An Animal Science Perspective on Crop Breeding and Selection Programs for Warm Climates. Cornell International Agriculture Mimeo No. 110. Ithaca: Cornell University.

16

The Roles of CRSP Social Scientists in Technology Evaluation and Generation

Hendrik C. Knipscheer

The objective of the CRSPs is to develop new technologies for Third World farmers and stockowners in order to increase food availability and income. One lesson learned from the green revolution is the importance of socioeconomic factors in agricultural R&D. Research policies now emphasize the social acceptability and economic profitability of technological innovations, as well as their biological or technical soundness. Today, socioeconomic analysis is encouraged, sometimes even mandated or taken for granted, as an integral component of the process of technology design, testing, and delivery.

This has led to new programmatic methods, most notably farming systems research and extension (FSR/E). Most of the CRSPs have utilized this new approach. FSR/E attempts to improve existing farming systems by means of technology. Specifically, it develops technologies *needed* by producers and *adapted* to their farms. It has been described as a multidisciplinary approach to small farm analysis, with social scientists participating in the ex ante evaluation of new farming systems or technologies (Norman 1978). But social scientists should and do play a number of different roles in the development of new technologies.

TECHNOLOGY EVALUATION

Technology can be broadly defined as a way of doing things. "New technology" implies a "better" way of doing things, or, in the context of international agriculture, a better way of farming. Better farming is farm management that brings producers closer to their goals, given their social, economic, and ecological environment. The decision to proceed with the development of a new technology implies that some evaluation of whether it is potentially "better" has been undertaken. Indeed, technology research can be regarded as a continuous process of technology design and evaluation.

In this process, biological and social scientists have traditionally tended to view their roles as, respectively, the generation and the evaluation of new technology. Social scientists typically lack the technical skills to participate directly in technology generation. However, they are expert in perceiving and analyzing the social and economic environments of producers. Hence, their crucial role in evaluation. A good example is DeWalt and DeWalt's (this volume) discussion of the introduction of new sorghum varieties in Honduras.

But, evaluations can be done in different forms and at different times. In fact, the roles of social scientists in this regard, as in the development of new agricultural technologies generally, have been changing and expanding (see Lipner and Nolan this volume).

While the importance of sociological variables in successful technology development has long been recognized, for some decades social analysts' input was generally incorporated only at the end of projects (ex post) to explain why things went wrong.[1] DeWalt (this volume) presents a classic example of this ex post role in his review of the Mexico Agricultural Program and its successors, where studies by social scientists were conducted after the fact. His chapter illustrates the loss of resources that resulted from the lack of ex ante analysis, as well as the limited impact of the ex post analysis.

During the last two decades, the pendulum has swung away from social scientists' participating solely in ex post analyses toward their becoming the preliminary (ex ante) investigators in applied agricultural research. For example, it is important to delineate the potential end-users of a given technology before it is designed or evaluated. Indeed, this is what determines the criteria for socioeconomic evaluation. Social scientists clearly have an important part to play in this definitional task (Jamtgaard; Uquillas and Garrett this volume).

More recently still, a consensus has emerged that social scientists should be involved *during*, as well as before and after, the entire process of technology generation. The timing of social analysis is critical if it is to have any impact. On technology-generating programs such as the CRSPs, therefore, social scientists now provide ongoing monitoring and feedback, as well as "before" and "after" evaluations of new technologies.

Today, anthropologists and sociologists also play a unique role as "brokers" between biological scientists who generate technologies and producers who ultimately use them.[2] Part of this role includes participating in on-farm experimentation and facilitating implementation of the research design (e.g., Cattle; Paolisso and Baksh this volume). However, the role of intermediary is difficult. It calls for understanding the beneficiaries, the technologies they currently use, and the new technologies being developed. In addition to being timely, the information that intermediaries collect must also be presented in the proper language—that is, in language that is comprehensible to scientists of other disciplines and, in the case of critical observations, diplomatic. Understandably, biological scientists have not always welcomed such observations. Many have been discouraged by negative social scientific evaluation of "their" new technologies. Many also question whether social scientists really provide a service, rather than an obstacle, to their work.

TECHNOLOGY GENERATION

Although the usefulness of the social sciences in technology evaluation is now recognized, technology generation is still considered the domain of biological scientists. This stance is linked to two main views of the technology generation process: "one step" and "black box." Both ignore the importance of participative approaches to technology generation.

One Step

Biological scientists often mistakenly view technology generation as a one-step process, a "eureka" experience. The FSR approach organizes research activities in phases: descriptive/diagnostic; technology development; evaluation; and then extension (Uquillas and Garrett this volume). This concept of research programming reinforces the idea that technology development is a one-step (one-stage/phase) process. In this paradigm, social scientists often find themselves stuck in the first phase: description (Coughenour and Reeves this volume).

Contrary to the standard FSR model, however, in reality technologies develop slowly and with marginal improvements over time. Technology generation is thus a continuous process of redesign and evaluation. In consequence, evaluation can take many forms, as displayed in Table 16.1.

It is evident from an examination of Table 16.1 that social scientists can contribute to *all* stages of technological development—notional, preliminary, and developed. As a matter of fact, involving social scientists and producers during the notional stage (e.g., during protocol or proposal discussions) leads to more efficient use of research resources. Although the FSR approach has proved very useful in integrating biological and nonbiological scientists within the CRSPs, the social sciences could doubtless have even more impact if a technology development paradigm were adopted instead.

TABLE 16.1.   FSR EVALUATION METHODS AND THE STAGES OF TECHNOLOGY DESIGN

Stages of Technology Design	Most Cost-effective Evaluation Method
Notional	Intuition Informal discussions Formalized discussions
Preliminary	Laboratory experiments Research-station field experiments Budgeting
Developed	Computer simulation experiments Unit-farms experiments Researcher-managed on-farm experiments Farmer-managed on-farm experiments

Source: Menz and Knipscheer 1981.

Black Box

Unfortunately, biological and social scientists alike share the conviction that the latter are not technology generators. This conviction can reduce the role of the social scientist to that of messenger—the bearer of good or, more often, bad news. This idea coincides with the view that social scientists' main role is brokering, or, as Paolisso and Baksh (this volume) formulate it, "articulation of areas of interest to biological scientists."

Actually, though, we know very little about how technologies are generated. Our ignorance in this area fosters a "black box" notion of the generation process, with biological scientists as the magicians. Yet defining the "magicians" or technology generators so narrowly excludes not only social scientists from the technology innovation process, but also the end-users.

Participative Approaches

Recently, the importance of input form producers into the technology design process has been acknowledged (Chambers 1985). Farmers and herders control large bodies of indigenous technical knowledge of their own. As one expert in this area observes:

> In most countries of the third world, rural people's knowledge is an enormous and underutilized national resource. . . . [T]here are innumerable skills and well-informed local experts. . . . Knowledgeable rural people are disregarded, despised, and demoralized by urban, commercial and professional values, interests and power.

For them to be better able to participate . . . one first step is for outsider professionals, the bearers of modern scientific knowledge, to step down off their pedestals, and sit down, listen and learn (Chambers 1983:92, 93, 101).

This stance acknowledges that farmers are experts on their own existing technologies and that they can directly contribute to the design of new ones. But this stance challenges the "magical" status of biological scientists (and their black box), as well as the position of social brokers, who suddenly find themselves wedged between two expert groups. Of course, social scientists, particularly anthropologists, are trained to overcome and communicate across such cultural boundaries. Yet even with this training, does the intermediary understand the technology she/he is talking about?

Ultimately social scientists can play a significant role in the process of technology development only by becoming subject-matter semispecialists, capable of translating between two expert groups. Several authors in this volume (e.g., Coughenour and Reeves) pay lip service to the need to follow the research of their biological colleagues. But only McCorkle offers a clear-cut example of a social scientist who becomes a subject-matter semispecialist, and who is therefore able to involve biological scientists and producers in a problem-solving dialogue.

Problem solving is what technology generation is all about. Producers can and should participate in problem solving both to select and to adapt new technologies to suit their needs. Kirkby and Matlon (1984) have provided excellent guidelines on how to engage producers in this process. The first guideline is to earn producers' respect.

LESSONS LEARNED

In light of the above discussion, how well have CRSP social scientists played their brokering role, be it in the old, ex post evaluation mode to in the new, continuous-involvement mode? To obtain an overview of the role and impact of CRSP social scientists in technology development, I have classified the studies described in this volume according to their technological orientation (Table 16.2). The chapters are groups by the following questions:

- Was the study oriented toward technology development?
- If yes, was it conducted in a multidisciplinary mode?
- Did the study involve producer participation?
- If yes, was this participation passive (e.g., only responding to questionnaires) or active (engaging in dialogue and problem solving)?

TABLE 16.2.   CLASSIFICATION OF CRSP SOCIAL SCIENCE RESEARCH

Research Studies[a]	Technology Development Orientation		Producer Participation	
	Unidisciplinary	Multidisciplinary	Passive	Active
DeWalt	*			
Lacy et al.	*			
Paolisso & Baksh	*		*	
Jamtgaard	*		*	
Coughenour & Reeves		*	*	
DeWalt & DeWalt		*	*	
Cattle		*	*	
Ferguson		*	*	
Uquillas & Garrett		*	*	
Wheelock et al.		*	*	
McCorkle		*		*

[a]As reported by the contributors to this volume.

Table 16.2 indicates that CRSP social scientists generally have been well directed. All have interacted with other social scientists, on the one hand; on the other hand, they have also worked in tandem with specialists in sorghum, cowpeas, goats, or whatever. As set forth in this book, the experiences of the CRSPs illustrate the usefulness of this intra- and interdisciplinary interaction. At the same time, however, Table 16.2 highlights two general areas of constraints to social scientists' role performance: disciplinary and institutional.

In disciplinary terms, as brokers on technology development projects, social scientists are making career sacrifices. By becoming subject-matter semispecialists and by gearing their language and publications to a multidisciplinary audience, they have gained recognition within their CRSPs, but not necessarily among their academic colleagues. Disciplinary groups often do not reward multidisciplinary research, viewing it as marginal or "maverick." Worse still, they may even "punish" it (Heberlein 1988).

Conversely, technical/biological scientists sometimes criticize the work of their social science colleagues as overly disciplinary and contributing little to new technology development other than some general information. For example, as an economist, I appreciate the chapter by Wheelock et al. on income elasticities for peanut products. As the same time, I can see how biological scientists might argue that the research resources devoted to this analysis could have been better applied to generating information relating more directly to new technologies.

Nevertheless, Table 16.2 suggests that CRSP social scientists have generally done a remarkable job of participating in multidisciplinary research. They have largely succeeded in balancing their act between achieving long-term academic career goals and serving as effective brokers to biological scientists.

Of course, multidisciplinary team research is never easy. Regional projects are difficult enough; multinational projects are even more so. In order systematically to identify the primary research activities that need to be implemented by each discipline and to integrate the multidisciplinary information generated thereby, an analytic framework is essential. The FSR paradigm provides one such vehicle. Experiences on the SR-CRSP show that in countries where the research team followed the general guidelines of FSR methodology, the program yielded the best results in terms of new technologies (although not necessarily in terms of numbers of research reports).

Institutional constraints also figure in the success of multidisciplinary efforts and the brokering process. One constraint is, typically, meager budgets for social science activities. The argument for this is that research institutions are technology factories; their primary mandate is technology generation rather than evaluation. They thus have an administrative bias that endows the technical/biological scientists with more status, power, control, and funds (Heberlein 1988) than are social scientists—who, again, are often cast in a "service" role. It is one of the virtues of certain CRSPs that the social science component is explicitly written into the program. This helps overcome both institutional and cross-disciplinary bottlenecks.

An additional lesson learned on the CRSPs is that, in view of disciplinary, institutional, and other constraints, the sites where CRSPs have worked with only one host country agency (rather than multiple agencies) have usually been more successful. Separate multidisciplinary research funds and external evaluation panels have also served as counterweights to negative institutional biases.

CONCLUSION

CRSP social scientists have been involved in technology generation in many ways. The conduct of their research, its direction, and its integration with other disciplines have varied across CRSPs, collaborating countries, and principal investigators. In retrospect, however, a number of strategies have made for more effective social science inputs: application of FSR methods; explicit inclusion of the social sciences in program design; collaboration with a single, strong host country institution; favorable budget mechanisms; and continual monitoring of social science performance in relation to the program as a whole.

Still, there is room for improvement. CRSP social scientists can be even more effective to the extent that they mobilize producer participation in the multidisciplinary research endeavor itself. To date, we have usually involved producers only passively. I firmly believe that more effort by CRSP social scientists to stimulate producers' active participation in research would also have led to fewer budget constraints. Active end-user participation is critical because it is also the ultimate test of whether institutional constraints have been overcome.

Presently, the SR-CRSP is conducting innovative research in this more interactive mode in Indonesia and Peru. This approach to technology generation has increased mutual understanding and appreciation between scientists (both social and biological) and producers. The result is applied research that is directly geared to user needs. This has been one of the major accomplishments of the social sciences in the CRSPs.

NOTES

1. This situation resulted in part from anthropologists' and sociologists' earlier unwillingness to become actively involved in applied research (Sutherland 1987).

2. This broker, or intermediary, role is relatively new to anthropologists and sociologists, especially when one considers that the first social scientists involved in multidisciplinary research were mainly agricultural economists.

REFERENCES

Chambers, R. 1983. *Rural Development: Putting the Last First.* London, Lagos, New York: Longman.

――――. 1985. Understanding Professionals: Small Farmers and Scientists. In *5 Essays on Science and Farmers in the Developing World.* S. A. Breth, ed. Morrilton, AR: Winrock International.

Heberlein, T. A. 1988. Improving Interdisciplinary Research: Integrating Social and Natural Science. *Society and Natural Resources* I(1):5–16.

Kirkby, R., and P. Matlon. 1987. Conclusions. In Coming the Full Circle: Farmers' Participation in the Development of Technology. P. Matlon, R. Cantrell, D. King, and M. Benoit-Cathin, eds. Ottawa: IDRC.

Mena, K. M., and H. C. Knipscheer. 1981. The Location Specificity in Farming Systems Research. *Agricultural Systems* 7:95–103.

Norman, D. W. 1978. Farming Systems Research to Improve the Livelihood of Small Farmers. *American Journal of Agricultural Economics* 60:813–818.

Sutherland, A. 1987. Sociology in Farming Systems Research. Occasional Paper No. 6. London: Agricultural Administration Unit, Overseas Development Institute.

About the Contributors

Michael G. Baksh is research anthropologist with the Nutrition CRSP's Kenya project, School of Public Health, University of California, Los Angeles, CA 90024. He also teaches anthropology at the University of California–Los Angeles, and at California State University, Dominguez Hills, and conducts cultural ecological research in the Peruvian Amazon.

Lawrence Busch is professor of sociology at the University of Kentucky, Lexington, KY 40546. He is co-author of *Science, Agriculture and the Politics of Research* and editor of several other volumes.

Virginia Caples is professor and associate dean of home economics at Alabama A&M University, P.O. Box 639, Normal, AL 35762. Her international involvement has been in the areas of nutrition education and family planning in Sudan, Tanzania, and the Caribbean.

Dorothy J. Cattle is assistant professor of biological anthropology in the Department of Sociology and Anthropology at Miami University, Oxford, OH 45056. Her research in Central America, Kenya, and the United States has applied biocultural perspectives to issues in nutrition, health, and natural resources development. In addition to serving in several administrative capacities on the Nutrition CRSP, she was the initial senior investigator in anthropology for its Kenya project.

C. Milton Coughenour is professor of sociology at the University of Kentucky, Lexington, KY 40546-0091. A past president of the Rural Sociological Society, he has conducted research on farming systems, resource development, and technological change in Sudan, Australia, and the United States.

Billie R. DeWalt is professor and chair of the Department of Anthropology at the University of Kentucky, Lexington, KY 40506-0024. He has done research on food policy, agrarian systems, and political ecology in Costa Rica, Ecuador, Honduras, and Mexico.

Kathleen M. DeWalt is associate professor of behavioral sciences and anthropology, College of Medicine, University of Kentucky, Lexington, KY 40506-0024. The 1986–1988 president of the Council on Nutritional Anthropology and a member of the Executive Board of the Society for Medical Anthropology, she is currently conducting research in Ecuador as part of the Nutrition and Agriculture Cooperative Agreement with the Nutrition Economics Group of OICD/USDA.

Anne E. Ferguson is the women in development specialist of the Bean/Cowpea CRSP, headquartered at the Center for International Programs, Michigan State University, East Lansing, MI 48824-1035. She has conducted anthropological research in Central America and Eastern Africa and is currently coprincipal investigator on the Bunda College of Agriculture, Malawi/Michigan State University/Bean-Cowpea CRSP Project.

Patricia Garrett is a sociologist with the Bush Institute, 300 NCNB Plaza, CB8040, at the University of North Carolina at Chapel Hill, NC 27599. She was coprincipal investigator at Cornell University on the Bean/Cowpea CRSP.

Keith A. Jamtgaard is a research associate in the Department of Rural Sociology at the University of Missouri, Columbia, MO 65211. He has spent nearly four years working with the Small Ruminant CRSP in Peru and has consulted on projects in Costa Rica, Bolivia, and Liberia.

Hezekiah S. Jones is associate professor of agricultural economics in the Department of Agribusiness, Alabama A&M University, P.O. Box 261, Normal, AL 35762. He has conducted research in Africa and the Caribbean that has focused on small-scale agricultural production and marketing.

Hendrik (Henk) C. Knipscheer is principal investigator on the SR-CRSP Economics Project and previous site coordinator for the project in Indonesia. An agricultural economist with 15 years' experience in Indonesia, the Ivory Coast and Nigeria, he is currently a program officer at Winrock International Institute for Agricultural Development, Route 3, Morrilton, AR 72110-9537, where he provides technical and administrative assistance to farming systems and livestock projects.

William B. Lacy is professor of sociology and director of the Food, Environment, and Agriculture Program at the University of Kentucky,

Lexington, KY 40506-0024. He is co-author and editor of several books and journal articles on the sociology of agricultural research and science policy, including two recent volumes on biotechnology.

Michele E. Lipner is a graduate research assistant and doctoral candidate in the Department of Rural Sociology at the University of Missouri, Columbia, MO 65211. Previously, she worked with the Small Ruminant CRSP's Management Entity at the University of California–Davis.

Paul L. Marcotte is a visiting research fellow at the International Service for National Agricultural Research (ISNAR), P.O. Box 93375, 2509AJ, The Hague, Netherlands, where he holds a Rockefeller Foundation Social Science in Agriculture Research Fellowship.

Constance M. McCorkle is research assistant professor in the Department of Rural Sociology, University of Missouri, Columbia, MO 65211, where she coordinates the Small Ruminant CRSP Sociology Project. Between 1972 and the present, she has spent more than five years in 12 Latin American and African countries conducting anthropological and farming systems research and advising on agricultural development projects.

R. E. McDowell, professor emeritus, Department of Animal Science, Cornell University, is currently visiting professor, Department of Animal Science, North Carolina State University, Raleigh, NC 27695-7621. He has conducted research and directed planning for international livestock development for the past 40 years and has spent a total of 14 years working in 21 countries of Africa, Asia, and Latin America.

Tommy Nakayama is professor and head of the Department of Food Science and Technology, University of Georgia, Griffin, GA 30223-1797. Between 1986 and 1988, he served as program director for the Peanut CRSP.

Michael F. Nolan is professor or rural sociology and associate dean, College of Agriculture, at the University of Missouri, Columbia, MO 65211. As director of UMC's International Agricultural Programs and principal investigator on the Sociology Project of the Small Ruminant CRSP, he has worked with development projects throughout Africa, Asia, and Latin America.

Michael Paolisso is an anthropologist at the International Center for Research on Women, 1717 Massachusetts Avenue NW, Suite 501, Washington, DC 20036, where he works on issues in gender, agricultural development, and health.

Edward B. Reeves is associate professor of sociology and anthropology at Morehead State University, Morehead, KY 40351 and coeditor of *Human Systems Ecology*. He has conducted research on farming and marketing systems in western Sudan and Appalachian United States.

Matt J. Silbernagel is research plant pathologist with the USDA Agricultural Research Service at Washington State University's Irrigated Agriculture Research and Extension Center, Prosser, WA 99350. A specialist in breeding beans for disease resistance and environmental stress tolerances, he has served as the principal investigator for the Bean/Cowpea CRSP Project between WSU and the Solsoine University of Agriculture at Morogoro, Tanzania, since its inception in 1981.

Bharat Singh is professor, Department of Food Science at Alabama A&M University, Normal, AL 35762. His work focuses on postharvest handling, storage, and processing of cereals and legumes.

Joyce M. Turk is livestock advisor in USAID's Bureau of Science and Technology, Washington, DC 20523, where she serves as program leader of the Small Ruminant CRSP. Formerly agricultural project officer and program analyst for the USAID/Sudan Mission, she has designed, implemented, and evaluated agricultural development projects in Indonesia, Kenya, Morocco, Peru, the Philippines, and Sudan.

Jorge F. Uquillas is a sociologist at the Fundación Ecuatoriana de Investigación Agropecuaria, Quito, Ecuador. He served as field sociologist on the Bean/Cowpea CRSP, representing Cornell University in its collaboration with Ecuador's Instituto Nacional de Investigaciones Agropecuarias.

Gerald C. Wheelock is professor of development sociology, Department of Agribusiness, Alabama A&M University, P.O. Box 12, Normal, AL 35762. He has conducted research on agricultural development and market structures in the semi-arid tropics of Asia and Africa; his current interests include the sociology of agriculture and resource conservation.

Index